HANDWRITING ANALYSIS
As a Psychodiagnostic Tool

HANDWRITING ANALYSIS
As a Psychodiagnostic Tool

A Study in General and Clinical Graphology

By
Ulrich Sonnemann, Ph.D.

*Associate Professor, New School for Social Research,
New York. Lecturer, Graduate Faculty, City College of New York*

With a foreword by
BELA MITTELMANN, M.D.

GRUNE & STRATTON
NEW YORK 1950

COPYRIGHT 1950
GRUNE & STRATTON, INC.
381 Fourth Ave.
New York City 16

Printed in U.S.A.
Bound by Moore & Co., Inc., Baltimore
in pyroxylin-impregnated,
water-repellent cloth

To Nell

FOREWORD

Recent investigations of expressive movements in psychology have prepared the ground for a broader scientific understanding of handwriting analysis and for a detailed discussion of principles and application of graphology. This is the task that Ulrich Sonnemann's book undertakes. In introducing it, I am happy to remember our commonly conducted courses in psychodiagnostic techniques at the City College of New York. In these courses numerous classroom experiments were conducted in "blind" graphological analysis, showing considerable agreement in general diagnosis and on specific clinical manifestations independently arrived at by the psychiatrist and the graphologist.

Much research and validation remain to be done in this field, but whichever graphological system is under investigation, it should be allowed to operate as a whole, with its principles of interrelatedness of various features of the specimen. This does not preclude the investigation of the validity of single diagnostic signs. However, the latter kind of investigation should be clearly differentiated from the former.

For the former type of investigation, it is to be welcomed that Dr. Sonnemann gives a critical revision of Ludwig Klages' graphological principles and offers a formulation of the way in which these revised principles can be further developed. Operating as a whole, graphology can take its place as a full equal in personality diagnosis with other projective methods, e.g., the Rorschach test, that have stood the test of time.

BELA MITTELMANN, M.D.

CONTENTS

FOREWORD vii

I. Introduction 1

The Nature and Purpose of Graphology, Its History and Main Assumptions 1

The Problems of Personality Psychology and the Theory of Expressive Movements 7

How Objective is Graphology? 11

II. The Graphological Method 20

Basic Concepts 20
The total motoric aspect: Contraction and release, 20. The total symbolic aspect: The quasi-spatial experience of the writing field, 21. The total interpretative aspect: Ambivalence and interdependence of indicators, 24.

The Sample as a Whole 25
The level of form quality, 25. Rhythm and regularity, Integration and fluctuation, 27. The Overall Arrangement, 36.

The Dimensions of Rating 39
Introductory note, 39. Extension, velocity, and impact, 40. The ductus, laterally and longitudinally: Sharpness and doughiness, connectedness and disconnectedness, 46. The vertical dimension: The three zones, 56. The horizontal dimension: *General dynamic aspects: Width, slant, total right- and leftwardness*, 65. *Static aspects I: the word*, 73. *Specific dynamic aspects: the forms of binding*, 76. *Static aspects II: the line*, 92. The dimension of background involvement. *Fullness and meagerness*, 102. *Elaboration and simplification; Ornamentation and neglect*, 106. *Distances and margins*, 111. General qualities of curve, 117. The signatures, special signs, and miscellaneous, 118.

The Interpretative Synopsis 134
　Age, sex, handedness, and the cultural background, 134. The arrayal of indicators on the contraction-release scale and according to their accessibility to conscious modification, 138. The work of determining, eliminating, combining: Evolving the finished analysis, 139.

III. **General and Clinical Applications** 144

　Twelve Lines from Joan: A demonstration of the graphological method 144

　A Problem in Personnel Selection 154

　Graphological and Psychiatric Concepts of Personality......... 168

　Main Types of Psychopathology and their Graphic Expressions... 173
　　Affective disorders, 173. Schizophrenic disorders, 181. Psychoneurotic disorders, 204. Intracranial disorders, 225. Miscellaneous, 233.

　Some Abnormal Samples and their Analyses.................. 244

SUMMARY 265
BIBLIOGRAPHY 269
INDEX 273

I. INTRODUCTION

THE NATURE AND PURPOSE OF GRAPHOLOGY
Its History and Main Assumptions

That something so "personal" as a person's handwriting should tell us something about his character, temperament, and state of mind is a simple and almost self-evident expectation. Long before any systematic inquiry into the psychology of handwriting was begun, sensitive observers of human behavior had come, independently of one another, to notice the persistent and inescapable mark of individuality in the handwritings of different persons. This raises an interesting question. Certainly, at the present time, a revival of interest in the psychological conveyances of handwriting is making itself felt among professional psychologists in this country, but why, at least in America (the development in Europe took a widely different course) did handwriting not receive its proper place in personality investigation long before our years? Why, at a time when in Europe the study of Klages' fundamental books on the subject had become required reading for students of psychology, was handwriting analysis in this country still left almost exclusively to the "quacks"—to be molded by them to their purposes and level of understanding? Let us take up these questions at their proper places, after having explored first what handwriting analysis is and wants and what assumptions and fundamental beliefs underly its now intricately ramified apparatus.

From the viewpoint of psychological investigation, handwriting offers itself to two different and distinctly separate ends. One is its utilization for psychodiagnostic purposes, the other for purposes of identification. Although materially overlapping with our subject in some areas of inquiry, the latter aim does not enter the scope of the present study, which is confined to graphology proper, i.e., the psychological analysis of handwriting for the purpose of exploring and describing personality.

At present, in pursuing their objective thus defined, graphologists can be grouped according to three divergent types of thinking and approach. One is a merely intuitive and impressionistic attempt, in the face of a given handwriting sample and by means of an empathy operating upon the visual experience of its total expressive qualities, to identify oneself with the originator and thereby gain insight into his character. While the attitude of an alert yet detached attentiveness for whole properties of visual pattern implied in such procedure is proving indispensable for graphological success with any method, the purely intuitive approach, since it does not involve any systematic controls, is subjectivistic to a degree of possible arbitrariness; it is, therefore, to say the least, unreliable.

A second approach, more recently proposed, leans heavily on the statistical method, not as a device for the ultimate validation of graphological personality pictures but as a participant factor in building up the graphoanalytic system itself. To test it, the concept of correlations between certain psychological trends and traits of handwriting is subjected to a statistical analysis of the group occurrences of quantitative reinforcements and reductions of such traits, and the results are then matched against such social, psychological, and clinical indicators as apply to the same groups. This approach, thus far, has been applied little in a practical sense. For reasons to be discussed in the methodological part of this study, it is believed to be no more adequate than the first-mentioned approach.

The third method—the one here to be expounded—is the fruit of many decades of a systematic study in handwriting analysis which in Europe was conducted by Ludwig Klages and by some of his followers, as well as more immediate predecessors. This study, as distinguished from the graphological dilettantism prior to their time, had been based on an investigation of expressive movements at large. What are expressive movements? To understand the achievements of Klages, we must cast a first glance at this most fundamental and most vital concept.

In a larger sense, all movements carried out by any organism at any time or place can be said to be expressive for the simple reason that their particular manner of execution, even if the purpose and environmental circumstances of the movement are "constant," varies not only from individual organism to individual organism but, within the scope of activity of a single organism, varies from one occurrence of the movement to any other. As no mathematically exact, automatic repetition of the same movement on the part of any organism is biologically possible, the element of uniqueness in every movement cannot be attributed to either the purpose or environmental circumstances of the movement but only to a structural principle within the organism which expresses itself in this very uniqueness. To the extent to which the movements of one organism, in comparison with the movements of any other organism, are altogether unique—to the extent to which they are bound together by analogies of structural characteristics—this global uniqueness on their part reflects the organism's individuality as a whole; to the extent to which the movements of the organism differ among each other, the uniqueness of every one of them reflects a particular state of the organism within the total temporal range of its individuality. The more distinct this temporal state, i.e., the more articulate the expressiveness of the movement, the more easily will it be understood by others observing it: for example, the facial expression of fright conveys the experience of fright with such persuasiveness that there can be no doubt about its meaning. This persuasiveness cannot be explained by previous experiences on the part of the observer with facial expressions of fright, since it follows from the axiom of uniqueness of every expressive movement that no such previous experiences, in a strict sense, can have occurred; associations with previous experiences of facial expressions of fright on the part of the observer, therefore, can be made only subsequently, on the basis of similarity; similarities, in turn, cannot be seen unless the things similar have actually been "seen" first, i.e., have been experienced in their wholeness and uniqueness without which no basis for spontaneous associations with previous experience can consequently exist.

   This requires the assumption that the element of expressiveness, i.e., of meaning, in organismic movements is a central, unifying factor which "organizes" the movement as the whole which is experienced by the observer, and that the observer is enabled to have this experience by the presence in him of a central unifying principle potentially corresponding to the one—"isomorphic" to it—that organizes the movement. This assumption, one of the basic tenets of Gestalt psychology, underlies the graphological method presented in this book as it underlies the theory of expressive movements altogether. The example that was chosen to illustrate it has purposely been a very plain one: the facial expression of fright is something that everyone in everyday life understands for what it is without having had to study expressive movements for the purpose. Understanding the meaning of a specific individual "gesture" in the handwriting of a person is exactly in the same order of experiences as the example that was given. The difference between the two is one in grade, not in principle: in order to be able to assess graphic movement psychologically, a higher degree of sensitivity for visual patterns than we may need in everyday life is required. The second requirement—the necessity for orderly thinking, for the purpose of organizing one's observations and utilizing them with the greatest possible profit—does not distinguish graphology from any other enterprise of science.

Yet, while scientific graphology unquestionably owes its existence to Klages, he himself is indebted to a line of predecessors which over nearly fifty years reaches back into the Nineteenth Century. Apart from such isolated hints as spontaneous descriptions of handwriting as characteristic of a certain personality which are scattered through the centuries and all national literatures, graphology as a systematic study came into being when Jean Hippolyte Michon in 1875 published his *Système de Graphologie*, which was the result of a decade-long comparative study based on letters Michon had received and on his personal acquaintance with their writers.

What Michon—followed by his more systematic but less talented disciple, Crépieux-Jamin—founded, was the so-called graphology of signs which after the time of these two Frenchmen degenerated into the kind of graphology still practiced today by many amateurs and charlatans in the field, although it may be said that the more typically amateurish approach at the present time appears to have become an inconsistent admixture of the "graphology of signs" with the wholly unsystematic attack on handwriting described in this chapter. To Michon, certain isolated hooks, loops, crossings, etc., represent definite qualities of character, and the character itself he believed to be the sum total of these. Due to his considerable personal powers of observation and combination, Michon's findings are not to be underrated, but his "système," once it was out of his hands, proved inadequate to such an extent that it caused the general view which disparages the psychological study of handwriting as necessarily unscientific—a view which up to the present time has essentially endured in this country. Its much earlier breakdown in Europe was due both to the considerable work of refinement and systematization achieved by the leading experts in the field and to new schools of thought which in Europe around the time of the first World War assumed a leading role in academic psychology itself.

Stimulated by Michon's findings, this development primarily took place in Germany, where Langenbruch, Busse, Erlenmeyer, and Preyer became its most influential promoters. Preyer's *Psychology of Handwriting* in 1895, despite its title, still presented no advancement in the psychological concepts but for the first time undertook a methodic analysis of the qualities and components of graphic movement. From then on, stimulated by graphological periodicals which were founded in Germany, the development grew faster. George Meyer's *Scientific Foundations of Graphology*, like most of the works here mentioned untranslated into English, was the first approach to handwriting analysis by a professional psychologist. Meyer's book is extremely conservative and more concerned with demonstrating the theoretical possibility of developing a scientific graphology than with actually doing so; he removes the naive specificity of Michon's interpretations, replaces them by more general concepts, but then fails to show the way to that critical specificity which after him was achieved by the philosopher and psychologist, Ludwig Klages.

All present day graphology with any claim to serving as a psychological instrument is indebted to Klages, who was the first one to formulate a general theory of expression. His main graphological works—*The Problems of Graphology*, 1910, *Handwriting and Character* (the most important one), 1917, *Expressive Movements and Creativity*, 1923, *The Foundations of Characterology*, 1928, and *Graphological Exercises*, 1930—not only stimulated many professional psychologists to take up handwriting research but achieved college status for graphology and prompted schools, clinics, guidance bureaus, business firms, and courts to seek graphological assistance for their varied purposes. Apart from Klages, most of the more outstanding modern work was done by Richard Saudek, whose works, with the exception of a treatise on American handwriting, were translated into English; by Max Pulver—*The Symbolism of Handwriting*, 1931, *Instinctual and Criminal Urges in Handwriting*, 1934, both untranslated—who introduced concepts of analytic derivation into the field; by Minna Becker who wrote an excellent book on children's handwriting in 1926; by Roda Wieser who also wrote on the graphic products of criminals; and by Johannes Walther who particularly excelled in the analysis of forms of binding. In this country, Zubin's and Hein-

Lewinson's monograph, which blueprinted the statistical analysis of single graphic traits mentioned before in this chapter, and Werner Wolff's more analytically influenced works have, in various fashions, taken up leads provided by the school of Klages.

At the present time, the influence of the Klages school still permeates the entire realm of graphological work and research. To a considerable extent, this not only may account for the merits of most of the works here mentioned but at the same time may explain their shortcomings. The growing influence which the Gestalt school has exercised on European psychology in the last twenty years paved the way for an understanding acceptance of graphology on the part of colleges and universities, but Klages, although near to that school in some aspects of his thinking, was too far from it in others to be able to develop his theory beyond certain limits. These limits, which derive mainly from his—highly dogmatic—philosophic theory of consciousness as a necessarily disturbing factor in the interplay of the forces of life in man, led to a simplification of his concept of graphic rhythm gross enough to disable him from understanding the basic difference between integrated and disintegrated states of personality as reflected in handwriting. His graphological system, in consequence, proved sufficiently inadequate for psychodiagnostic purposes to necessitate a revision of some of his most vital—but also most distorted—concepts by the author. In the present book, this revision has been formulated in the chapter on rhythm and regularity, integration and fluctuation. It has been put into operation both in the systematic part, which undertakes to rebuild the structure of the rating dimensions, and in the clinical chapters, which, while offering preliminary findings, are the fruits of many years of observation and experience in the field.

THE PROBLEMS OF PERSONALITY PSYCHOLOGY AND THE THEORY OF EXPRESSIVE MOVEMENTS

The significance of all expressive movements as relevant indicators of character has been touched upon before in our discussion. Viewed in some of its specific aspects, the concept of the "isomorphisms," or analogies of system properties, implies the existence of lawful, meaningful, and inevitable connections between a person's psychological makeup and forms of behavior; these connections would seem to ascribe to the behavioral forms a morphologic and aesthetic unity closely similar not only to the unity of form in individual organisms, but also of "style" in artistic creations, of "patterns" of thought and culture in social and ethnological entities and of many other "physiognomic" phenomena related to these realms. Personality, according to this concept, functions as a configurational whole which is extended in the dimension of time but in which the parts are primarily not determined by their succession in time (causative determination) nor by any other direct mutual relations between any two of them; rather is there continuous operation of an underlying common principle of system action to which the individual facts of behavior (in both its physiological and psychological aspects) can be traced and to which they must be traced in order to be understood. A principle of system action, such as that governing the organismic total process, is not an aggregate of several two-factor relations but represents a fundamentally different logical category: in two-factor relations and their aggregates, the relata are independent, each of them, of the dimension of their distribution; in systems the component parts are whatever their positions in the system determine them to be; their dimension of distribution thereby itself becomes constituent to the system. While two-factor relations and their aggregates do occur in organismic functioning, they never involve the entire organism; rather are they to be understood as special and most simplified manifestations of a principle of system action which is relatively independent of the principle of system action governing the organismic total process and is restricted to its temporal dimension. Regarding this process as a whole and following Andras Angyal (*Foundations for a Science of Personality*), who has been most instrumental in developing these categories, three main dimensions of personality functioning can be distinguished.

1. A dimension of progression in which personality functions are determined according to the law of finality underlying their temporal order in the conscious pursuit of goals.

2. A dimension of depth in which personality functions are determined according to the unconscious organismic needs they correspond to.

3. A transverse dimension in which personality functions are determined according to their order of mutual coordination.

In terms of expressive movements, the dimension of progression is represented by the degree of consistency of effort and direction; the dimension of depth by the degree of impulse release; the transverse dimension by the degree of rhythmical integration. Both impulse release and rhythmical integration are functions the operations of which tend to escape the person's conscious control; consistency of effort and direction does this to a lesser extent but can be consciously manipulated only at the expense of impulse release and rhythmical integration, a fact which allows of an easy detection of any such manipulation. Expressive movements, in other words, are the more revealing and actually the more expressive the less conscious an individual is of their expressive qualities as he is executing them. It is primarily for this reason that handwriting is a system of expressive movements of particular psychological value: the writer, while being aware of the school pattern which he uses and while consciously focusing on the contents he wishes to convey by his writing, is hardly aware of the way in which he individually modifies the pattern and, in general, not at all of what such modification may imply. Whatever dim awareness he may have of "his" handwriting diminishes to the degree to which the contents of his writing occupy his thoughts and generate and absorb his emotional impulses.

One of the most fundamental laws of expression appears to be postulated by this particular nature of the impulses of movement: their potency to "impel," both in terms of impact and directional consistency, increases and decreases reciprocally to the introspective attention which the consciousness of the writer—left unabsorbed, to the extent of that attention, by his external pursuits—is giving them and is thereby diverting from its proper—spontaneity-generating—goals. This is the reason why, among types of handwriting samples, letters and manuscripts are generally preferable for psychological analysis to copies of given texts and—even more so—to any specimens produced with the awareness of subsequent graphological exploration.

Regarding the goals *spontaneously* aspired for in expressive movements, the goal of expression, of which the organism is unaware to the extent of the aspiration, in turn ought to be differentiated from the conscious purpose of the movement. In handwriting, this conscious purpose is determined by the task of performing, graphically, certain letters, words, sentences, and whole texts; the goal of expression, by the writer's inner experience as he is carrying out this task. It follows that, in expressive movements, in terms of total organismic experience, goals of the following two general categories appear to be simultaneously in operation: (1) the *purposive* goal of the movement, determining the aspect of behavior within the progressive dimension of personality; (2) the *expressive* goal of the movement, determining the aspect of behavior within the depth dimension of personality.

In addition to these, a third general category of aspiration, only potentially operative, can be constituted by impulse impediment brought about by diversion of conscious attention towards the self. In accordance with the law of expression above stated, it seems to result from a conflict between the purposive and expressive goals of the activity and to affect personality functioning in its transverse dimension, the dimension of coordination.

In order to illustrate the dichotomy of purposive and expressive goals, daily life examples of movements strongly dominated by either one of these at the expense of the others may be useful. The highly mechanized movements of a worker employed on an assembly line are determined by purposive goals to an extent of rendering their expressive goal-directedness certainly negligible although not by any means nonexistent; the spontaneous gesture of horror, warding off from his face a danger not actually involving his person, by which he reacts to the sight of an accident incurred by another worker at a distance, is determined by his inner experience to an extent of rendering its purposive goal-directedness at least as negligible.

While, in either case, the dominance of one type of goal-directedness is found at an extreme, most of the activities of daily life are far more balanced in regard to the purposive and expressive goals they serve. In accordance with this situation, one of the major practical advantages for psychological analysis offered by graphic movement consists of its combined and fairly equal allowance for goals of both general categories. Apart from its relatively close analogy to the dominant structure of most life situations, this also seems to facilitate an ample and well-ordered supply of psychological indicators. Quite in distinction from other expressive movements, handwriting presents the observer with a fixed record, a handy and readily available trail of such movements, whereas a study of gait, for example, in order to be conducted systematically, would require rather extensive cinematographic recordings.

HOW OBJECTIVE IS GRAPHOLOGY?

All science, regardless of its subject matter, has developed on an original basis of systematization of everyday empiric knowledge. The graphological method, pursuing, within a particular domain, the common human activity of recognizing, classifying and interpreting behavior, makes no exception to this rule. The layman in graphology will hardly have a feeling of unduly committing himself by calling an extremely disorderly handwriting disorderly, nor an extremely regulated one orderly, but he may be inclined to call farther reaching statements speculative, thereby uncritically defining the limits of his own sensitivity for expressive properties as the dividing line between objectivity and subjectivity.

Yet, while this attitude explains the frequency with which graphology has been indicted of "subjectivism," it does not answer the question how "valid" the graphological method actually is; and the reproach that graphologists are simply not sufficiently concerned with the task of objectification has often been made. In view of this criticism, it may be useful to point to the work of validation already done and to explore the question of how experimental settings for further validation and group research, in order to be meaningful, should be constructed. In this country, the experiment in 1919 conducted by Hull and Montgomery, which turned out disastrously (if not for graphology, for whatever was probed in this experiment), is frequently referred to by opponents of the method. It was, however, unscientific from the viewpoints of graphological and experimental theory alike. The method tested by Hull and Montgomery dealt with the upward and downward alignments of words, the widths of little m's and n's, and the lengths of t-bars, all thought possibly to correspond to certain definite traits of character and their individual variations, but this was still Michon's graphology of signs which at that time, eighteen years after the publication of Meyer's work, nine and two years, respectively, after Klages' first publications, was already outdated. The experimental setting, objectively not less questionable, was a college fraternity, a close-knit unit of students largely homogeneous in their attitudes, backgrounds, and standards of value, all untrained in the role they were to assume in this experiment, which was to rate each other's character on some of those traits assumed to correspond (always one trait to one characteristic of writing) to the graphic marks which

Hull and Montgomery selected and which they undertook to measure quantitatively. Inadequate on both its graphological and experimental sides, the undertaking could not be expected to yield results any more meaningful than was the method by which it approached its objectives.

Single experiments in blind graphological diagnosis, testing out trained workers of the Klages, Pulver, and Saudek schools, have frequently been conducted in Europe. The results in a large majority of instances matched, and in many cases completed, the available social and clinical evidence so highly that at least in regard to the validity, if not the reliability, of the method the original skepticism of the investigators was greatly reduced; it was felt that on a basis of pure chance an infinite number of possible personality descriptions could result from experiments with handwritten copies of standard texts in which only the age and sex of the writer, but nothing else, was given; and that, in consequence, highly specific personality descriptions, agreeing, in their very specificity, with the social and clinical picture and arrived at independently by different workers using the same method of approach, could leave no doubt that this method was valid. However, the need for securing a fair degree of reliability also was felt as the method developed, and it led to the many objectification experiments which, in Germany, were undertaken mostly by the Institute for Industrial Psychotechnics and, in this country, were reported by Allport and Vernon in their book on expressive movements. The experimental setting here was provided in most cases by the work ratings of individual employees according to their employers' judgments on the one hand, graphological ratings of their corresponding qualities (such as honesty, reliability, efficiency) on the other. The correlations arrived at by the use of point scales were all highly above chance, most strikingly so on those experiments which involved graphological ratings by Saudek, Couvé, von Kuegelgen, and particularly by Seesemann, whose graphological ratings of employees showed a 93 per cent correlation with the judgments of employers.

But successful objectification experiments involving graphology were by no means limited to Europe. Mention may be made here of Ruth Munroe's "Three Projective Methods Applied to Sally" and "A Comparison of Three Projective Methods" (the latter with Stein-Lewinson and Schmidl-Waehner) which, with very encouraging results, undertook comparative studies of "blind" personality descriptions derived, independently of each other, from the Rorschach method, Waehner's art technique, and graphology.

While all these results can be considered as first steps on the road toward a global objectification of the method rather than as conclusive evidence of its reliability, they are believed to be highly encouraging, considering the complexity not so much of the method itself as of its subject matter, personality. The fundamental problem of the attainment of objective criteria against which personality descriptions—on the basis of graphology as of any other technique—can be meaningfully checked grows even more intricate when the relatively simple situation presented by ratings of personality on certain traits of social functioning which lend themselves to point scales is left behind, and we enter the field, clinically of far greater interest, of total personality assessments graphologically derived. In order to establish a correct frame of reference for objectifying such assessments, we must know first what general order of phenomena they describe, since only this knowledge will enable us to look for the corresponding order of phenomena in reality.

Preceding the systematic analysis of the sample in the various dimensions of rating which are being applied to it, the examiner focuses upon the sample as a whole, totally eliminating its contents from the field of observation and allowing the latter to turn into a pattern of movement trails. In the passive yet attentive visual experience of this pattern, the specific social functions of writing have ceased to play any role for the observer, and any intellectual activity on his own part has as yet not started to function. In this phase of the investigation, and by virtue of it, the examiner not only can gain an overall impression of the sample but can allow single or recurrent characteristics to catch his attention; and the same holistic view is again taken at the end of the investigation where it serves the restoration of a proper total frame of reference into which the various data of observation can be fitted, which determines their relative characterological significance—their "position" in the personality system—and which may have become lost in the process of concentrating upon single graphic details and areas of rating. The phenomenon here approached is clearly not one or the other "trait" but personality as a functional unit; hence, only personality as a functional unit can be the proper objective criterion against which to check graphological findings. This does not exclude the graphological examination of personality concerning specific lines of social functioning (the European experiments above referred to were all centered around examinations of this type) but it does exclude any direct and isolated graphological judgment on single "traits": judgments of this kind must be inferred from the whole personality structure and must not be based on singled-out qualities of handwriting interpreted outside of their given texture.

It follows that quantification procedures in graphology (possibly not in graphology only), in order not entirely to miss their points, ought to be carried out on the level of entire personality evaluations (or specific statements inferred from them) rather than on the level of any specific interpretative assumptions: the latter, in their individual application, are always tentative, always implying a certain range of characterological meaning. The extreme positions within their range, in terms of social and moral value, can be diametrically opposed to one another, and the fixation of definite traits of personality grossly indicated by any one dimension of rating is always arrived at by taking into account no less than the entire configuration of indicators within and beyond that particular dimension. All other procedures are necessarily atomistic and are not objective, insofar as they dogmatically tend to dictate the conditions under which their objects of investigation shall surrender to scientific cognition, instead of letting these conditions be determined by the nature of the phenomena to be investigated. In a functional whole, the component parts have no significance apart from their position within that system of functioning. When a melody is transposed into another key, not a single note in it retains its identity; the melody, however, does. In the same way, entirely different concepts of "traits" in terms of social behavior, even though their potential scope is significantly limited by the personality structure itself, may apply to the same individual in different life situations and from different angles of external observation; it requires the picture of the entire structure to recognize its identity.

This means that quantification of single graphic traits may here and there be meaningful for purposes of procedure, in order to assist the investigator in orienting himself to his field of observation, but it would be utterly arbitrary as a basis for direct psychological interpretation and for comparative statistical studies based thereon. This is confirmed by the inner situation of grapho-analytical work itself, and an example may illustrate it. "Pressure" in handwriting is understood generally to indicate concentrated energy for work and goal-directed pursuits, available roughly to the degree of the pressure. The atomistic method of investigating this assumption would set up a scale for the quantitative measurement of pressure, apply it to handwriting samples, tentatively interpret the degrees of pressure as degrees of externally available energy, check the interpretation against social and clinical evidence, and expose itself to considerable surprises: beyond a certain point of intensity, the trend of psychological meaning for "pressure" reverses itself, indicating, at the rate of its further reinforcement, the presence of inhibitory internal rather than challenging external obstacles to be overcome by such display of force. The exact location of the point of reversal on the scale of degrees of intensity is, in turn, variable and dependent upon the individual configuration. The situation is further complicated by the fact that the pressure present in the sample may or may not be displaced into movements normally calling for motoric release and that other qualities may modify the interpretative basis for it in a virtually infinite number of possible ways which totally escape orderly quantification and in order to be understood must be traced to the common principle of system action underlying them. For while of course it is possible to circumscribe in theoretical terms the overall meaning of a graphic quality like a certain degree of pressure independently of indicators modifying and specifying it, the resulting concept would be far too general and characterologically embracing to correspond with any positive and differential qualities of personality behaviorally observable, and would therefore not lend itself to validation experiments involving such observation. Apart from the necessity of conducting experiments of this kind on a basis of total personality pictures only, it follows that graphological work, to be conducted systematically, must organize its observations by qualitative classification of expressive properties, and that neither eye training for such properties nor a critical balancing-out of their interpretative values can be replaced by mechanical measurements of single quantitative aspects.

The objectivity of any method of investigation, ultimately, depends upon the nature of its object. Personality not only is not an aggregate of quantifiable traits of behavior; it differs from the objects of physical science also by its far closer interweaving into the investigator's own existence, thereby causing it to be experienced by him in ways fundamentally different from those in which he perceives any objects of physical science. As, inevitably, value judgments already enter the cognition of his object sphere on the perceptual level, the concept of the object itself, personality, is much less firmly established, in proportion to any testing methods devised in its regard, than the concept of physical forces or chemical elements is in proportion to testing methods devised for their measurement. A concept of personality which would be independent of human standards of value—which may vary greatly from interpreter to interpreter—does not exist. Many differences among personality pictures arrived at by psychological methods applied to one and the same case by different examiners are due neither to an inadequacy or inaccuracy of the methods used nor to different ways of using them but to different standards of value causing differences of the interpretative focus.

Insistence upon quantification of single graphic traits, rather than removing this difficulty, would remove the given context in which alone these traits have any meaning. As a validation procedure required from the view point of alleged scientific objectivity and aiming at comparative studies of such "quantified" traits, it would imply a contention that phenomena constituting individualities in a strict sense cannot be subject to scientific cognition. This would be an uncritical extension of the metaphysical position of Positivism to subject matters tending to cast a shadow of doubt on that position rather than an argument speaking in the voice of experience. Not only the personalistic psychologies but any studies dealing with the morphologic, aesthetic, "topographic," and historic dimensions of reality and proceeding by way of concepts adequate to the nature of the—always "unique"—phenomena observable within these dimensions would thereby be declared invalid. If we try to analyze what, in our direct experience, makes up our concept of the "personality" of someone we know, we find the principle linking all the elements entering into it provided by a certain qualitatively unified way of his own confined exclusively to his person and answering a "how" rather than "what" type of question. The subject matter itself, personality, then, as a psychological and not as a social category, can only be defined on the basis of this quality of the "individual gesture" which is exactly the one the analysis of expressive movements sets out to investigate.

The problems of validation of findings arranged in the form of total personality pictures, or of specific inferences from them, are therefore the same in graphology as in any of the currently so prominent projective techniques. The Rorschach, from a strictly statistical viewpoint, has not been sufficiently validated either, but neither has the statistically oriented school of psychology been able to provide sufficiently objective criteria of validity in this realm. However inconclusive, from a viewpoint stressing mechanical reliability as a criterion of evaluation of psychological techniques, the adherents of this school who deny the existence of relationships between personality and handwriting may judge the recorded experimental successes with the graphological method, they have failed to explain these successes which so poignantly contradict their denial. The frequent claim that successes of this kind are due to a special "intuitive talent" of the graphologist not only is inconsistent with the basic tenets of the "objectivistic" school but is a masterpiece of uncritical thinking. If, in a controlled experiment in which the investigator had access to nothing but a sample of handwriting of strictly noncommittal content, he is able successfully to describe the psychological makeup of the originator of that sample, his "talent," regardless of how we define it, is bound to operate on the exclusive basis of the subject's handwriting; whatever accurate and specific findings, therefore, he is able to make in regard to that subject, must, in some way, in the situation here depicted, have been contained in the handwriting sample, and in nothing besides.

The academic "resistance" to graphology, therefore,, considering the strength which it has shown in the past, is likely to find its chief explanation in less rational motives than have been cited explicitly by opponents of the method. In the author's opinion, one of the most obvious among these motives is the typical scientists's comparative lack of specific aptitude for the adequate perception of pattern qualities which the typical student of art and aesthetics has no difficulty in recognizing in all their distinctness; rationalizing for this deficiency, the scientist is easily tempted to ascribe the "vagueness" of his own experience of such qualities to the experience object. A second presumable motive operating behind the "resistance" to graphology, however, and one which may be more serious in the long run, is the widespread tendency in our time to popularize and "simplify" psychological methods to an extent which is incompatible with their nature and which no chemist or physicist would tolerate in his realm. As a tendency on the part of graphologists and pseudo-graphologists themselves, this has accounted in the past for the scores of irresponsible approaches to the subject which have caused so much damage to its reputation; but the strange fact exists that, once the "objectivist" investigates this subject with some apparent good will, he usually nurtures that same tendency by trying to adapt graphology to his own ways and level of psychological understanding. Nor is this attitude necessarily restricted to the "objectivistic" school. The craving for short-cuts, which is already making itself felt in recent forms of Rorschach teaching and related propagations of knowledge, is necessarily at odds with the intricate thought processes required in the systematic analysis of handwriting. True, owing to the easy procurement of the materials for inquiry, graphology's considerable economic advantage over most of the current psychodiagnostic methods is obvious; but while, on the whole, it takes far less time to do a graphoanalysis than it takes to do a Rorschach, the grapho-analysis requires a much higher effort in terms of perceptual and intellectual concentration. This brings it in conflict with a mentality which, in the sense of the old graphology of "signs" and of the summative procedures in present day psychological testing, wants "lists of diagnostic indicators," where every graphic trait has its allegedly definite significance, where trait names can simply be checked off and where intellectual effort is avoided as much as possible. If the graphologist gives in to this mentality—inconsistent with the principles of his method as with the nature of personality itself—he is lost; he has allowed the "objectivist" to denaturalize graphology and turn it into a bogey, and he must not be amazed if then this bogey, in experiments like Hull's and Montgomery's, is all too easily knocked down.

How, in view of this situation, can graphological findings be objectified conclusively? We have seen already that no validation can be meaningful unless it is undertaken on the basis of whole personality descriptions or of single statements inferred from such descriptions, but the question of the "valid criterion" remains yet to be answered. In the author's opinion, and in accordance with his whole preceding argument, the only possible criterion of indisputable relevance for the objectification of personality descriptions is the recognizability of the described subject's identity by persons who know him well. The only sound solution, then, appears to be matching experiments, in which a group of personality descriptions derived on the basis of "blind" graphological analysis are plotted against the group of the subjects described and in which the "judges"—who have to be thoroughly acquainted with the personality of each of them—are asked to determine the identity of the subject of each of these descriptions.

Such matching experiments can and should be tightly controlled. They can and should be subjected to the most rigorous statistical analysis. Yet, in order also to answer the question of the reliability of the method as such—i.e., independently of the individual graphological worker—such experiments would have to involve a larger number of psychologists thoroughly trained in the graphological method. At the present time, no such group appears to exist in this country. That the day may not be distant when it will not only exist but when its skills—in education, in social work, in vocational guidance, and, most of all, in psychiatry and clinical psychology—will finally have proved themselves beyond doubt is the author's hope and confident expectation.

II. THE GRAPHOLOGICAL METHOD

BASIC CONCEPTS

The Total Motoric Aspect: Contraction and Release

The writing movement is continuous only in terms of the dependence of each of its components on an overall purpose; it is discontinuous in terms both of the direction of movement and of the speed with which it proceeds. The former is obvious from the necessity of producing the directionally complex forms of letters; the latter from the necessity of separating words. Both necessities affect the continuous release of motor energy not only by way of their own direct requirements for discontinuity, but also by way of the organism's inability to meet these requirements to exactly the extent implied in them: the directional complexity of letters, apart from making it more difficult to maintain an overall continuity of direction than a simple horizontal movement would, involves centrifugal as well as centripetal movement components which, in being carried out, tend to surpass their directional complexity as intended by the school pattern; the dynamic complexity of word separation involves the necessities not only of stopping and starting again but also of slowing down and speeding up again; finally, the directional discontinuity tends to enhance the dynamic one for the very same reason of the involvement of centrifugal and centripetal components and of the necessity to control them. The writing activity, being discontinuous, is differentiated by the alternation of contraction and release of the finger muscles participant in it, an alternation which is necessitated by the varying requirements of direction and speed.

The first and most general dichotomy of all components of the graphic movement, then, divides them into movements of contraction and movements of release, and, with the single exception of the level of form quality, there is no graphic characteristic within any of the dimensions of rating which cannot be classified in either of both groups. Since the total direction of movement in all occidental handwriting systems is a horizontal one, the principle of differentiation applying to it can be expected to operate in a vertical direction and to manifest itself most plainly in those movements making up the structural skeleton of all handwriting, the upstrokes and downstrokes: in normal handwriting unaffected by emotional blockings, the former represent the most basic movements of release, the latter of contraction. Psychologically, emphasis on contraction relates to ego emphasis with its possible implications of relative increases in volitional, emotional, and concept control; emphasis on release relates to object emphasis with its possible implications of relative increases in spontaneity, impulsivity, and fantasy life. Differential determination of lines of emphasis as indicated by increased contraction or release depends primarily on the dimension of rating within which these increases are encountered; a classification of dimensional ratings according to their positions on the sides of either contraction or release, as it presupposes a discussion of the rating dimensions themselves, will follow later in this book.

The Total Symbolic Aspect: The Quasi-Spatial Experience of the Writing Field

Handwriting, from the viewpoint of reality, lies in a two-dimensional plane, penetrating the third dimension only insignificantly and in such a way that the penetration does not essentially partake in its visual appearance. From the viewpoint of direct experience on the part of both the writer and reader, however, handwriting is a spatial phenomenon. This is not meant in any figurative but in a literal sense. The writing field is experienced in such a way as to convert it into a projection of space on a two-dimensional plane very similar to the space projections in paintings and drawings: we speak of slanting or perpendicular handwriting, of falling lines, of spacious loops, of "space" that is left for marginal notes, of upstrokes and downstrokes, even though these strokes, with the usual position of the writing paper, are in reality not performed upward and downward but away and toward the body; finally, the qualities of the stroke itself particularly tend to create an illusion of depth, and the word "body" as a whole is being experienced as distinctly and plastically set off against its white "back" ground: to our immediate experience of it, the handwriting is *elevated* above the paper, it is seen as standing in space; it "makes room," the room which surrounds it, and thus its quasi-spatial nature is reflected in the spontaneous terms commonly applied to its movements.

This situation implies the projection into graphic movement of a realm of inner experience within which the projector orients himself in unconscious symbolic analogy to his orientation in space, this orientation, in turn, following the same directions of space-analogous symbols as more or less all conceptual thinking does. Were we but to mention the common verbal concepts employing—by virtue of an immediate inner experience which repeats itself in all individuals using such terms and without any conscious figurative intent on their part—the analogy of vertical directions, their number would seem endless in no matter what language, and examples like "rising in someone's esteem" or "feeling low," "superimposed" or "subliminal," may suffice at this point, since any reader will find it easier to continue than to terminate the series. Symbolically, then, if we imagine handwriting to be divided by a system of coordinates with the writing line as abscissa, all movements falling below this line are to be thought of as related to such experiences as in the writer's own system of inner orientation implies the general concept of "below," all movements falling above this line as related to such experiences as imply the general concept of "above." The latter rule, however, requires some qualification: since the mass of the interconnected horizontal movement itself consisting of the short letters and those parts of the long letters corresponding with the vertical extension of the short letters does not fall evenly on both sides of the writing line but on its upper side only, "above" is meant to designate all movements rising above the upper edge of these short forms. The latter constitute the so-called "middle zone" of the handwriting; those movements falling above or below it, the "upper" and "lower" zones, respectively. In the symbolic thinking underlying, without known exceptions, all human cultures, experiences related to the static concept of "above" or the dynamic one of "upward" are all those implying the concepts of God, heaven, day, the light, the spirit, freedom from gravity, from physical bounds, the world of ideas, of forms, of individual perfection, consciousness; experiences related to the static concept of "below" or the dynamic one of "downward" are those implying the concepts of animal, earth, the dark, the demonic, night, matter, gravity, the flesh, the world of collective and vegetative forces of life, of instincts, of the formless, and of dreams; in the paternalistic cultures, furthermore, the concepts of "father" and "man" are experienced as related to the first, those of "mother" and "woman" as related to the second of these groups. Relative emphasis on either of the two peripheral zones of handwriting accordingly is an evidence of the relative emphasis, in terms of inner orientation and attitude, on the corresponding sphere of experiences; while relative emphasis on the middle zone, since its represents the zone of actual and contiguous graphic progression, evidences relative emphasis on activity per se, in distinction from any primarily "experiencing" inner attitudes. An elaboration of these statements, in terms of both the possible modes of movement distribution and of their psychological interpretations, again requires a discussion of the corresponding dimensions of rating.

While the vertical dimension of handwriting thus relates to the person's self-orientation to available values, the horizontal dimension relates to his orientation to reality, which involves the choice of objectives and behavior in their regard, in brief, the processes of externalization. In the western cultures, writing as a total activity is rightward directed, and this modality seems to accord with the emphasis on purposeful and goal-directed activity, in brief, on the *future*—a fact which, in distinction from the oriental cultures using directionally different systems of writing, is characteristic of the occident. Presupposing the use of the right hand—the special criteria applying to the left-handed will be discussed separately—any movement of the arm-hand system swinging away from the body in a natural and unstrained manner necessitates the following of a rightward direction which graphologically is therefore identified as the direction of contact

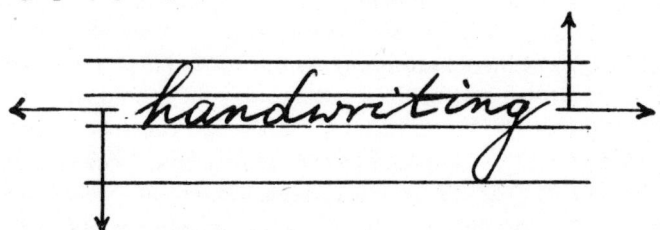

FIG. 1 (7%).* The writing field and its directions

and of externalization per se, while emphasis on leftward movement is interpreted as significant of contact avoidance and of concentration, in whatever manner and aim, upon the self. Furthermore, since the actual progress in time of the writing activity follows its spatial progression towards the right, the right side is identified as a symbolic correlate to

* Original samples reduced by % given in legends.

the concept of "future" in the writer's own inner experience; and emphasis on the past, again regardless of its manner and motivation, would correspondingly be indicated by an accentuation, in terms of the distribution of the writing movement, of leftward components. Further differential studies of graphic movement distribution, however, in its horizontal even more than in its vertical dimension, again presuppose an investigation of handwriting in a considerable number of more specific areas (fig. 1).

The Total Interpretative Aspect: Ambivalence and Interdependence of Indicators

The tentative nature of single indicators within any one dimension of writing has been pointed out in the foregoing. Their function could be defined as one of setting the limits beyond which their positive and specific value cannot be expected to fall. Their actual determination, however, depends upon the entire configuration. In the grapho-analytical procedure, this dependency becomes operative in a two-fold manner.

Since the psychological meaning conveyed by a single graphic quality such as "narrowness" covers a large number of simultaneous applications to specific lines of personality functioning, of which only a few and very general ones are viewed as invariably and all others as only potentially valid, positive conclusions in regard to potential applications can only result from a combination of the psychological tenor of "narrowness" with other indicators potentially applying to the same line of personality functioning. Indicators, in brief, are *interdependent*. They are *ambivalent*, inasmuch as each of them in turn implies the whole range, from extremely positive to extremely negative shades of meaning, of possible moral, social, and cultural values attached to each of such general concepts as "stubbornness" or "adaptability," "impulsivity" or "self-control." For example, the general personality characteristic of a "high self-esteem" would be differentiated into its possible versions of either "playful vanity" or "rigid conceit" by the principle of *interdependence;* it would be differentiated, in terms of the degree to which it is either "empty" or backed-up by actual personality value, by the principle of *ambivalence*. Fixation of the exact meaning in terms of personality value conveyed by either single or combined graphological indicators is dependent primarily upon the writer's sense of values as conveyed by the handwriting itself, i.e., on its *level of form quality*.

THE SAMPLE AS A WHOLE
THE LEVEL OF FORM QUALITY

The aesthetic quality of a given handwriting sample provides the frame of reference for the proper interpretation of all dimensional findings and is therefore one of the guiding criteria in graphological work. The concept has little to do with the calligraphic concepts of penmanship as promoted by handwriting teachers in accordance with the varying national school patterns: except for persons of low education or intellectual development and little opportunity of graphic communication, to whom attainment to the school pattern appears to remain a lifelong focus of attention, the school pattern in its exact sense is individually abandoned at the age of puberty at the latest, and the rate, the final extent, and the specific direction of that abandonment closely parallel the corresponding lines of the personality development itself.

The reasons for this abandonment, particularly for the very great extent of it observable in the handwritings of leading figures of the nineteenth century and of our time, may partly have to be sought in the modern school patterns themselves which, in comparison with those before approximately 1830, appear relatively unsatisfactory from an aesthetic viewpoint. This is also supported by the relatively far greater average closeness to the school patterns of their times apparent from the letters written by many outstanding persons of the centuries prior to the indicated approximate date, a fact which significantly coincides with the general breakdown of "style" in other areas of the culture. The difference in this respect between those times and our own is fairly marked and is too general to be accidental; it may reflect the greater security which the more stable values of past ages were able to afford the individual by allowing him a greater personal identification with the culture.

The criterion of form quality relates to the extent of genuine spiritual aspiration and self-demand attained in personality development; it denotes the degree of articulateness to which a value system has become integrated in the inner life of the person. In terms of graphic qualities, it can be defined as the relative degree of originality of form in combination with its relative degree of aesthetic balance. While it is readily admitted that, technically speaking, ratings in this area are of necessity subjective, caution is recommended in regard to conclusions from this fact.

While the laws of aesthetics, on account of the nature of the aesthetic situation itself, manifest themselves in the realm of personal experience only, nevertheless they do not apply to this realm but apply to that of the aesthetic objects; otherwise, no communication of aesthetic experiences, and no interpersonal consistency among them, would be conceivable. The correlations among personal choices of the aesthetically more or less balanced of a number of given objects are known to be high, and the same applies, as many experiments have shown, to laymen's judgments of levels of form quality in handwriting as compared with each other and with the judgments of graphologists. This, of course, applies mainly to the ratings of the grosser differences in quality, and it seems to apply somewhat more to judgments on aesthetic integration than on originality. Regarding the latter subcriterion, much again appears to depend on eye training and a sharpening of the general sense of quality; the function of final discrimination here involved does not, however, require any unduly extraordinary abilities; essentially, it is the same which, for example, would enable an observer to tell, without too much hesitation, a 1280 gothic or 1680 baroque church from their 1880 imitations.

A remaining margin of "subjectivity" in determining form levels may be disclosed by more minute variations in their point scale arrayals by different raters. The variations, however, reflect not the arbitrariness of personal selection but the nature of the object here investigated itself. With different tables of values, the phenomenon of personality lends itself to a variety of possible evaluations. Beyond a certain maximal point of interconsistency these evaluations may more or less widely diverge. Personality thus differs from the objects of physical science by the fact that beyond that maximal point the perspective of recognition becomes not merely a medium for the perception of objective properties but the frame of reference separated from which these properties have no meaning at all. The difference between the talents and temperaments of A and B can "objectively" be stated; any statement, however, about which of the two is the "better" man will of necessity by "subjective." This does not mean that it has to be in any way arbitrary, in any way meaningless from an epistemological viewpoint; it simply means that the criteria "good," "better," etc., *themselves* imply human values; any of their applications, therefore, is "objective" or "inobjective" only with respect to a given system of values, the presupposition of which underlies the statement. In the author's experience, this situation is easily demonstrable by more scrutinizing experiments with variations in point scale arrayals of graphic form levels carried out by different judges. If, after having—"blindly"— scaled the handwritings of subjects I to X, the same judge has an opportunity of personal acquaintance and conversation with the subjects themselves and then is asked to scale them on the basis of these "direct" approaches to their persons, his point scale arrangement, in almost all instances, will nearly coincide with his previous—graphological—one. Whatever variations there may be will on the whole be far smaller than the variations between his previous graphological arrayal of the ten samples and those graphological arrayals of the same ten samples carried out by other judges. This constellation strongly points towards the "objectivity" of the form level criterion in the only sense in which, in its regard, the concept of "objectivity" can be meaningful at all, i.e., with the individual judge's given system of values serving as the inevitable—the "objectively" irreplaceable—frame of reference. From this it follows that a more conscious and explicit awareness—if it could be attained—of their different standards of value on the part of different trained investigators could be expected to reduce areas of interpretative disagreement between them to a minimal and clinically insignificant point (figs. 2-15).

Rhythm and Regularity, Integration and Fluctuation

Like all life processes, the alternate phases of contraction and release do not follow each other with mechanical precision but in a more complex order of succession which results from the simultaneous operation of the two mutually opponent principles of repetition and of change: similar, not identical, intervals follow each other; their variations, in turn, show a tendency, more or less strong, to repeat themselves in equal intervals; this repetition is subjected to a counter-tendency causing it to occur in units of more or less fluctuating lengths; and so forth. This quality of the contraction-release cycles relates them to all phenomena which are articulated in the dimension of time by means of a structural order of themselves rather than by the mere imposition upon them of an abstract and static principle of time division. Reconciling the divergent principles of periodicity and fluctuation, this structural articulation is essentially identical with what in music is called "rhythm," in distinction from the "time" or "measure" of the music: the "measure," in itself only an

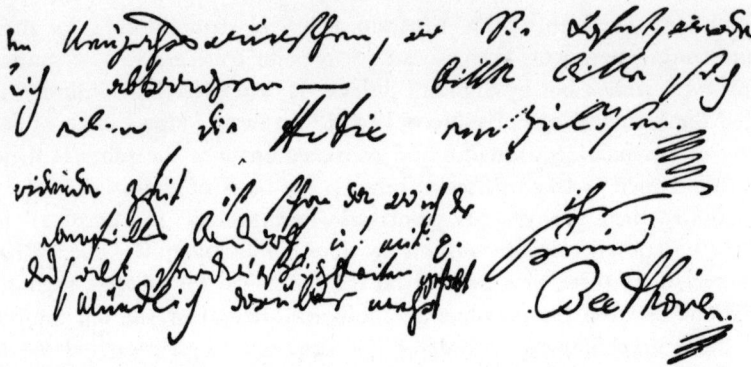

Fig. 2 (31%). Exceptional form level

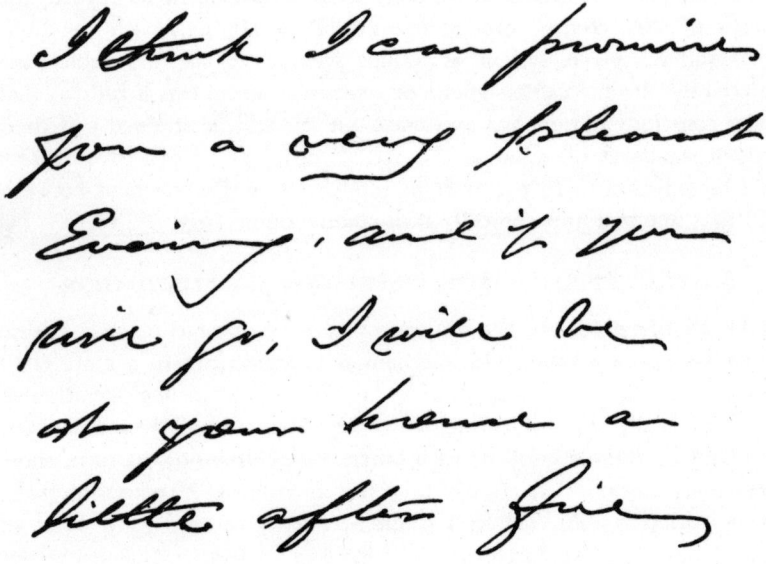

Fig. 3 (7%). Superior form level

Figs. 2-15. Levels of form quality

abstract and static principle, marking identical divisions of the temporal path along which a work of music proceeds, nevertheless corresponds with one of the two principles of rhythm, that of repetition; yet it is not

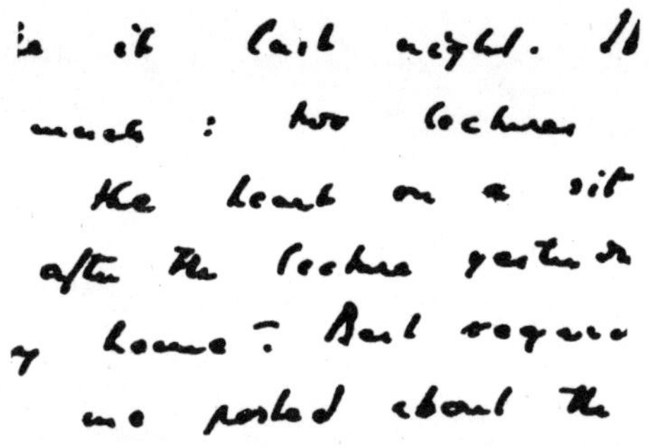

SAMPLE AS A WHOLE

[handwriting sample]

FIG. 4 (7%). Superior form level

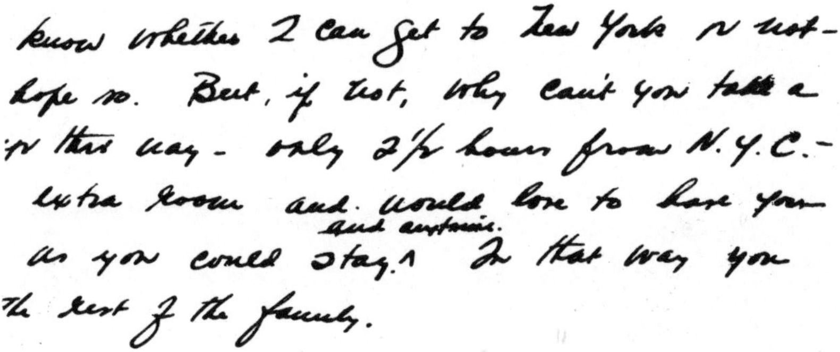

[handwriting sample]

FIG. 5 (3%). Good form level

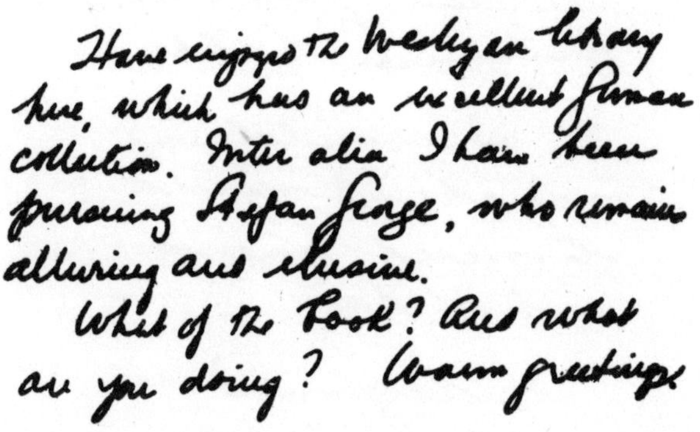

FIG. 6 (7%). Good form level

[handwriting sample]

FIGS. 2-15. Levels of form quality (cont'd)

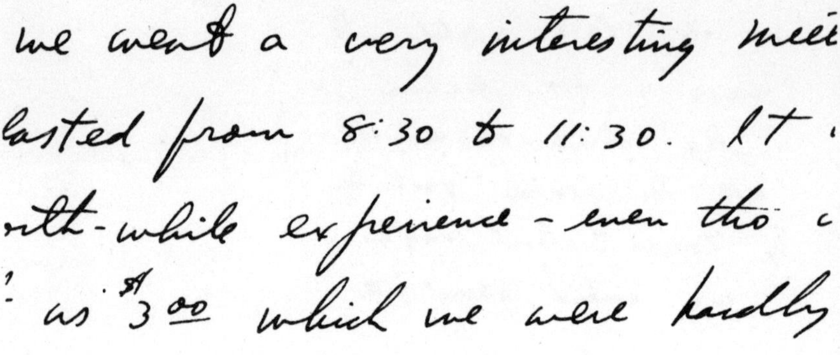

we went a very interesting mtil
lasted from 8:30 to 11:30. It
rth-while experience - even tho a
as $3.00 which we were hardly

FIG. 7 (17%). Fair form level

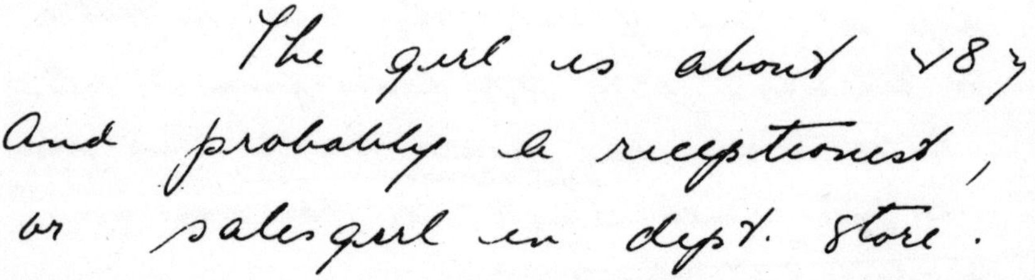

The girl is about 18,
and probably a receptionist,
or salesgirl in dept. store.

FIG. 8 (17%). Fair form level

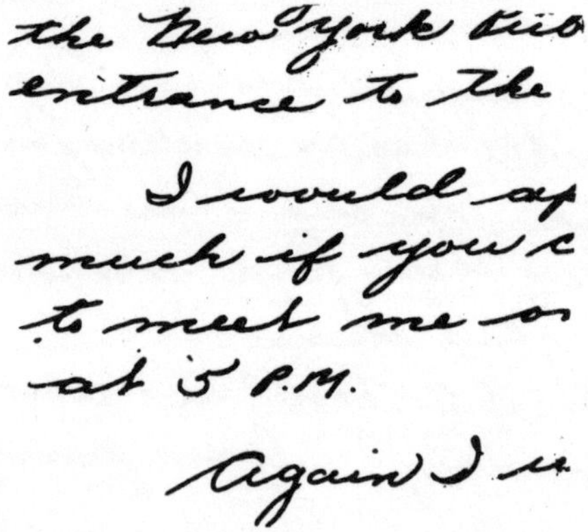

the New York the
entrance to the

I would ap
much if you c
to meet me o
at 5 P.M.

again I u

FIG. 9 (7%). Mediocre form level

FIGS. 2-15. Levels of form quality (cont'd)

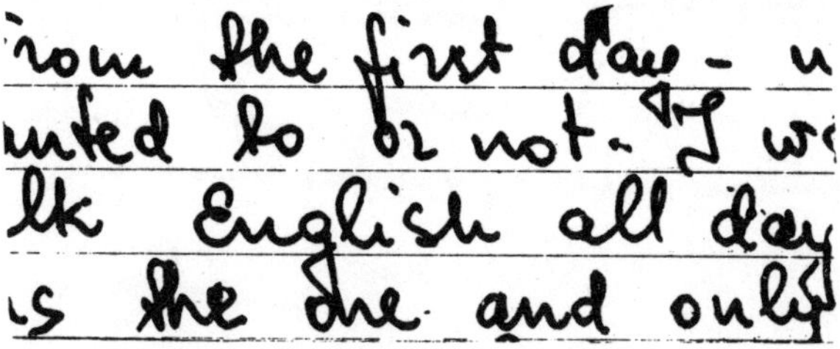

Fig. 10 (7%). Mediocre form level

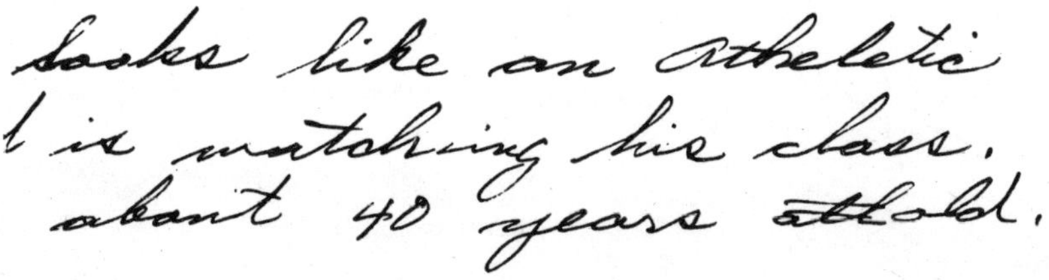

Fig. 11 (26%). Essentially inferior form level

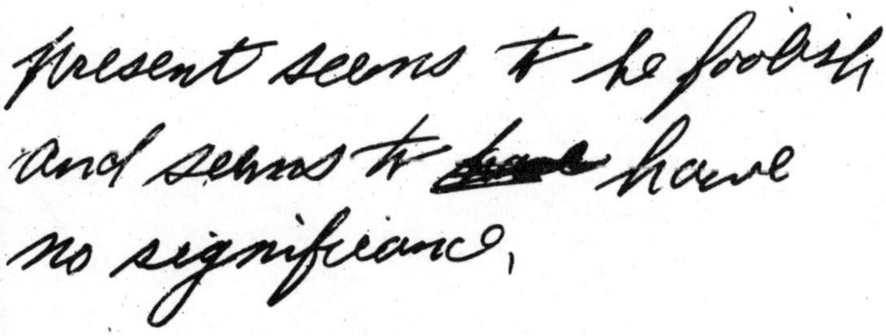

Fig. 12 (26%). Essentially inferior form level

Figs. 2-15. Levels of form quality (cont'd)

identical with the rhythm of the music per se which by varying means, such as syncopation, follows its second principle, that of change, to counter-balance the element of sameness implied in the first. Thus, by using the repetitiousness of the identical divisions for purposes of varia-

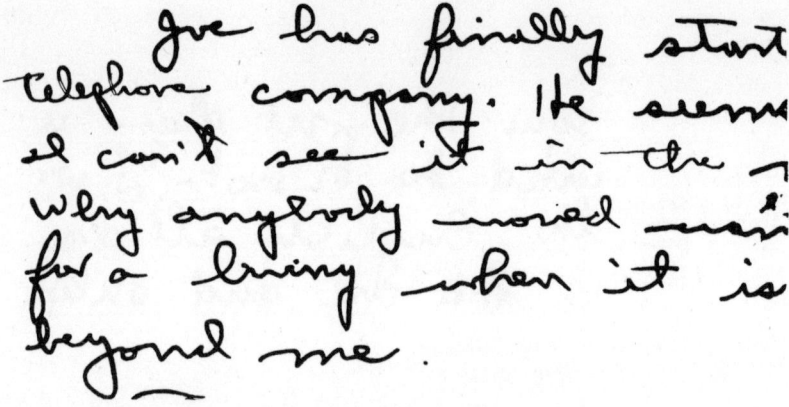

Fig. 13 (7%). Definitely inferior form level

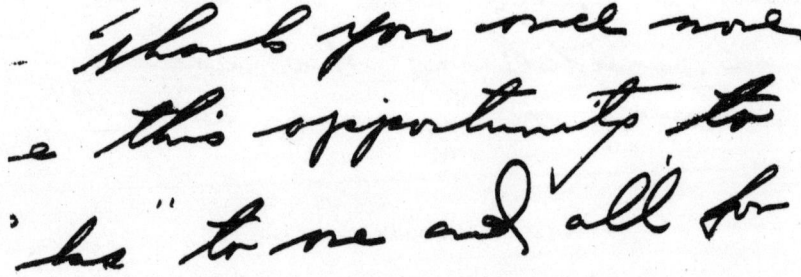

Fig. 14 (7%). Definitely inferior form level

Fig. 15 (7%). Very inferior form level

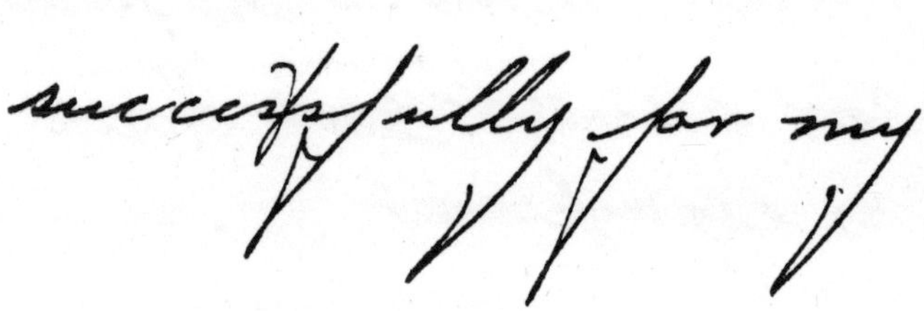

Figs. 2-15. Levels of form quality (cont'd)

tion within each repetitive time measure, the measure is integrated and the enlivening effect of "rhythm" brought forth.

Applying this concept to the corresponding elements of the writing activity, we encounter the static principle of repetition on the part of the contractive, that of change on the part of the released movements. Visually, this is strikingly suggested already by the simplest form of their alternation, a series of up and downstrokes as in little n's and m's, where the pressure-accentuated downstrokes have the synaesthetic effect of "beating time." The writing process is centered upon them: if we erase all downstrokes, the remainder will hardly even suggest the sight of handwriting; if, instead, we erase all upstrokes, not only this general "graphic" character of the remainder but even its legibility is essentially found preserved (fig. 16). Obviously, then, as the contractions reveal themselves as the

FIG. 16 (7%). Relationships of downstrokes to essential structure

proper immediate objectives of the writing movement in each of its segments, they appear to represent a principle of conscious volitional control which can be said to set the path for the writing activity as a whole process and to which the release impulses have to "adjust" themselves in order to integrate it into contiguous movement. This constellation implies two conclusions. First, the movements of contraction can be expected to reveal the consciously exercised functions of volitional control, the movements of release, the adaptability of the life process as a whole in regard to this control; the emotional reactivity of the personality structure as determined by its unconscious layers is thus revealed by the movements of release. Secondly, the greater the constancy of the control imposed upon the movement, both in terms of its contractive components proper and of their intervals, the more "regulated" appears the handwriting and the more "controlled" can the writer be expected to be; correspondingly, the lesser this constancy, and consequently, the more freely flowing the handwriting, the greater spontaneity on the writer's part can be assumed.

Klages' dichotomy of "regulated" and "rhythmical" handwritings, as roughly corresponding to disharmonious and harmonious personalities, oversimplifies this situation, and it is in this area of his system that the author feels compelled to take exception, since the difference in concepts is neither a merely technical nor a terminological one but is highly fundamental. The entire "vitalistic" school of thought, headed, in France by Bergson, in Germany by Klages, interpreted consciousness per se as a disturbing force in the free interplay of impulses, as a force directed against life and life's rhythm itself. In accordance with this basic view, Klages came to consider expressive movements betraying a high degree of conscious control—such as "regulated handwritings"—as symptomatic of lacking integration, regardless of the *kind* of conscious control betrayed. Obviously now, Klages' concept of consciousness generalizes observations which are valid only for the one specific type or case of conscious control commonly implied in the term "self-consciousness"; the impeding effects on emotional and motor impulses exercised by self-reflecting and introspectively-observing attitudes are generally recognized and, in terms of their specific impact upon expressive movements, have been discussed in an earlier chapter. "Consciousness," however, apart from such reversal of its normal direction, primarily implies the awareness of, and focusing upon, an external object of cognition or objective of will; in normal functioning, it is simply a necessary attribute of the human organism's directedness towards its goals and, as such, qualifies and conditions rather than impedes a spontaneous flow of affect. The attribution of a disintegrative effect to "conscious control" should in consequence be reserved for those expressive moments which indicate an affect-repressive display of such control; or, more generally, which indicate conflict due to an unreadiness of the emotional impulses to sustain conscious volition in its chosen directions. In terms of the writing movement, a situation of this kind is not necessarily manifested by "regulation," which in itself only shows the consistency with which conscious volitional forces are displayed; instead, it is manifested by difficulties of coordination—in the form of strokes either unduly abrupt or unduly involved—arising from a more or less pronounced inability of the organism to adapt itself to these forces. Such difficulties imply that the organism experiences its own element of conscious volition like a "foreign body" that imposes demands upon it, rather than, as normally, experiencing its relationship to this element as one of identity.

"Regulated" handwritings, in consequence, *can* be satisfactorily rhythmicized also, provided that the regulating forces of consciousness are graphically integrated—in other words, that their low degree of fluctuation does not appear as the artificial effect, more conflagrating than harmonizing with the recognizable impulses of release, of any kind of self-coercion; while highly fluctuating handwritings, correspondingly, *can* be quite unrhythmical: the typical graphic trail of the psychopath, for example, combines lack of rhythmical integration with considerable irregularity.

Rather than being able to accept Klages' simple dichotomy of rhythm versus regularity, we are in need of two mutually independent criteria, the relative degree of fluctuation and the relative degree of integration. Apart from their level of form quality, all graphic products can be determined according to these two criteria, the clinical application of which greatly tends to clarify the existing multitudes of types both of normal and pathologic personality.

Klages' dichotomy, however, retains its value inasmuch as it applies to graphic rhythm at least in one of these two dimensions, the dimension of fluctuation. By application of the ambivalence principle to either "regulated" or "released" handwritings, and worded in simple terms of character description, the following first table of potential traits of personality is derived.

TABLE I
Degree of Fluctuation

"Regulated"		"Released"	
Dominance of Control		Dominance of Emotion	
+	−	+	−
Self-denial	Constriction	Warmth	Lack of balance
Self-conquest	Coldness	Impulsivity	Lack of direction
Firmness	Poverty of emotions	Vivaciousness	Lack of purpose
Resolution	Stereotypy	Creativeness	Fickleness
Endurance	Quality of being "boring"	Self-adjustment	Lackadaisicalness "Weakness of will"
Ability to concentrate	Self-neglect		Distractability "Anarchy of drives"
"Hierarchy of Drives"	Self-coercion		
	Lack of self-adjustment		

In the graphoanalytic procedure, a proper perception of rhythmical properties, very much like that of the level of form quality, depends largely on eye training and a good general sense of visual characteristics. Some basic rules can, of course, be given. A handwriting will be called the better integrated in a rhythmical sense the more the element of repetitiousness of the contraction-release phases in it, regardless of the strength of the contractions, appears as the product of a spontaneous flow of the impulses of movement, and the more the elements of fluctuation in it, regardless of the scope of the fluctuation, show gradual rather than abrupt changes. To determine the degree of regularity even simpler rules evolve from the general analysis of the contraction-release cycles made at the opening of this paragraph. On the basis of this analysis, the criterion of regularity can be defined as the combined relative constancy of the lengths of the downstrokes in the middle zone, of the distances between their foot points on the writing basis, of their directions, and of the amount of pressure displayed in their execution (figs. 17-21).

The Overall Arrangement

In addition to the two guiding criteria of the level of form quality and of the rhythmical properties of handwriting, the overall arrangement of the text is essential in helping the graphological worker to orient himself to his field of observation and in starting him on his way toward the closer investigation of graphic details which in turn is indispensable for the dimensional studies to follow.

FIG. 17. Rhythmical and regular

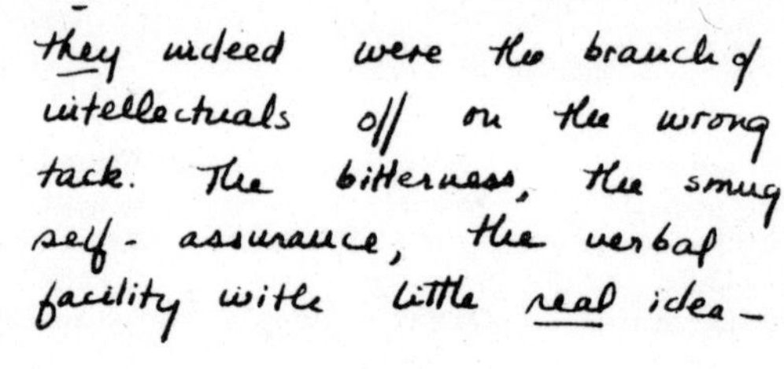

FIGS. 17-20 (31%). Rhythm and regularity

The most common dimension-setting qualities of arrangement, such as orderliness versus disorderliness, neatness versus smeariness, suggest their own general meanings and thus do not seem to warrant any elaborate analysis at this point. Both these qualities and the psychologically more complex ones of crowding versus dispersion, margin-emphasis versus

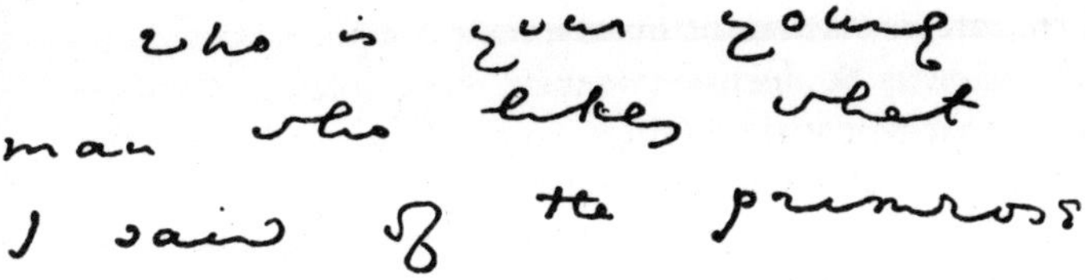

SAMPLE AS A WHOLE

[handwriting sample: "who is your young man who likes what I said of the primrose"]

FIG. 18. Rhythmical and irregular

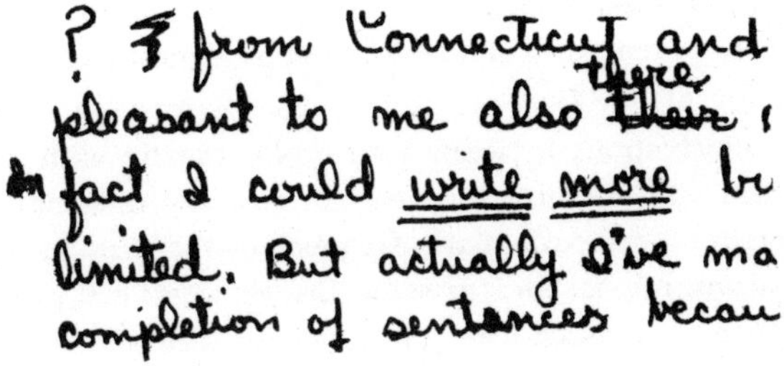

FIG. 19. Arhythmical and regular

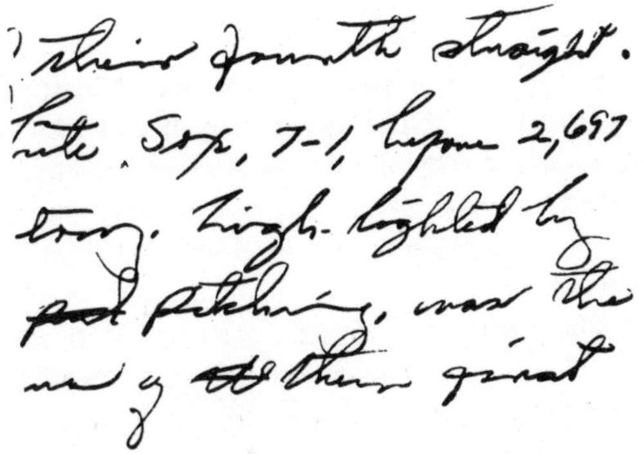

[handwriting sample: "? F from Connecticut and pleasant to me also there, in fact I could write more be limited. But actually I've ma completion of sentences becau"]

[handwriting sample: "their fourth straight. rate, Sox, 7-1, hopes 2,697 trong. Singh-lighted by post pitching, was the un of all their great"]

FIG. 20. Arhythmical and irregular

FIGS. 17-20 (31%). Rhythm and regularity (cont'd)

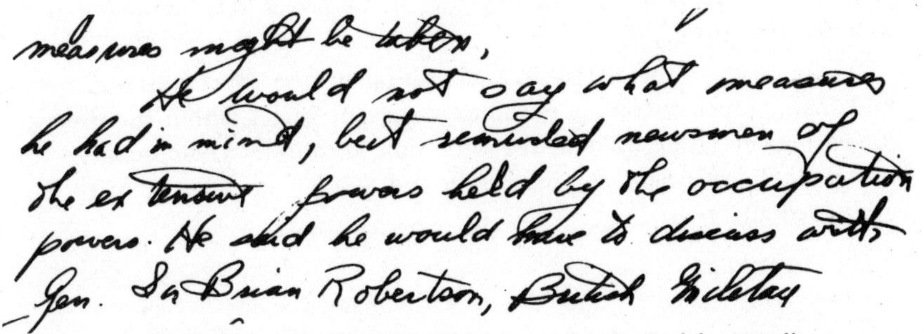

[handwriting sample: "measures might be taken. He would not say what measures he had in mind, but reminded newsmen of the ex tensure frwas held by the occupation powers. He said he would have to discuss with Gen. SaBrian Robertson, British Militay"]

FIG. 21 (42%). Rhythmical disturbances on a fair level of form quality margin-neglect, etc., are derivations of more specific components of movement which will separately be discussed at their proper places. Crowded handwriting involves the potential meanings, positively, of a rich and more intensively reflecting and elaborating than extensively spreading ideomotor production, negatively, of lacking articulateness of ideas; dispersed handwriting, positively, of good abilities of conceptual survey over a large field of subject matter, negatively, of wanting thoroughness and, in early schizophrenics, of a fear of logical derailment working towards the isolation of words.

Fluctuations between both types, usually with a very superior level of form and significantly irregular but at the same time highly rhythmical qualities, are particularly frequent in the manuscripts of independent and unconventional and in some cases exceptionally creative but also disharmonious personalities (Beethoven, Balzac) and also in those of the clinically manic-depressive. General emphasis on margins, particularly of the upper and left-hand sides, relates to an aesthetically articulated sense of personal distance and distinction; a more ample discussion of margins will follow later. Absence particularly of the upper margin and lack of distance between lines reflects a lack of self-reliance, an anxious holding-on to environmental positions already secured; several lines of possible graphological interpretations, among which a more or less developed "stickiness," i.e., obtrusiveness, in interpersonal relations, may be mentioned, diverge from this general concept. The habit of filling in particles of text, if predominant, and particularly if it does not spare the margins, resembles the frequent tendency of certain persons to renew, in the hallway, or already at the door of the partner's house, a conversation with him already terminated; in its less harmless interpretative versions, it reflects a completion craze operating at the expense of consistent time economy and well-ordered procedure.

While most of the characteristics making up the overall arrangement find their proper systematic positions at specific places within the diverse dimensions of rating, they at the same time constitute whole qualities of the graphologist's field of observation and attack and, as such, merit his undivided attention.

THE DIMENSIONS OF RATING

Introductory Note

The theory of expressive movements holds that personality structure, being a qualitative concept, can never explain what an individual does unless attention is focused on how he does it. Qualitative analysis of behavior, in turn, reveals personal preferences for certain gestures and gestural qualities and omission or suppression of others. Since handwriting offers the individual the entire scale of possible gestural emphases and disemphases, it can be expected to reveal his personal profile of expressive articulation with particular distinction.

The system according to which this profile is analyzed is suggested by the principal properties of graphic movement themselves and, in accordance with their given order, is classified in the dimensions or areas of rating to follow. Findings within these areas are not to be understood as "particles" of personality structure but as particular aspects, each implying a specific angle of observation, of personality as a whole. Dimensional ratings as given in the following apply to the extreme degrees of the graphic traits in question at either pole of any particular dimension, i.e., to prototypes; in their application to actual sample analyses they have to be treated, therefore, as tendencies approximating the prototype to a degree dependent on the articulation of the trait in the handwriting examined, on its fluctuation, and on its possible alternation with tendencies pointing in an opposite direction.

The revision of the Klagesian concept of graphic rhythm which has previously been pointed out results in a number of deviations from Klages' system as far as the application and focus of characterological concepts are concerned. Except for these deviations, for considerable differences in emphasis as well as in the psychological rationale of most of the basic dimensional interpretations, and for a more elaborate inquiry into the proportion between the middle and peripheral zones, the tables of characterological trait names presented for each of the main rating areas (including the one for "regulated-released" already presented) generally follow those which have been given by Klages in *Handschrift und Character* and have proved a solid and indispensable foundation in decades of graphological research in Europe. However, in accordance with the previously stated difference in the concept of rhythm (respectively, of personality integration), the range of character tendencies listed has been widened to cover pathological trends wherever a potentiality for such trends was found to be directly implied in any one of the chief "dimension"-setting properties of graphic movement.

EXTENSION, VELOCITY, AND IMPACT

Viewed only in themselves, independently of their environmental field and the criteria of direction implied in it, all movements can be defined in terms of their extension, velocity, and impact. In a previous chapter, the vertical dimension of handwriting was defined as the one representative of the person's orientation in the realm of available values; the horizontal one as representative of his orientation in reality. In both instances, movement is viewed directionally, in reference to a field not involved in the movement itself. Regarding those of its properties constituting, in a narrower sense, its own identity, graphic movement, accordingly, must be considered in terms of the three above-named criteria. Psychologically, since no external point of reference is implied in them, their application can be expected to inform us about the person's self-experience *regardless* of its differentiation in terms of any specific experience of reality, and of his aspirations *regardless* of their differentiation in terms of available values. The size, speed, and pressure of the handwriting, in consequence can be expected to yield important psychological clues in respect to that basic organismic potential of the person generally called temperament.

While the size of the handwriting evidently derives from the extension of the fingers engaged in the writing movement, the greater psychological and technical complexity of the two other criteria seems to warrant a word of comment. While it is true that exact measurement of *speed* in writing is possible only by controlled experiment (which would involve the setting-up of conditions liable to interfere with the person's time disposal and with his normal degree of attention to the task), the writing trail itself offers sufficient clues for a reasonably reliable estimate of the speed of production. The visual criterion here is the "sweep" or "slenderness" of the stroke, and its validity is verified by the well-known fact, of great importance in handwriting identification, that writing trails *cannot be copied:* while every other quality of the writing but the speed of it can, the time required in this painstaking task is so extensive, its performance so slow that the resulting clumsiness of the stroke offsets the entire effect of the formal accuracy of the imitation. "Clumsiness" here does not necessarily imply thickness. Rather does it mean a lack of smoothness of the lateral edges as well as of consistent direction of the stroke in each tiny section of its course, an observation which the magnifying glass or the microscope readily confirms but which in most instances and by most observers can be made without their support.

Concerning the third of the named criteria, that of pressure—graphically disclosed by swellings of the flow of ink with resulting widening and darkening of the strokes—its psychological representation of the total impact of the movement appears from an analysis of all the muscular pressure involved in the process. Basically, three lines of pressure: of the lower arm against the table, of the fingers against the writing implement, and of the writing implement against the paper, can be distinguished. Of these, however, only the one last named has any concrete and lasting effect and is, in addition, the only one directly subject, due to its close attachment to the tangible and visible results of his activity, to the writing person's own experience. The total impact exercised by the writing movement psychologically culminates in the graphic pressure proper and is therefore assessed in accordance with its strength.

The general significance of the three dimensions at hand, as pointed out above, can be specified for each of them on the basis of a simple realization of its potential gestural implications. In symbolic experience, "big" and "important" are interchangeable terms, as are "small" and "negligible," and such expressions as "greatness" and "grandeur" in their figurative usages, "magnanimity," a "grand gesture," a "narrow" mind, all betray the same general complex of associations. Size, therefore, is graphologically taken as a measure of the person's spontaneous self-estimate, of his feeling of self-importance—regardless, again, at this level of the investigation, of any supplementary and qualifying criteria which would inform us about the particular function of the personality around which it is centered, or about the conscious attitude ensuing on it, or about its basis of justification in terms of values and accomplishments; however, it ought to be realized that, as the elevation of any position over its environments determines how much of them is "overlooked" from there (both in the sense of "survey," positively and generally, and of "failure to notice," negatively and specifically), the level of self-experience is decisive also for the person's ex-

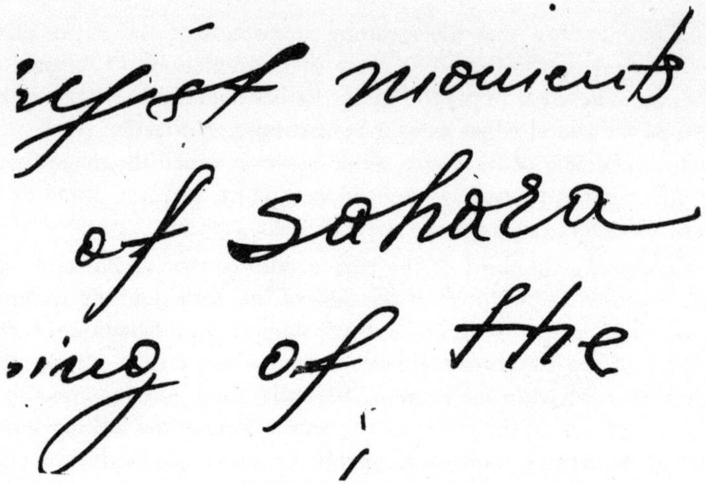

FIG. 22. Very large

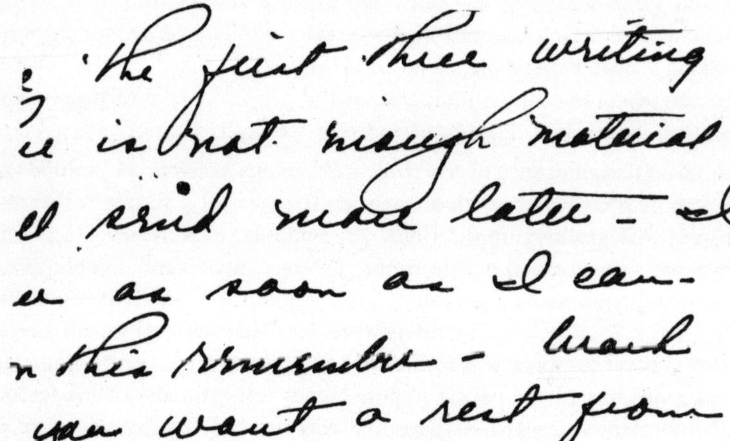

FIG. 23. Medium

FIGS. 22-24 (7%). Size

ternal experiences at least in regard to the basic set of his aspirations: it determines how widely or closely his focus on reality ranges, what "size" of objects and objectives, of tasks and challenges, he perceives and how

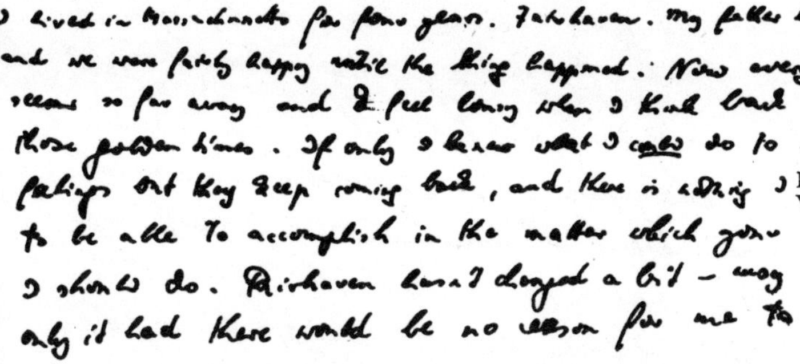

DIMENSIONS OF RATING

[handwritten text:]
I lived in Massachusetts for some years. Father... My father & and we were fairly happy until the thing happened. Now every seems so far away and I feel lonely when I think back those golden times. If only I knew what I could do to ... pulling out they keep coming back, and there is nothing to be able to accomplish in the matter which you I should do. Richhaven hasn't changed a bit — may only it had there would be no reason for me to

FIG. 24.
Very small

FIGS. 22-24 (7%). Size (cont'd)

sizable his scope of attack on reality, if not the force of the attack, is likely to be (figs. 22-24). While "size" thus relates to self-experience and total aspiration in a static sense, self-experience and aspiration in action reveal themselves in the dimensions of pressure and speed.

Let us discuss "pressure" first. As the necessary dynamic condition of self-experience is the experience of a resistance encountered and overcome, the amount of effort directed against the resistance can serve us as a measure of the intensity of that experience on its two sides of "ego" and "obstacle," which thus reveal themselves as interdependent; therefore, for general empiric purposes, the externally available amount of volitional energy would indeed seem to be indicated by the absolute degree of pressure present. Theoretically and clinically, however, this identification of ego-force with externally available energy as an assumedly necessary one would be uncritical, since the experience of resistance does not reveal the objective nature of the obstacle which can have the form of an intrapersonal impediment as much as of an external challenge. To what extent a certain degree of pressure represents externally available energy, to what extent the presence of inhibitions or blockings, depends on how well the various displays of pressure are rhythmically integrated into the total configuration, the revelations of which thus once more prove decisive (figs. 25-30).

The reasoning process for the interpretation of the relative speed takes an exactly opposite course. The more forceful our movements, the greater the obstacle "rightly" or "wrongly" experienced; the faster our movements, the more imposing the goal-image experienced in proportion to, and in spite of, all experienced obstacles; the lesser, in consequence, the

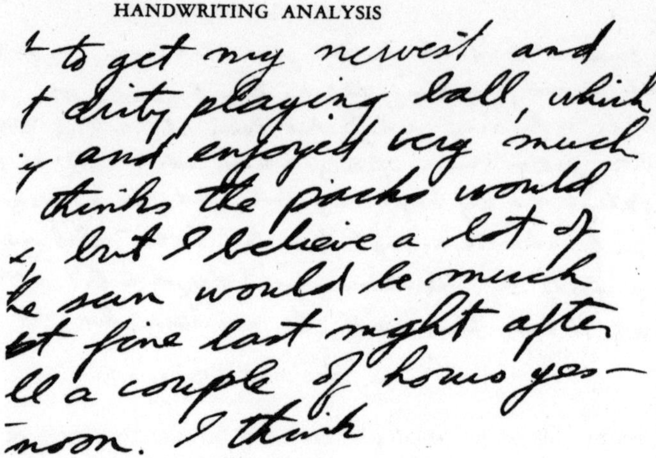

FIG. 25. Strong

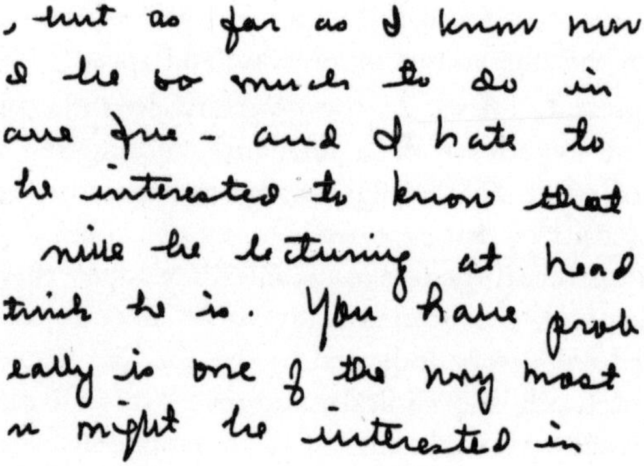

[handwritten sample]

FIG. 26. Medium

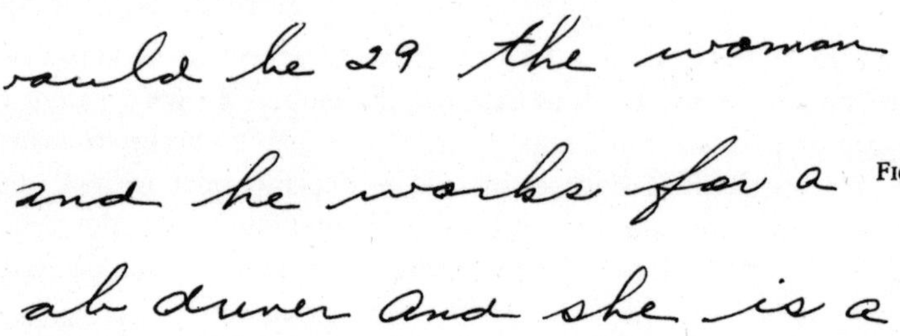

[handwritten sample]

FIG. 27. Frail

[handwritten sample]

FIGS. 25-27 (31%). Pressure

ego's awareness of the latter (which includes self-awareness), and the greater the ego's identification with its goals and the resulting flow of spontaneity. Again, total configurative considerations focusing upon the

DIMENSIONS OF RATING

Fig. 28. Fast

Fig. 29. Medium

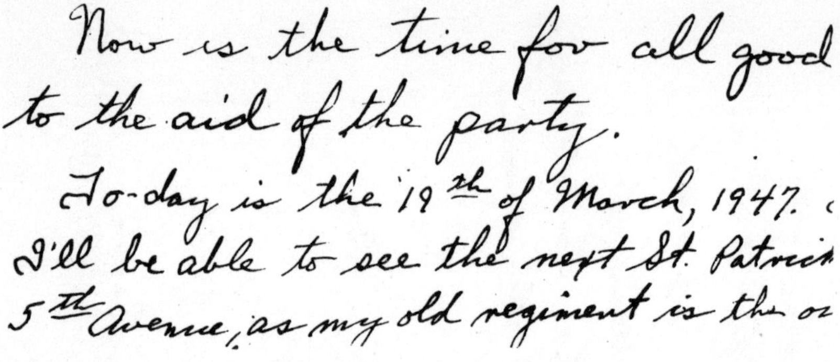

Now is the time for all good to the aid of the party.

To-day is the 19th of March, 1947.

I'll be able to see the next St. Patrick 5th Avenue, as my old regiment is the o

FIGS. 28-30 (26%). Speed

degree to which the other qualities of the writing stand up under the acceleration usually following the first few lines of a text prevail in the interpretative assessment of the relative speed; applying both the principle of interdependence and the principle of ambivalence to the results of our analysis, we arrive at table II, worded in plain personality-descriptive terms, for the possible conveyances of size, speed, and pressure.

THE DUCTUS, LATERALLY AND LONGITUDINALLY: SHARPNESS AND DOUGHINESS, CONNECTEDNESS AND DISCONNECTEDNESS

A central position between the dimensions discussed in the previous chapter and those involving directional principles is occupied by qualities of the stroke not implied in its basic motoric make-up, yet not transcending into the system of quasi-spatial orientation governing the writing structure as a whole.

Apart from the criterion of pressure which is modulated by the contraction-release cycle, the stroke is characterized by a certain degree of "absolute," i.e., relatively constant, thickness. While the latter, to a certain extent, depends upon the writing implement, the average variation among the different effects upon thickness exercised by the existing variety at least of the more common writing implements remains substantially below the variation in thickness attained by a numerically corresponding variety of writers of divergent characterological make-up using the same pen. While this is believed to be attributable to individual compensatory

TABLE II

Extension, Velocity, and Impact

Size

Large		Small	
+	−	+	−
Pride	Conceit	Modesty	Lack of self-confidence
Independence	Arrogance	Humility	Over-scrupulousness
Generosity	Pretentiousness	Devotion	Fear
Chivalry	Grandiosity	Tolerance	Inferiority feelings
Noblesse	(Megalomania)	Peacefulness	Despondency
Enthusiasm	Exaltation	Adaptability	Submissiveness
Courage	Domineeringness	Carefulness	Docility
Farsightedness	Inconsiderateness	Conscientiousness	(Compulsiveness)
Leadership	Lack of care and caution	Scrutiny of observation	(Self-torture)
Long-term planning	Project-making	Accuracy	
"Great concepts"	Vagueness of concepts	Ability to concentrate	
Talent for organization and survey	Thinking in generalities		
Ability to build	Poorness of observation		
	Distractability		
	Neglect		

Speed

Fast		Slow	
+	−	+	−
Agility	Restlessness	Leisure	Inactivity
Vivaciousness	Flightiness	Self-collection	Inertia
Need for change	Rashness	Foresight	Sluggishness
"Temperament"	Haste	Carefulness	Hesitancy
"Élan"	Superficiality	Steadiness	Irresolution
Passion	Unsteadiness	Sense of facts	Laziness
Zeal	Planlessness	(Concrete thinking)	Lack of temperament
Purposefulness	Unreliability		Slowness of thinking and reaction
Goal-mindedness	Excitability		"Pedestrian"
Inner engagement in task at hand	(Loose thinking)		(Dullness)
Interest and initiative			(Concretistic thinking)
(Low reaction time)			
(Quickness of thinking)			
(Intelligence)			
(Abstraction)			

Pressure

	High		Low	
+	−	+	−	
Energy	Obstinacy	Adaptability	Lack of energy
Tenacity	Stubbornness	Propensity for new enterprises	Lack of resistance
Determination	Aggressiveness		
Endurance	Self-aggressiveness	Sensitivity	Lack of determination
Assiduity		Easy abreaction	
Self-consistency	Irritability	Easy adjustment	Lack of stamina
Steadiness	Repressed, uncontrolled and explosive impulsivity	Elasticity	Yieldingness
Self-control			"Weakness of will"
"*Active* indifference"			*Passive* indifference
			Lability
Depth of emotion	(Inhibitions)		Superficiality
Controlled impulsivity	(Blockings)		Forcelessness of affect
	(Paroxysmal character)		Flatness of affect

adjustments to the pen deriving from the tendency—underlying all expressive movements—of organisms to structure their environments according to their needs, it is not denied that the remaining margin of technically conditioned variability is sufficiently broad to suggest extreme caution in operating this criterion. With progressive training of the eye, however, this margin is narrowed down farther by a number of qualifying observations which more or less allow one to determine whether thickness is resisted or indulged in; thinness escaped or held on to.

The different terms just applied to an individual's possible reactions toward both poles of the dimension already convey its psychological polarity, which the reader will have no difficulty in realizing by following the diametrically divergent directions of inner experience they suggest. The sensual nature of the broad, heavy stroke, the "fleshlessness" of the thin, sharp stroke are immediately evident. While, for systematic purposes, the discussion of this criterion had to be separated from that of the fundamentally different one of pressure, the interrelation of both in the actual sample are extremely close and intricate but also revealing. Obviously, the thicker the stroke, the lesser the opportunity for the contraction-release cycle to appear in the form of modulated swellings of pressure; correspondingly, the thinner the stroke, the greater this opportunity. "Doughiness"—the graphological term for the product of thick, heavy strokes—thus appears as a result of motor energy applied in a manner of diffusion, yet, as it derives from a particular way of holding the pen rather than from any particular degree of muscular energy, it cannot be taken as a measure of the degree of this energy but only as a modality of displaying it in action; while sharpness, vice versa, thus appears as a product of motor energy applied, regardless of its strength, in a manner of concentration (figs. 31-34).

This analysis suggests the interpretation of doughiness-versus-sharpness in the general terms of sensual and sensorial dispersion or decentralization versus ego-linear constraint. The term ego-linear is chosen, negatively, because no other and sufficiently broad category to convey the true scope of possible significance here implied exists; positively, because all shades of possible significance applying to ductual "thinness" have this in common that the organism to which they pertain is dominated by the experience of self in the dimension of progression and, either on account of positive orientation to the goal or a feeling of "being driven from behind" or a negative evaluation of the given environment or any combination among these three, experiences all "lateral" stimuli more or less as disturbances. The following table of potential character traits is thereby suggested.

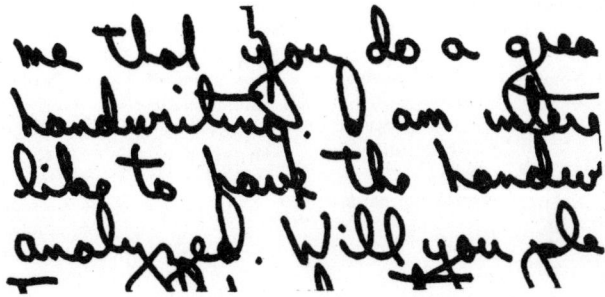

FIG. 31. Doughy

FIGS. 31-34 (7%). Doughiness and sharpness

TABLE III

Ductual Dispersion

Doughiness		Sharpness	
Sensuality Love of pleasure Indulgence in present moment Intensity of reality experience Accent on visual and tactile orientation Intensity of imagery "Thinking in images"		Spirituality (regardless of level) Restraint and reserve Asceticism Speculativeness Intensity of thought experience	
+	**−**	**+**	**−**
Warmth Earthiness Realism Wide scope of available experiences Capacity of enjoyment "Joie de vivre" Readiness for new situations Ability to absorb shock Sense of color Sense of humor "Democracy of needs"	Crudeness Roughness Brutality Uninhibitedness Lack of self-discipline Susceptibility to sensual distraction Readiness for "temptations" "Excesses" Indulgence in sexual day dreaming Anxiety, free floating (Propensity for narcotic stimulation) "Anarchy of needs"	Refinement Sensitivity Idealism Emphasis on logic Personal articulateness Economization of strength Unswervingness of purpose Sense of discrimination Sense of nuances Sense of irony "Narcissism of minutest differences" "Hierarchy of needs"	"Pallor of thought" Coldness Resentment Inability to enjoy Lack of realism Narrow scope of available experiences Low threshold for shock and narcotics Rigidity Inner remoteness Indulgence in day dreaming pertaining to achievement and social rank Anxiety, obsessional ("Loss of reality") (Auditory hallucinations) (Delusions of persecution) "Tyranny of one need"

As a particular ramification of possible negative meaning for doughiness, stealthiness and concealment, "hushing over," visually and psychologically suggested by the disclarifying effect of smeary excesses of the quality, filling-in of loops, etc., may be mentioned. "Bad conscience" in the sense

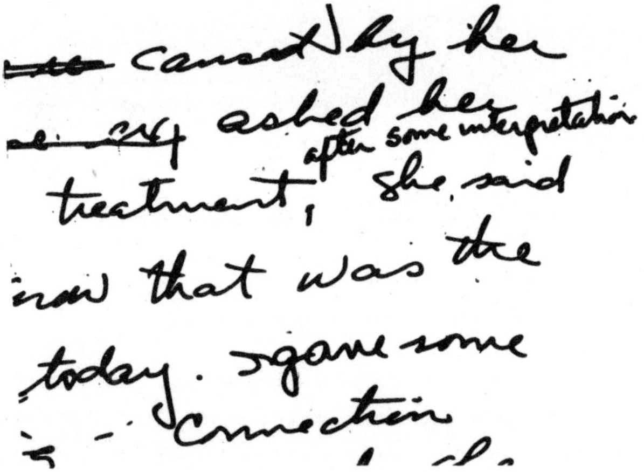

DIMENSIONS OF RATING

FIG. 32. Moderately doughly

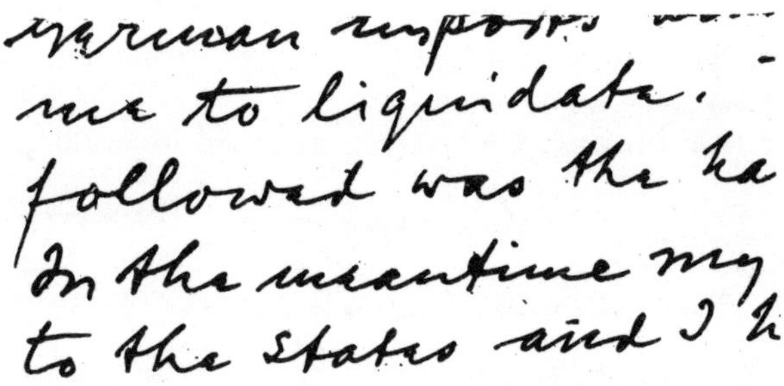

FIG. 33. Moderately sharp

FIGS. 31-34 (7%). Doughiness and sharpness (cont'd)

of guilt experiences more immediately connected with feelings of anxiety than is true in the case of obsessional and paranoid "guilt" is already implied in some of the traits for doughiness (especially that of "free-floating anxiety") which are listed under the minus sign and which derive from the implications of positive sensual indulgence conveyed by that quality. Incidentally, another sign for the essential unity of personality structure, in itself and in its motor-expressive aspects.

The longitudinal characteristics of the stroke, apart from their particular direction and gestural qualities, can be assessed in terms of the relative readiness of the writer to produce his words more or less by one contiguous

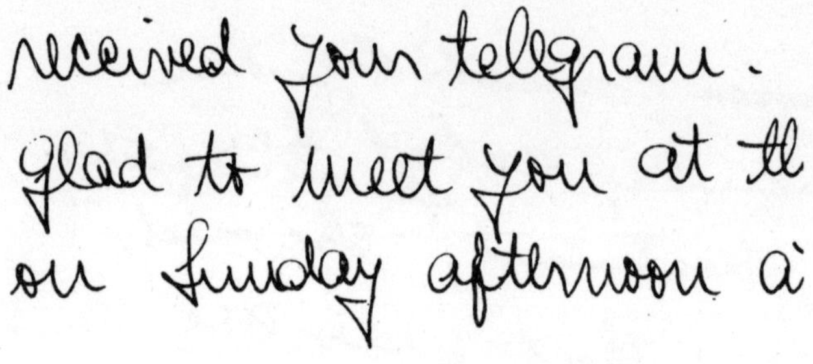

FIG. 34. Sharp

received your telegram. Glad to meet you at tl on Sunday afternoon a

FIGS. 31-34 (7%). Doughiness and sharpness (cont'd)

movement of the pen, or else to proceed in a more or less disconnected fashion. The psychological principles here in operation are, in general terms of "gesture," the tendency of "disconnectedness" to isolate, enclose, collect, conserve, fence off, secure, rest, wait, contemplate, put aside, accumulate, maintain, nurse, sow out, and let grow, of "connectedness," to bind, mix, bring together, arrange, tackle, organize, compromise, tear away, take along, break through, advance, keep up, entertain, stop never, attack, conquer, flee the past, drive on, make things and make them go.

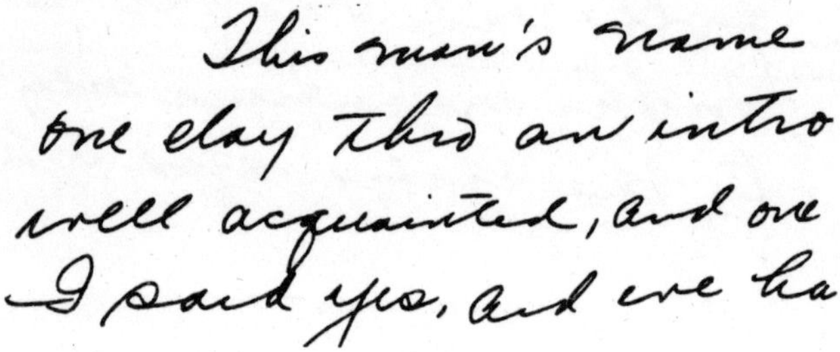

This man's name one day Thid an intro well acquainted, and one I said yes, and we ha

FIG. 35 (26%). Ordinary connectedness

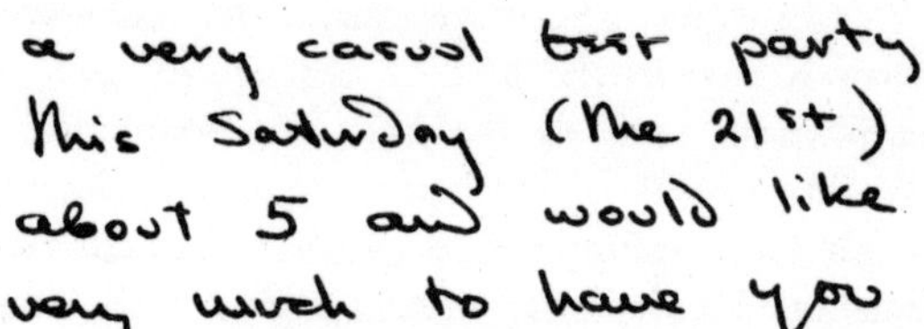

a very casual beer party this Saturday (the 21st) about 5 and would like very much to have you come. It's not necessary

FIG. 36 (26%). Connectedness and disconnectedness in balance

FIGS. 35-40. Degree of connectedness

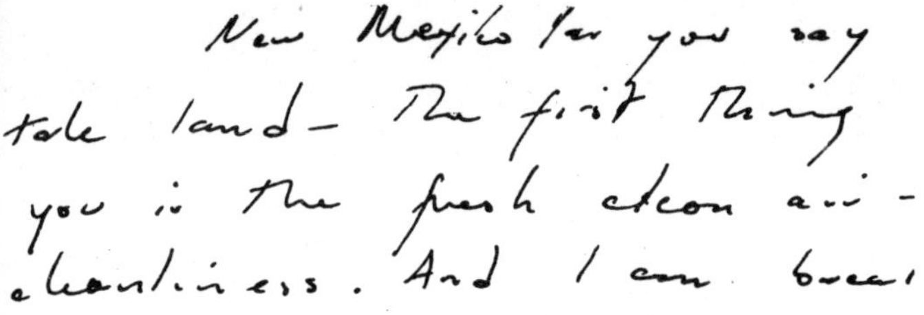

FIG. 37 (26%). Advanced disconnectedness

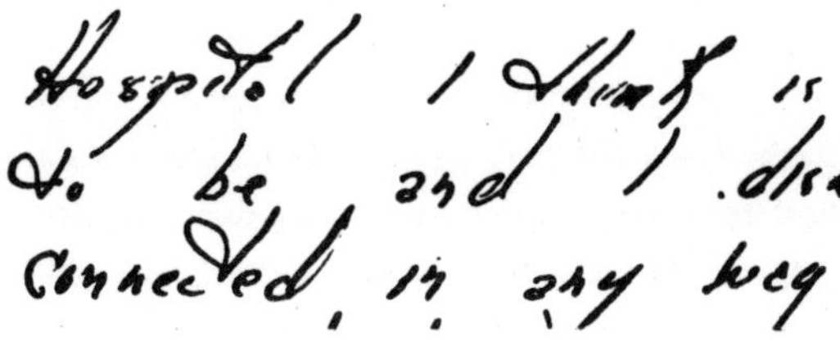

FIG. 38 (26%). Isolation of letters

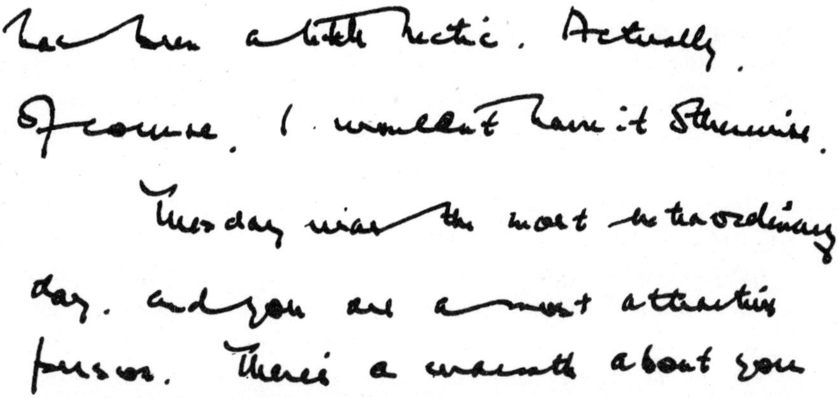

FIG. 39 (7%). Connective trend interlacing words

FIGS. 35-40. Degree of connectedness (cont'd)

The relation between connectedness and disconnectedness and entire attitudes and outlooks on life is evident and is believed to be verifiable by social and ethnological studies of handwriting; and not only the degree of either one of these traits and its various possible fluctuations but again also the total of all other indicators is differentially decisive in regard to their specific psychological significance (figs. 35-40).

FIG. 40 (7%). Interlacing of words with word-internal disconnectedness

FIGS. 35-40. Degree of connectedness (cont'd)

The particular relation of the degree of connectedness to the functions of *memory* follows from the foregoing: between the extreme positions of flight from the past and perseverative fixation on it all nuances can occur and are further differentiated by the pertinent criteria provided within the dimensions of zonal emphasis, total right-and-leftwardness, fullness, and emphasis or disemphasis on the word-initial upstrokes, the significance of which will later be expounded. Disconnected handwritings (not considering those using script) can be fragmented to a degree of piecemeal presentation of the single letters, or even beyond that mark (some types of hebephrenia; also frequently in senility—the disconnecting tendency, in accordance with its psychological meaning, generally tends to increase with age); they can, on the other hand, operate in such a way that letters are being regrouped and the school pattern as a whole restructured in an original and aesthetically satisfactory personal way which does not convey the impression of fragmentation at all but rather, to the graphologist, one of "new wholes," and to the unaware, by operation of the closure effect, again one of "whole words." Increases in connectedness linking entire words are negatively (and comparatively rarely) to be interpreted as signs of flightiness of ideas; positively, they can disclose a particularly accentuated sense of combination and are frequent in the handwritings of military, political and chessboard strategists, but also, especially in conjunction with specific word-interior occurrences of disconnectedness, in the handwritings of creative writers and artists of the more speculative and avant-garde than conservative and meditative types. A table for potential character trends indicated within the dimension of connectedness-disconnectedness follows here.

TABLE IV

Degree of Connectedness

Connected		Disconnected	
Extensity of thinking and working		Intensity of thinking and working	
+	−	+	−
1) "Abstract thinker" Deductive thinking and systematic work Logic, fighting its way through facts Consistency of linear reasoning Steadiness of work Planning Precaution	1) Poverty of ideas Thinking in secondhand concepts Poor observation Lack of initiative Lack of creativeness Dependency of judgment Lack of originality "One-track mindedness" Disinclination for risks Overadaptability Stereotypy	"Empiricist" Wealth of ideas Intuitive and inductive thinking Observations seeking their arrangement by logic Consistency of whole concepts Initiative Imaginativeness Independence of judgment Presence d'esprit Wit Inventiveness Combination II (in observing) Good memory accentuating the conservation of impressions Desire to collect Desire for controlled changes Caution	"Jumpiness" and perseveration in thinking ("spastic" thinking) Lack of self-criticism Lack of logic Lack of abstractive ability Thinking in "impressions" Lack of forethought Frequent changes of projects Lacking adaptability Stinginess Fearfulness ("Concretistic" thinking)
2) Sense of calculation and strategy Combination I (in planning) Aggressiveness I Desire for adventurous changes Audacity	2) Flighty and superficial thinking Speculativeness Negligence Restlessness Aggressiveness II Lack of leisure Squandering Thinking in words Shortness of memory Blindness for observations Tactlessness Carelessness Inconsiderateness		

The Vertical Dimension: The Three Zones

In an earlier chapter, extension of handwriting in the dimension perpendicular to that in which it proceeds as a whole was defined as being subject to the person's orientation in the realm of available values. The respective possible emphases or disemphases on either the upper or lower zones were interpreted as relating to the corresponding general spheres of inner experience, and the degree of the vertical development of the middle zone was defined as representing the degree of emphasis on activity per se, in distinction from any primarily "experiencing" inner attitudes.

The situation thus revealed points toward two separate ratios, one of which applies to the proportion between the peripheral zones, the other one to the proportion between both of them and the middle zone.

Let us discuss the latter one first. As my pen moves toward the right, I experience directional impulses which can be subsumed under the two general categories of horizontal progression and vertical organization. The first one is guided by the image of a goal toward which my activity as a whole in its external realm of relations is moving; the second one is guided by the necessity to carry out this activity in such a way that it will convey to a real or imaginary reader what I want it to convey. This means that operative in the activity, in addition to the external goal, is an internal one with which I am identifying myself and which, in terms of direction, to the extent of the identification, tends to counteract the demands of the external. On the conscious side of the process, this goal simply consists of forms of letters to be produced; in order to produce them, however, I have to disturb my total set which, being horizontally oriented, can be expected to react negatively to the disturbance by attempting to reduce vertical diversions to a minimum. The more rigid the set, the stronger this attempt; the more elastic and the more harmonious, in consequence, my total emotional household, the more balanced, in its vertico-horizontal proportions, the product. This already implies two conclusions, but in order to arrive at the first one we still have to elaborate on the concept of "external goal" which applies here. Evidently, this goal—since specific directional aspects are not involved in the dimension of movement here discussed—is no particular one of any kind in the form of a concrete image which would correspond to an emotionally positive inner experience, but is merely the general one of "getting ahead," "getting through," "getting it finished"; in brief, the writer is focusing upon the future *per se*. This may be temporary and may be due to having little time, being in a hurry, etc., but if at the same time the speed of the writing shows no significant increase, its implication evidently is the more general one that the person feels uncomfortable in his condition at hand and is trying to escape its stresses, a conclusion which in turn is consistent with the concept of rigidity which before was found useful for explaining the phenomenon of vertical reduction in terms of the specific motoric reactions bringing it about. Our first conclusion, then, is that a greater balancing-out of the distribution of movement components between the two dimensions, in brief, a vertically substantial development of the middle zone, would indicate a positive inner focus of the writer, with its implications of self-enjoyment and intensity of emotional experience, upon the activities as such in which he is engaged, in distinction from the inner focus merely upon the general direction of possible goals—i.e., the future—as indicated by vertical reduction of the middle zone. Our second conclusion will be that a loss of the inner balance required for a positive experience of the "present moment"—a loss of which "rigidity" is just one aspect—would, vice-versa, show up in the form of that very reduction.

Here, however, the question arises in proportion to which factor that reduction shall be assessed. Obviously, in order not simply to enter the dimension of size which only potentially—in the case of small-sized handwriting—implies some shades of meaning pertaining to "reduction of the middle zone," some standard of assessment for the relative degree of that reduction is needed. Two possible standards suggest themselves. One would be the horizontal extension of the short-form movements of release, in other words, the width between the downstrokes in the middle zone. This standard enters into the dimension of left-rightward extension to be taken up later rather than into the one here at hand: the very concept of "middle zone" implies the existence of points of comparison available in the vertical. The peripheral zones, the upper and lower ones, therefore, impose themselves as the only sensible standard, yet before using it we have to face a possible objection. Does the process of vertical reduction not involve the long forms themselves? Our answer is that it does in specific instances which leave horizontal points of comparison as the only ones available and therefore enter into the area of observation mentioned above—the assessment of the relative width, rather than the assessment here under discussion. For our present purpose, the only fact important is that in a great number of handwritings with shrinking of the middle zones, the upper and lower lengths not only are not also reduced but show a particular quantitative accentuation (figs. 41-43).

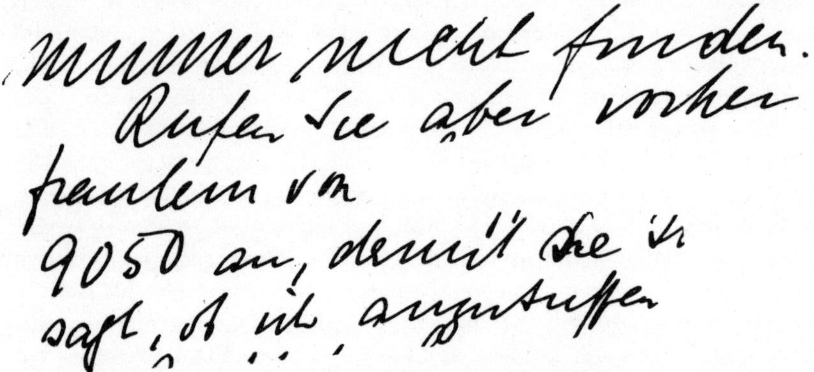

[handwriting sample in German]

FIG. 41 (7%). Middle zone overextended

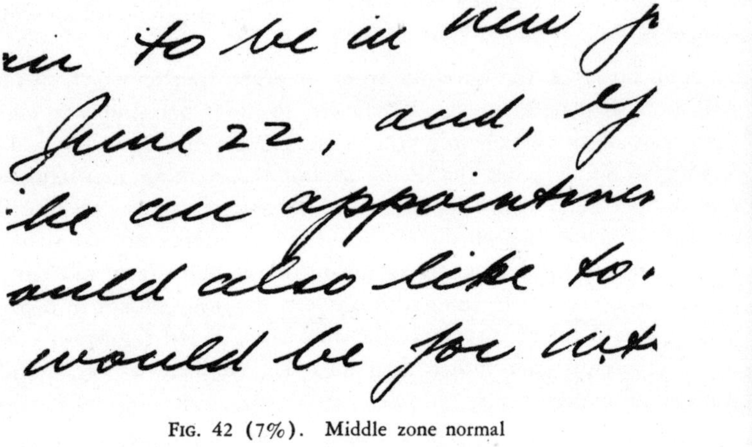

[handwriting sample in English]

FIG. 42 (7%). Middle zone normal

FIGS. 41-46. Vertical dimension

In order to understand this observation, we have to remember that the middle zone is the only one in which horizontal movement is contiguous. In consequence, disturbances of the horizontal urge would primarily affect this zone and only potentially and indirectly the peripheral lengths. The function of the latter in terms of the aesthetic and motoric articulation of the entire writing structure is one of a lateral balancing-out of the rightward-directed movement, very similar to the arm movements of a rope walker balancing his activity by means of a stick. This analogy again is not to be understood as a figurative one, but as the appearance of one Gestalt principle manifesting itself in two materially rather than structurally different types of situation. The thinner the rope,

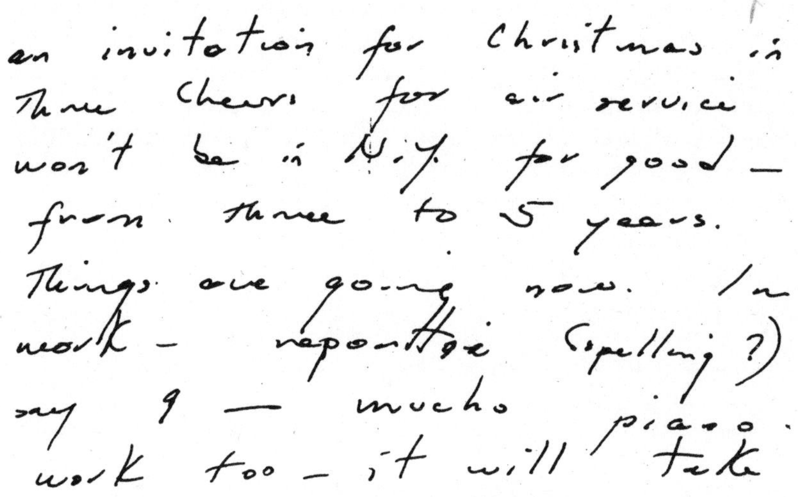

[handwriting sample:]
an invitation for Christmas is
Three Cheers for air service
won't be in N.Y. for good —
from three to 5 years.
Things are going now. I'm
work — reportage (spelling?)
say 9 — mucho piano
work too — it will take

FIG. 43 (7%). Middle zone shrunk

FIGS. 41-46. Vertical dimension (Cont'd)

the more the emphasis in the entire process of rope-walking is bound to be placed on these balancing movements and to come about by spontaneous adjustments of the organism to its situation rather than by reasoning processes on the part of the rope walker. Correspondingly, the thinner the middle zone in the handwriting, the more articulated will the writer's need be for peripheral accentuation, unless other resources of security not here under discussion should help him out. Psychologically, the writer's orientation in terms of available values—represented by the vertical dimension as pointed out previously—can be said to serve a function of balancing necessary to the person's orientation in reality, an observation which any analysis of actions and attitudes will confirm. Where the middle zone is accentuated, where the relative extension of the peripheral extremities thus is limited, the writer's inner balance is sufficient to allow him a limitation in awareness of the values guiding him; while with loss of that balance this awareness grows, implying a growth also in the psychological (as, correspondingly, in the graphic) remoteness from "himself" as a "real" ("horizontally progressing") person experiencing these values; as their distance increases, they function less and less as positive and ego-immanent forces of motivation and more and more as extraneously fixated "authorities" imposing themselves upon his inner experience. Their psychological meaning, thus, is disintegrative, at least in tendency, and again is consistent with the implications of tension and stress already shown in the analysis of vertical reduction proper. Graphically, their representatives, the peripheral zones, can be said to "squeeze" the middle zone, representative of the ego; psychologically, in accordance with this analysis, the following total picture is derived.

TABLE V

Vertical Dimension I

Middle vs. Peripheral Zones

Broad Middle Zone Moderate "super-ego" development		Low Middle Zone High "super-ego" development	
+	−	+	−
Inner balance	Lack of drive	Drive	Restlessness
"Harmony"	Lack of self-demand	Articulateness of values	Irritability
Leisure	Lack of self-criticism		Tension
Self-enjoyment		Idealism	Anxiety
Power of emotion	Lack of articulate values	Humility toward own ideals	Rigidity
Contemplativeness			Envy
Attentiveness		Conscientiousness	Guilt feelings
Observation		Self-demand	Resentment
Orderliness		Self-criticism	Animosity
Firmness		Ambition	Negativism
Sense of form and beauty		Farsightedness	Over-critical attitudes
		Power of abstraction	Aggressiveness
Smoothness in social relations			Self-punitiveness
			Dearth of positive emotions
Adaptability			Constriction
Elasticity			(Hysteria)
Diplomacy			(Compulsiveness)
			Poverty of inner resources

Middle Zone Over-Extended
Low "super-ego" development

+	—
"Powerful personality"	Moral ego-centricity
Realism	Cynicism
Strong-willedness	Domineering tendencies
Capacity of organization	Shortsightedness
Leadership	Inability to delay pleasure
Richness of inner resources	(Psychopathy)

The term "super-ego" as used in this table might conceivably seem to contradict earlier statements regarding the specific significance to the writing person's inner experience of the symbolic value of either of the peripheral zones and might be understood to imply a confinement of the term to the psychological interpretation of the upper zone only. A naive application of psychoanalytic concepts to handwriting might suggest this, and a misinterpretation of the upper and lower zones as representatives either of "super-ego" and "id" or else at least of "conscious" and "subconscious," respectively, might result and has resulted, with distorting consequences, here and there in amateur graphology. In order to clear up misunderstandings of this type, we have to be constantly aware of the following.

While personality functions may involve the total functional system of the organism to a greater or lesser extent, it always involves the entire personality in its dimension of depth, all "layers" of the structure partaking, each in its way, in the function. This forbids the assignment of statically defined sections of a product of personality functioning, such as a handwriting trail, to any one layer and requires the share of the "layers" to be inferred from its dynamic properties.

The dynamic properties being subject, apart from the "temperamental" criteria applying to them, to directional ones, the graphological placement of the aforementioned concepts of psychoanalysis depends simultaneously upon the direction of movements and on the static direction in which, from the viewpoint of a central position representing the ego not as "part" of the personality system but as its organizing principle of action, the components of movement trails are located. A consideration of the "zones" involves only the latter, and, in addition, involves them in only one aspect, the vertical one. In its vertical aspect, handwriting is determined by the person's experience of the symbolic values of the "zones";

such experience in turn, involves conscious as well as unconscious layers. Differentiating the object of experience from experience as a psychological process, the "zones" would then relate to the objects in their directional relationships to the experiencing and all the while temporally-progressing ego, as "paternal" and "maternal" stabilizers of its course, rather than to the processes themselves; they would indicate the person's orientation in terms of vectors connecting him with what he symbolically experiences as being "sky" and as being "ground"; they would show the distribution of these vectors in their projection upon the "screen" of inner experience by showing the projection of this distribution upon the writing field (figs. 44-46).

This means that a graphological "translation" of the mentioned concepts of psychoanalysis will have to wait until further dimensions have

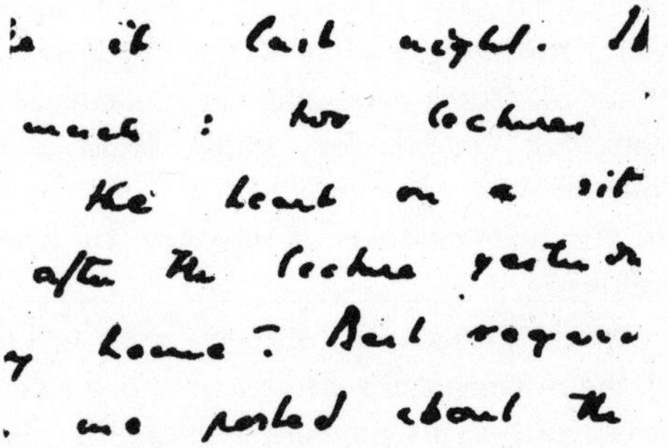

Fig. 44 (7%). Upper zone exceeding lower

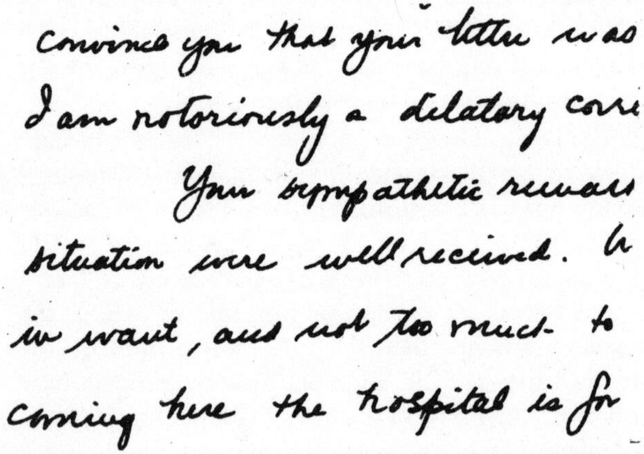

Fig. 45 (7%). Upper and lower zones in balance

Figs. 41-46. Vertical dimension (Cont'd)

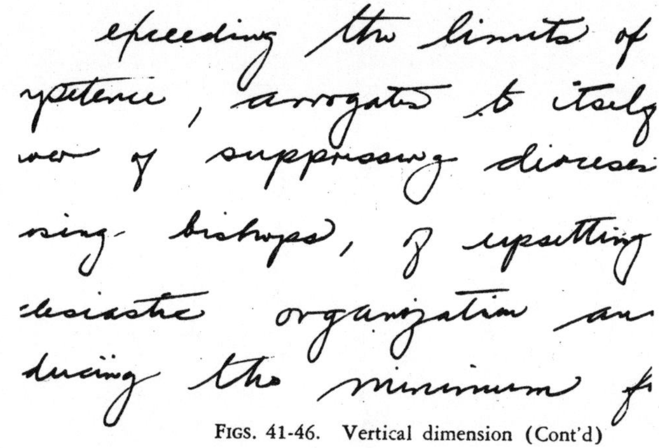

[handwriting sample]

FIG. 46 (31%). Lower zone exceeding upper

FIGS. 41-46. Vertical dimension (Cont'd)

been investigated, but also that the possible indicators within the dimension of vertical ambi-peripheral distribution can now be arrayed without danger of involving concepts extraneous to its proper scope of meaning.

TABLE VI
Vertical Dimension II
Upper vs. Lower Zone

U > L "Platonic" character		U < L "Chthonic" character	
Intellectual and imaginative *motility*	Exaltation	Earthiness	Immobility
Spiritual temperament	Superficiallity (in social and value relations)	Warmth	Pedantry
Idealism	Lack of "roots"	Realism	Clumsiness
Enthusiasm	Lack of objectiveness	Practical and technological inclinations	"Pedestrianism"
Conscious emphasis on freedom, self-determination and independence	Elusiveness	*Power* of imaginative forces	"Materialism"
	Fickleness		"Sensuality"
	Forgetfulness		Voraciousness
	Flightiness	Thoroughness	Greed
	Adventurousness	Accentuation of memory functions	
(In art:) Expressionism		Conscious emphasis on necessity, responsibilty, obligation	
Generosity		(In art:) Impressionism	
Ambition		Self-reliance	
Form-mindedness		Matter-mindedness	

Fig. 47 (18%). Wide

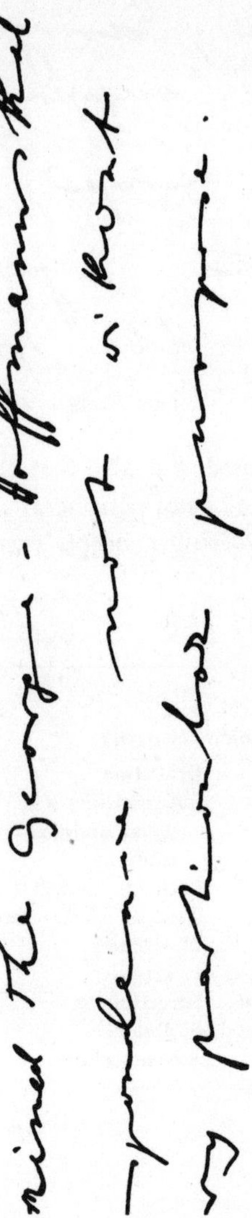

Fig. 48 (18%). Artificial wideness

Figs. 47-50 (18%). Width

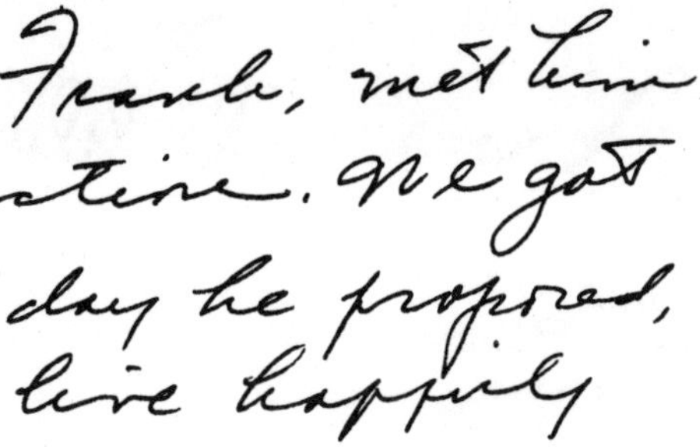

FIG. 49 (18%). Medium

FIG. 50 (18%). Narrow

FIGS. 47-50 (18%). Width (Cont'd)

THE HORIZONTAL DIMENSION

General Dynamic Aspects: Width, Slant, Total Right- and Leftwardness

Entering upon the most manifold of all the dimensions of the writing movement, along which this movement as a total process takes place and which has previously been defined as representing a person's system of orientation in terms of his reality contacts, we find a first group of sub-criteria suggested by the overall nature of this movement.

The first one of these is the horizontal extension per se which, in its

FIG. 51 (7%). Leftward slant, marked

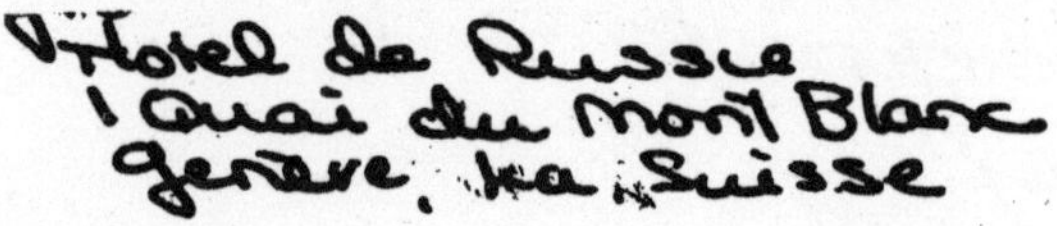

FIG. 52 (7%). Leftward slant, moderate

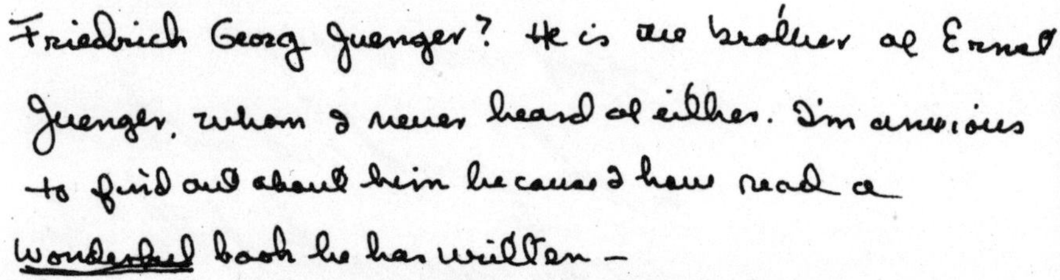

FIG. 53 (7%). Perpendicular with slight leftward slant

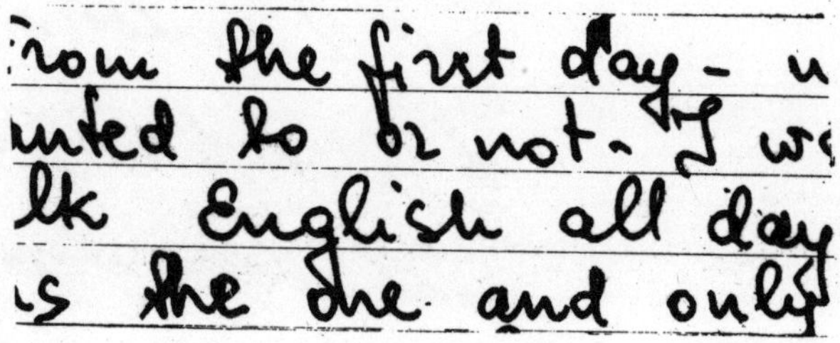

FIG. 54 (7%). Perpendicular

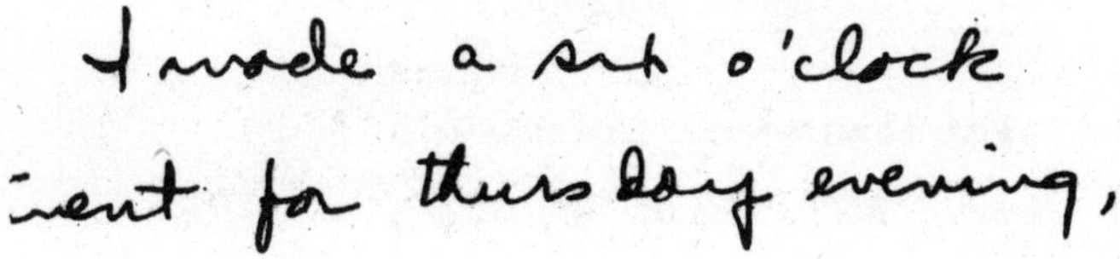

FIG. 55 (7%). Perpendicular with slight rightward slant

FIGS. 51-58. Slant

relation to the vertical extension, can only be assessed according to the width between downstrokes, in the middle zone, as proportionate to their lengths. The second one is the relative slant of the letters, their direction in terms of the angles they form with the basis, or writing line.

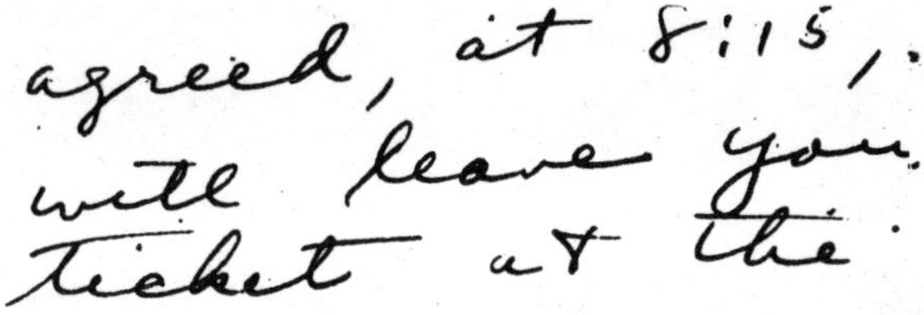

DIMENSIONS OF RATING

FIG. 56 (7%). Rightward slant, moderate

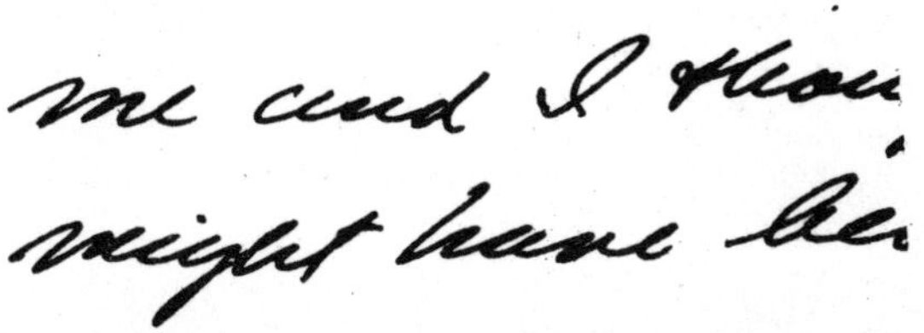

FIG. 57 (7%). Rightward slant, accentuated

FIG. 58 (7%). Rightward slant, extreme.

FIGS. 51-58. Slant (Cont'd)

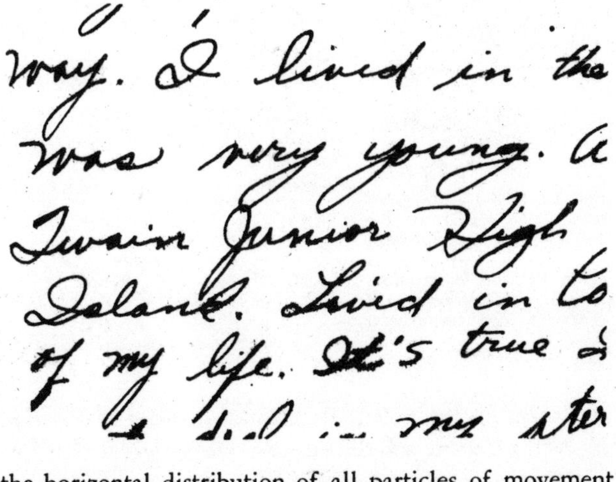

FIG. 59 (31%). Increased total leftwardness

The third one is the horizontal distribution of all particles of movement directed either rightward or leftward, considered in their total amounts and relative to a cross of coordinates made up by the writing basis as the abscyssa and any line perpendicular to it as the ordinate (figs. 47-62).

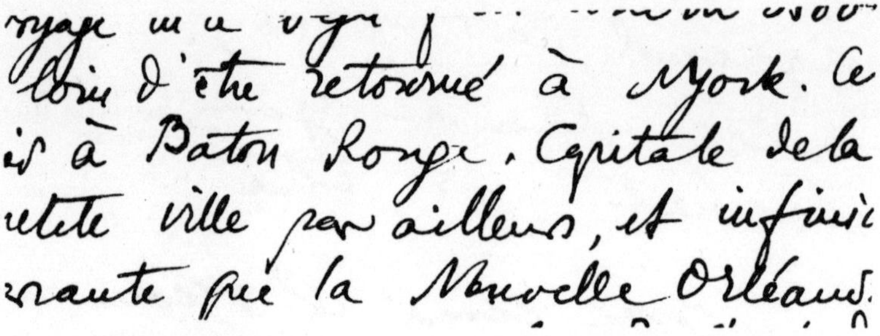

[handwriting sample]

FIG. 60 (7%). Leftwardness and rightwardness in balance

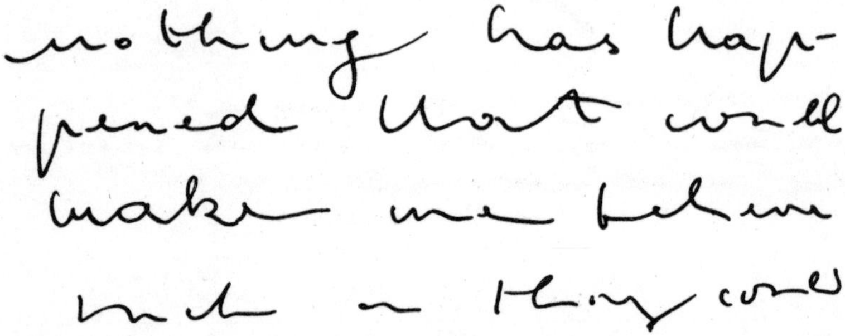

[handwriting sample]

FIG. 61 (31%). Increased total rightwardness

FIG. 62 (7%). Increased total leftwardness in the first name of the signature of a patient with feelings of guilt and frustration, general secretiveness of character, and obsessional trends

[signature sample]

Analyzing the potential gestural qualities of the movement as implied in each of these sub-dimensions, we arrive at the following definitions.

The degree of the *width* represents the degree of impulse externalization per se; more specifically, its relation to the personal *sense of economy* is obvious already from a consideration of its direct effect upon the rate of absorption of paper.

DIMENSIONS OF RATING

The degree of *slant* represents the degree to which the ego "inclines" toward (respectively, leans back from) its objectives (goals, partners, subject matters—either real or imaginary), in other words, the degree of self-identification with these objectives and hence that of *communicativeness*.

The degree of total rightwardness represents the degree to which impulse externalization per se and communivativeness *in their given degrees* can proceed without stirring up counter-impulses directed towards the self.

In order to assess the latter meaningfully, we have to realize that our writing system itself is rightwardly directed. This postulates a frame of reference implying a greater basic allowance for rightward than for leftward movements.

The following tables of potential character trends indicated by dynamic qualities of writing within the horizontal dimension can therefore be drawn up.

TABLE VII

Horizontal Dimension I

General Dynamic Qualities

Width

Wide		Narrow	
+	−	+	−
Spontaneity	Lack of self-control	Restraint	Over-cautiousness
Impulsivity	Rashness	Self-control	Inhibitedness
Drive	Carelessness	Reserve	Distrust
Elan	Neglect	Moderation	Suspicion
Zeal	Impatience	Self-consistency	Anxiety
Courage	Inability to delay	Cautiousness	"Embarrassment"
Boldness	Lack of thoroughness	Considerateness	Calculation
Striving	"All-out" attitudes	Tactfulness	Manipulation of attitudes
Goalmindedness	"Head through the wall"	Contentment	Self-containment
Socialmindedness		Sense of economy	Hidden ambition
Sociability	Elusiveness		Negativism
Motility of expression	Uncautiousness		Jealousy
	Adventurousness		Malice
Active ambition	Inconsiderateness		Cunningness
Frankness	Conventionality		Deceitfulness
Freshness	Gregariousness		Reluctance to give
Desire to give	Lack of economy		Avarice
	Tactlessness		
	"Freshness"		

Direction of Letters

Rightward Slant

+	−
Dominance of social feelings	Lack of control and restraint
Ability to love	Immoderateness
Passion	Lack of good measurement
Devotion	Lack of discipline
Self-sacrifice	"Happy-go-lucky"
Adaptability	Lack of leisure
Dexterity	Impatience
Social ease	Haste
"Doing a thing for its own sake"	Restlessness
Verbal articulateness	Distractability
Communicativeness	Over-adaptability
Optimism	Over-susceptibility to external promptings
Sociability	Self-inconsistency
Curiosity	Excitability
	Aggressiveness
	Verbosity
	"Rhetorics"
	Over-optimism

Quality of the Perpendicular

+	−
Dominance of intellect (regardless of capacity)	Lack of empathy
Control and restraint	Coldness
Caution	Quality of the "unemotional"
Imperviousness	Pitilessness
Self-collection	Lack of external interest
Foresight	Indifference
"Personal distance"	Self-containment
Self-consistency	Egotism
Contentment	Rigidity
Sense of dependence	Shut-off qualities
Pride	Uncommunicativeness
Unswerving attitude	Pessimism
"Weighing one's words"	
Skepticism	

Leftward Slant

+	−	
Self-conquest	Self-consciousness	Arrogance
Self-denial	Self-coercion	Dearth of emotions
Introspectiveness	Forced behavior	Egotism
Freedom from illusions	Stiltedness	Fear of committing oneself
	Affectation	(Blockings)
	Artificiality	Quality of the unapproachable
	Manipulation of attitudes	Cynicism
	Pretentiousness	
	Conceit	

"Manipulation of attitudes," as listed under the minus sign for narrow handwriting, can reach as far as to simulate, owing to a certain chosen "attitude," the basic quality of impulse externalization itself. In this case, the manipulation would effect movement components according to

Total Relative Right- and Leftwardness

Prevailing Total Rightwardness "Extraversion" in its proper sense		Prevailing Total Leftwardness "Introversion" in its proper sense	
+	−	+	−
Adaptability	Dependency	Sense of self-account	Self-centeredness
Sense of enterprise	Weakness	Independence	Selfishness
Dexterity	"Easily influenced"	Determination	Over-sensitivity
Empathy	Suggestibility	Self-loyalty	Accumulation of affect
Helpfulness	Forgetfulness	Sense of self-preservation	Resentment
Unselfishness	Lack of contemplativeness	Reflexiveness	Cruelty
Altruism	Lack of economy of forces	Contemplativeness	Jealousy
Goodness	Agitation of impulses	Meditativeness	Envy
"Humanitarianism"	Fickleness	Accentuation of memory functions	Egotism
Desire to give	Precipitation of judgment	Self-collection	Sentimentality
	Blindness for danger	Lyrical propensities	Compulsion to appropriate
	Wastefulness	Ability to appropriate	Desire to take (Narcissism)
	"Spreading oneself thin"		

the degree to which awareness of the rightward progression is implied in their execution. This means that letters themselves would remain relatively unaffected, while their connections would be lengthened. In the literature and in graphological practice, this sign is referred to as *artificial wideness* and is interpreted as one of the most distinct manifestations of a calculated type of sociability.

Since the principles which govern the width, slant, and total right- and leftwardness of handwriting are the same which determine the field of interaction between the human organism and his environment in general, it may be worthwhile to define their relationship to certain basic concepts of present day holistic psychology. Referring again to Andras Angyal's *Foundations for a Science of Personality,* we recognize his "trend toward autonomy" in the combined graphic trend toward *wideness* on the one hand, increased total *leftwardness* on the other. Since "wideness" and "leftwardness" operate in opposite directions, this seems to require a more ample comment. The tendency to master as fully as possible the heteronomous power of the environment evidently calls for rightward extensivity—i.e., wideness—in graphic movement, but rightward extensivity alone would be mere self-exposure without the presence of movements positively establishing and securing the position of the person as one of independence, of "autonomy" in front of the "field"; and heteronomous forces, accordingly, will the more be found to be in actual dominance over the life of the person the more his handwriting tends toward a combination of narrowness with increased total rightwardness in its movements. Regarding the role of the letter directions, finally, the rightward slant as an indicator of the personal need for *communication* clearly relates to all those human tendencies which *incline* toward experiences within the general area of emotional participation, of group integration, and of spiritual communion, i.e., in Angyal's terminology, to the *trend toward homonomy,* reduction in which, in consequence, is graphically represented by a corresponding reduction in rightwardness of the direction of letters. Exempt from the latter rule are only personality systems characterized by a highly static hierarchy of values in whom the trend toward homonomy is itself almost fully internalized and is graphically operating toward a particular intensification of the *form quality.*

While the three general dynamic qualities of the horizontal dimension represent sharply distinct aspects of expressivity, their interrelations in terms of the physical possibilities of distribution of graphic movement are all the more indicative of their common dependence on the personality organization; at least if we restrict our view to a consideration of middle zone movement it can be stated that the positional values of any two of them are bound to determine that of the third. This is clearly demonstrable by any attempt at deliberate changes of one's handwriting in any two of these aspects; e.g., a combination of rightward slant beyond a certain degree with narrowness beyond a certain degree results inevitably in increases in total leftwardness of the trail. If, on the other hand, we go to such an extreme as to undertake a complete omission of leftward movement, the demand for two positional values as determining the third is reduced to a demand for only one: regardless of the width of the writing, such omission is not possible without turning any original letter direction into a leftward slant. This total situation is only in accordance with a phenomenological analysis of the interrelations of the corresponding aspects of personality organization itself: e.g., a conjunction of a strong trend toward homonomy with strong inhibitory restrictions in the externalization of basic organismic impulses can neither be found nor be conceived without the presence of an emphatic introversiveness of the character; a total constriction of the inner life of the person can neither be found nor be conceived without a corresponding constriction—with all its implications of emotional coldness and standoffish egotism—of his trend toward homonomy; etc. While it is clear that peripheral movement may modify any configuration of middle zone horizontal dynamic aspects, it is also clear that such modification can neither extend to the width of the writing nor serve a more than compenastory function in either of the two other areas; moreover, in at least one of them, the area of the letter directions, such compensation will of necessity result in rhythmical inconsistencies reflecting corresponding ones of the personality structure itself.

The situation thus revealed is informative on a number of accounts. For one, it serves to demonstrate vividly three basic tenets of the holistic concept of personality dynamics, the impossibility of interpreting relationships between different manifestations of the psyche in terms of either a machine theory or causal genetics, the supremacy of a unifying principle of system action from which all single manifestations of the psyche radiate, and the correlation existing between the "good order" thus provided for the operations of the psyche and the order of self-distribution of phenomena in the physical world. Beyond these more general implications, however, the interdependence of the three named aspects is of special significance in view of the intricate and by no means necessarily antagonistic relations it reveals—relations important particularly for an understanding of human creativity—between the strength and inner organization of the trend toward autonomy on the one hand, the strength and specific direction of the trend toward homonomy on the other. As, in psychological literature, the former trend may thus far have been defined too narrowly, while the latter has altogether been treated too little and with a far too exclusive attention to personality's relations to its concrete and immediate social environment, the disclosures of the writing field imply a direct suggestion for further exploration in the indicated direction.

Static Aspects I: the Word

Applying the principles of quasi-spatial symbolic experience to the experience material in its given over-all units, the single words, we encounter the dimension representative of the person's self-experience in his approach towards the environment. From our previous analysis of rightward movement per se, applying its results to the word body, it follows that the word represents a trail of contacting movement, from which we can infer the symbolic placement of the ego at the beginning, of the contact objective at the end of the words; the word beginnings would therefore relate to the self-experiencing ego, the endings to the manner in which contacts in life are made or avoided. As the accentuation of the experience of interruption between words beginning with minuscles, or small letters, particularly if they are short forms, is relatively subliminal, emphasis must be placed on interruptions preceding majuscles, or capital letters. This implies attention to these word beginnings themselves as well as to those word endings immediately preceding an interruption of this kind, since the person's inner preparation for the comparatively "heavier" task ahead which the capital letters represent already accentuates his closure of the preceding word in a manner of greater finality of his inner attitude; even apart from this special condition, however, closures are generally of greater relative indicativeness than minuscular beginnings.

The consequences this situation implies for a detailed application of all dimensional criteria to the left-rightward phaseology of the word are as fruitful as they are inexhaustible. Neither here, as we have not yet taken up in our discussion a number of the criteria involved, nor within the limited framework of this book altogether, can there be attempted a halfway complete description of all the possible combinations applying here. Yet, one particular aspect of this phaseology seems important enough to be mentioned: since the writer, due to the interruptions imposed by the confines of the word, is more aware of his activity as such at both the beginnings and ends of words, analysis of the word-interior is of particular importance for investigation of impulses tending to escape his consciousness (figs. 63-64). Furthermore, an over-all analysis at least of majuscular beginnings imposes itself at this point, both on account of its particular importance for clinical work and in view of the especially distinct graphic physiognomy which majuscular beginnings derive from the fact that their very make-up involves the vertical dimension, the dimension of available values, thus accentuating their significance as representative of the ego in its self-relationships.

A table for the rating of ego-emphasis, with its possible positive and negative implications, is provided at the end of this chapter. It is clear that this tabulation had to be restricted to the degrees of total quantitative emphasis placed on capital letters, but also, that other and more specific,

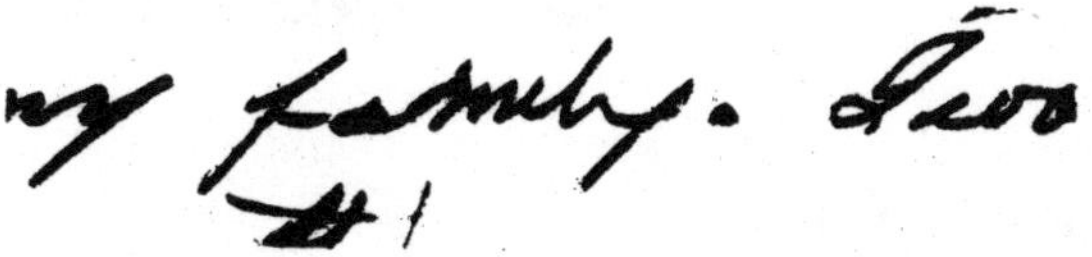

FIG. 63 (7%). Impulses of defiant self-enclosure in an incipient schizophrenic

FIG. 64 (7%). Sharp alternation of impulsivity and constriction in an hysteric patient

FIGS. 63-64 (7%). Word interior

yet not less important aspects of majuscular articulation suggest their analysis. Not to speak here of any particular form qualities entering into this subject, the movement impulses underlying the directional articulation of capital letters in either the vertical or horizontal dimensions largely co-determine their psychological meaning. As the reader is already more familiar with the principles of expressive movement analysis, an application of these principles to specific majuscular forms, against the background of their overall interpretative position in the system, will cause him no great difficulties. As a guiding empirical instance here the fact may be mentioned that capital letters of excessive height combined with excessive narrowness are generally found in the handwritings of ambitious students and young scientists who nurture high spiritual aspirations in conjunction with an over-sensitive ego, and who socially are timid and emotionally more or less inhibited (figs. 65-67).

Another observation which may be of interest in this connection, is the sometimes observable tendency to enlarge minuscular beginnings of words to a degree approaching or attaining the proportions of capital letters. Without particular effort on the interpreter's part, this characteristic reveals itself as relating to self-assertive impulses manifesting themselves with special propensity in situations objectively not calling for them.

FIG. 65

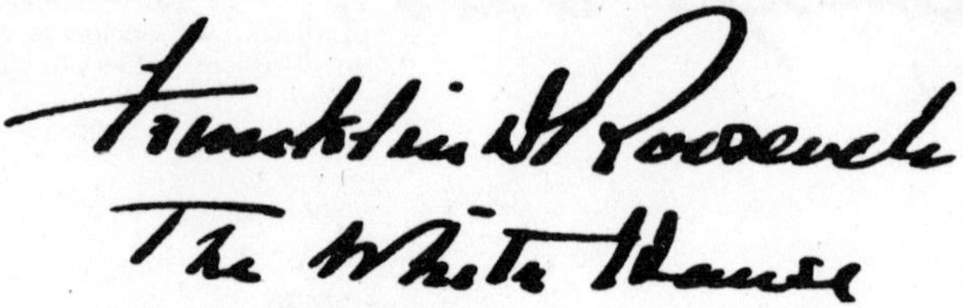

[handwritten: Dear Doctor—]

[handwritten: Franklin D Roosevelt] FIG. 66

[handwritten: The White House]

FIG. 67

[handwritten: This is the record]

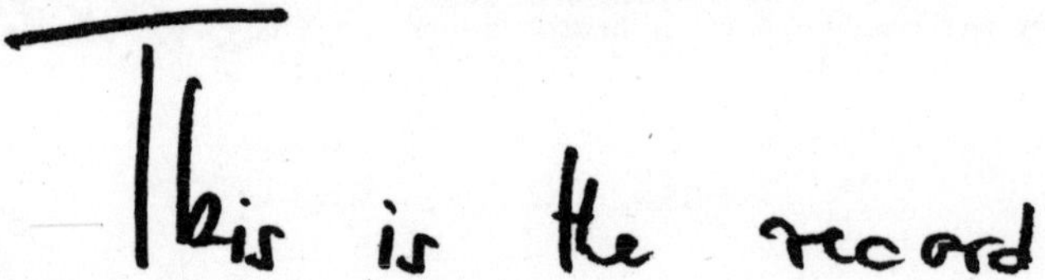

FIGS. 65-67 (7%). Various types of ego emphasis

TABLE VIII

Accentuation of Capital Letters

Ego-emphasis

Dignity	*Vanity*
Identification with higher values	Self-assertiveness
Spiritual self-awareness	Pretentiousness
Desire for greatness	Boastfulness
Sense of distinction	Arrogance
Sense of honor	Conceit
Leadership	"Superiority complexes"
Pride	"Grandeur"

Specific Dynamic Aspects: the Forms of Binding

In distinction from patterns of printed script, the letter forms making up school patterns of handwriting are shaped in such a way as to lend themselves easily to the act of linking them into contiguous left-rightward movement; the shape of the linking parts themselves, however, in the way in which the school patterns prescribe it, is not determined by any strict necessity immanent to the movement. Since the task of binding letters together can, with essentially equal mechanical facility, be accomplished in various different manners, it, more than any other element of handwriting, invites the person's "typical gesture" to show up. In view of the nature of the letter forms, a precise criterion for where the letter ends and the "form of binding"—also termed "connective type" here and there in the literature—begins cannot be defined but neither does it appear necessary: the individuality of the movement is the same in all its part-elements, letters as well as forms of binding; the latter, however, not only show the person in those phases of impulse externalization bringing about, due to the necessities of "tying up," of "stepping forward," his typical gesture and thus, in a highly crystallized version, his individuality itself, but these forms of binding, more clearly than the forms of written letters proper, lend themselves to qualitative analysis and classification.

The typical gesture itself is more or less removed from the relatively neutral forms of binding of the school patterns, a fact which, if sufficient "background" data are given, can serve as a criterion for assessing the degree to which personality development has led away from such cultural attitudes as were immanent to the "style" featured by the writer's education. Apart from handwritings more or less sticking to that relative graphic and psychological neutrality of the school, samples can be grouped according to the more or less distinct prevalence in them of one of the following four main forms of binding (fig. 68): the *garland*, the *arcade*, the *angle*, the *thread*.

FIG. 68 (7%). Prototypes

angle

garland

arcade

thread

FIGS. 68-86 (7%). Forms of binding

In order to reach an understanding of their meaning, a first and simpler dichotomy seems necessary: all handwriting is more or less angular, more or less curved. The symbolic implications of "angularity" and "curvedness" from the viewpoint of direct experience are relatively well-known, and so is the consistency of these implications regardless of the element in which they manifest themselves: Wolfgang Koehler's experiment with "Maluma" and "Takete" will be remembered by many. Expounding these qualities here can therefore be restricted to a necessary minimum.

The two qualities of angularity and curvedness can be said to involve, as its inescapable attributes, the totality of our reality experience. The more complex phenomena combine both of them in varied manners and proportions; the more "elementary," however, the phenomena the more are they articulated in one way or the other: it is impossible to associate angularity, for example, with clouds, curvedness with lightning. Within the life-lifelessness, animal-plant, masculinity-femininity, polarities, "life," "animal," "femininity" are inescapably more on the side of the curve; not less inescapably, "lifelessness," "plant," "masculinity," more on the side of the angle. The two qualities, therefore, are psychological realities of the first order, the phenomenological essence of which, in assessing movement, we only have to relate to the specific articulation, in terms of their polarity, of any given movement, in order to understand some of the most fundamental qualities of the specific inner experience that particular movement conveys: inescapably, the straight line necessitating the angle in order to allow of directional changes is on the side of firmness, determination, hardness, finality, fight; the curved line, providing the directional change by itself, on the side of yieldingness, elasticity, smoothness, reconciliation, softness; the straight line on the side of pushing, aggressing, aiming, hitting; the curved line on the side of compromising, joining, engulfing, embracing. Regarding the psychological backgrounds proper, Klages has been instrumental in clarifying the situation: "A movement evidently comes out the straighter the more exclusively its motivation is dominated by the image of the movement goal; the more angular, the more it carries this exclusiveness over to a new goal determining a change of direction; the more curved the more it does not obey the goal image as much as a need for combining and uniting." (*Handschrift und Charakter*, p. 83). It follows that definite attitudes, definite forms of wishing, wanting, giving, taking, doing, are conveyed by the forms of binding, but also, that a relative lack of definite attitudes would be reflected by the more or less complete absence of a distinct and articulate form of binding and to the extent of that absence. The latter observation is basic to an understanding of one of the mentioned main forms, the thread; concerning the others, it becomes clear that two of them, the garland and the arcade, each representing a specific combination of angularity and curvedness, should be preceded in our discussion by the far more elementary *angle*.

On the basis of what has already been said about it in the foregoing, angularity could be interpreted as *necessitating* an uncompromising approach to his environments on the part of the writer. Obviously, however, the indicator can be restricted already in this, its seemingly basic significance, by the principle of interdependence, here operating in the form of other indicators primarily provided by two of the three general dynamic aspects of the horizontal dimension, i.e., narrowness or prevailing total leftwardness, or any combination of them; "unreadiness to compromise" can be modified by caution, diplomacy, self-preservation to such an extent that its behavioral picture is clouded even though the mentioned realistic character traits may seem to articulate rather than abate this "unreadiness" once we take a more distant view of the life course and focus upon the person's actual achievements. Yet, since "unreadiness to compromise" and "diplomacy" remain logical opposites, we have to look for an even wider and more basic category to cover "angularity"; we find it provided by a realization of the type of inner experience underlying this form of movement. Unreadiness to compromise—in the sense only of inner experiences having the form of such unreadiness—no longer necessarily implies uncompromising behavior, but does imply a primary orientation toward *violence*, i.e., the abrupt display of concentrated energy for the solution of conflicts. This in turn implies that the ego-reality relation itself is being experienced under the primary form of conflict allowing only of "up" and "down" strokes, in brief, of "either-or" decisions in the sense of an inescapable inner alternative the writer faces: he pursues his life course, not necessarily uncompromisingly —his compromises, however, if otherwise indicated, are more likely to have the form of patience, self-restraining moderation, awaiting his hour, etc., than that of yielding in his ultimate goals—but he does, in any case, pursue it as a successive execution of *decisions* of whatever kind and content, each engendered by the experience of a conflict situation and each generating the impetus which he needs to drive on towards the next one.

This generative capacity of the typical angular writing movement is confirmed by a consideration of the type of action here involved on its physiological side also. Except for angular trails so overcontrolled that their execution is carried out with particular slowness—in which instance the combined presence of slowness and angularity will suggest a special case of deliberateness and artificiality both motivationally and from the viewpoint of visual experience—the performance of straight and at the same time sharply terminated movements of the fingers is not possible without the emergence of a counterimpulse. Like all bodily movements of this kind, they are subject to processes of involuntary muscular recoil, i.e. to proprioceptive reflexes deriving from compensatory innervations of the "passive" muscle and relieving its previous intracentral block (Sherrington's "secondary induction" phenomenon), an effect which will be the stronger the faster the movement happens to have been. The necessity to control this recoil is basic to all co-ordinated volitional movement but the manner of conducting this control is characterologically revealing. The particular attitude of the producer of the fast angular trail toward the task of control can be defined as an inclination to master the reflex by utilizing it, without any attempt at suppression, in its full natural force and approximately also in its given direction. The psychological implications of this behavior are manifold. One aspect of the complex here encountered is that his displays of motor energy are fed directly by the force of impulsivity, that obeying the latter and controlling it are one in his experience, and that between internal needs and external "role" no antagonism or even separation is allowed, a constellation which in turn implies, negatively, that he has little awareness of his position in the social environmental field, positively, that he is strongly inclined to become as fully as possible absorbed in his actions and interests, inclined to "do a thing for its own sake." On the other hand, since it follows from our analysis of his way of mastering the proprioceptive reflex that experiences of the fullest impulse release and of the fullest volitional concentration must succeed each other in him in the briefest intervals conceivable, a particular propensity for extreme and rapid changes of set is indicated, a conclusion which in turn implies a predisposition on his part, negatively for inner conflict, positively for the accentuated "self-steering" so inherent in the dynamics of creative thought.

A further conclusion postulated by this inner situation of the angle-writer is his basic *moralism,* not in the sense of any necessary level, type, or quality of his morality—which of course can range (according to the form level and criteria from other dimensions) all the way from very high to very low—but in the sense that his inner experiences are articulated according to an imperative need to say *yes* or *no*. In brief, incessantly, even in his most ordinary functions of daily life, as already known to relate to the middle zone of handwriting, the angle-writer is compelled to orient himself according to values, regardless again of what type and quality: the relation of "up" and "down" strokes in the middle zone to the peripheral zones of the vertical dimension is likewise quite compelling and only shows the complex here discussed from one more of its manifold aspects. The resulting total psychological picture of graphic angularity has now to be developed in its contours to lead to the table of potential character traits provided for it at the end of this sub-chapter.

In view of its rigidity of impulse coordination—which by no means necessitates an ineffectiveness of the latter—the nearest relative of the angle among the other main forms of binding is clearly the arcade; their differences, however, are at least as large as their similarities. In the angle, the contraction-release cycle is so accentuated by the person's experience of its poles that no room for transition between the two remains. This takes away from the movements of release the quality of "flowing" necessary for their full conscious articulation as experiences of release; in consequence, and in accordance with all the other aspects of character structure suggested by this form, the angle-writer is hypothecated as repressing such inner demands for conscious release-experiences as, being a human, he necessarily encounters. Analyzing now the arcade in the one aspect of its gestural profile comparable with the aspect of angularity just discussed, we find a widely different structure. In the arcade, contraction is built up articulately and released briefly but, due to the experience of an obstacle *surmounted,* a position *secured,* which its gestural profile suggests, the release turns out to be a downflow of used-up energy allowing the writer a moment of rest: unlike "release" in the angle, where each line, being a straight dash, tends to shoot beyond its goal unless arrival at that point results in the immediate reception of a new push in the opposite direction, release in the arcade, notwithstanding its briefness and if certainly less so than in the contractive phase of the arcade movement, is still *consciously articulated*.

The stated motoric experiences of difficulty-to-stop and resting-easily for angle and arcade, respectively, are easily available to anyone desiring to experiment with both forms himself. The arcade, according to this and all other indications, relates to an experience of pausing after a point of resistance has been taken *not* by hitting but by surrounding, overcoming, persuading, appropriating, depending, cultivating it; concerning the "appropriation," "defense" and "cultivation" facets, its gestural resemblance with a hand reaching out graspingly but also protectingly or caressingly is obvious. The arcade, quite visibly, is a gesture of closure, of either setting confines to one's realm, not to be trespassed by what or whoever is beyond them, or else carrying these confines forward in action. The angle-writer, if only at the price of a continuous action without peace and pause, still has intercourse with the environment: experiencing ego and environment as necessarily conflicting counter-poles, he thereby still is united with the environment in one way, for both share in "disunity," which to him is the only "real" experience; to the arcade-writer, the environment is "real," i.e., matters, only as far as he has power over it, and he himself is "real" only is as far as he can have peace, i.e., release his tension, which he cannot do but after having incorporated some environment in one of his articulately built-up movements of contraction.

The arcade, thus, is a gesture of ruling as well as fencing-off, and its scope of possible positive meanings, radiating from this basis, is thereby determined. Some of its implications may not at once be obvious; one is a certain feeling of an inner void or vacuum, and of the need to elude that vacuum by the concave perimetric movement of the semi-circle, which it conveys and which is applied in the gestalt quality of the arch itself which is essential to it and from which its name derives. The determining expressive quality of the arch, if we clarify it in our inner experience, is a maintenance of definite and stable form or rule, i.e., in terms of symbolic meaning, of reality itself, *"in spite"* of the void which it bridges. That gives it a demonstrative character: the arch "represents," and from this its great role in the architecture of the Roman empire, all-time model of the imperialistic state, becomes understandable. The arcade, therefore, is frequent both in the handwritings of members of ruling social groups dominated by the obligation of representativeness of attitude which their origin and status impose on them, and of schizoid and schizophrenic individuals shutting themselves off and, in their seclusion, facing the maintenance of a feeling of reality as their primary life problem.

Embracing all these related shades of meaning in one category, we can define the arcade as the most specific gesture of ego-articulation. In the interest of clarity, the difference between it and the aforementioned ego-indicators is stressed. Regulation and pressure indicate an accentuation of volitional control in total personality functioning. Sharpness indicates a hierarchy of drives implying an accentuated experience by the ego of its inter-actions with the self and the environment but no necessary experience of *distance* from either. Perpendicularity is a gesture of abstention from emotional tie-ups with the environment. A low middle zone shows the ego functions accentuated by the need to escape discomforting inner stresses; a broad one shows the ego functions in a state of relaxation and of harmony with the self and its resources. Total leftwardness emphasizes the person in his relations to his past, his inner experiences, his material and instinctual resources, i.e., the self rather than the ego. Majuscular emphasis indicates an aggrandizement of the ego *image* as well as a strengthening of its motivating power. The arcade, finally, is an indicator of the ego exercising with emphatic increase in the experience of *distance* its most critical and self-constituent function as a *screen* between the self and the environment.

With an analysis of the *garland* this picture totally reverses itself. Where the arcade closes off, the garland opens up; where the arcade rules, the garland submits; where the arcade appropriates and protects, the garland gives out and lays open, exposing itself to the environment and drawing it in rather than imposing itself on it. This is corroborated by following some other of its aspects, all of which again converge towards the same psychological essence of its total expressive quality. In the arcade, the position of rest is at the bottom, immediately following the contraction, after the "surrounding of an obstacle"; in the garland, it is "suspended in air," after a long-drawn movement of release and preceding the here extremely short one of the new downward contraction. The implication of *confidence* in the choice of the resting place cannot escape us. The garland writer is at home *in* the world; the arcade writer's "home" is a place of security *from* it. To the arcade writer, the ego is basically more real than the environment; to the garland writer, the environment basically more real than the ego. To the arcade writer, the reality of the environment itself, which his gesture incorporates, depends upon the incorporation, i.e., upon the ego; to the garland writer, the ego is real only inasmuch as it experiences the influx of reality in its—to him—ultimate sense, i.e., of the environment. That in turn implies that the garland writer's inner orientation is dominated by emotional rather than ego functions, and it explains the garland's far greater frequency, suggested also by one aspect of its form character, in the handwritings of women than of men. Its relation to the affective psychoses likewise is evident from this premise. Regarding its possible negative implications, the varying shades of *parasitism* suggested by again other aspects of its form character, those of the taking hand and of "sucking," may be mentioned.

Where articulateness of character has either never come about or else gives way to disintegrative processes, its crystallized expression, the person's "typical gesture" becomes indistinct: the *thread* is a manifestation either of original attitudes more or less worn off or, as in some mental diseases but also, in form of a threading "tendency," in nervous, more or less chronic fatigue, of a basic inner state of indetermination beyond which the person has never progressed in his course of instinctual, emotional, and moral maturation, and which accordingly implies the total ambivalence of personality value characteristic of the inner and external condition not only of the pathoform problem children of society but also of its real and potential geniuses: in the latter case, the thread does not appear as the product of a wearing off of the other, so-called archaic, forms of binding, but as a capricious, more or less unruly alternation among them. Accordingly, for a proper evaluation of the thread as an indicator, it is decisive whether this graphic manipulation appears as a creative chaos bringing forth alternate archaic forms of binding, each in an articulate and original manner suggesting the continuous succession of divergent or antagonistic psychomotor forces each strong enough to enforce the person's total momentary identification with them at their times of evolvement—in which case one speaks of "primary thread"—or whether the picture is that of disruption, of "threading" in the more literal sense of a refusal to "commit oneself" by way of any articulate form—a refusal which essentially follows *only* the rightward impulse and thus the line of least resistance; combinations of both types are, of course, as possible as are combinations of both types of inner conditions here indicated. In the second case, that of "secondary thread," the inevitable result of such wearing-off of all form is always a reduction of the middle zone which, depending upon the strength of the super ego forces, can be absolute or relative, i.e., may or may not involve the peripheral zones also. At any rate, our previous discussion of the vertical dimension bears heavily upon an understanding of the thread as a type of graphic manipulation which, in one of its aspects, can be said to try to avoid an orientation in the realm of available values. This avoidance can either—where the peripheral components are also reduced—involve the person's total outlook on the self and the world, or it can, where the peripheral components, representing unabsorbed inner demands, are hypertrophied and where only in the middle zone vertical movement is kept at a minimum, be limited to an involvement of the daily life activities and the spontaneous attitudes actually assumed in their regard which are represented by the middle zone's contiguous rightward extension; in the latter case, a specification of the indications of stress conveyed by lowness of the middle zone suggests itself in the sense of an attribution of such stress to functional nervous disturbances.

More generally speaking, the secondary thread writer is not dominated by an identification with his activities as such in the sense of a meaningful experience of their phases, nor by a need for self-organization, self-fulfillment, personal and social articulateness *while* proceeding toward his goal images in the dimension of time, but evidently is dominated by the experience of having to get ahead in this dimension somehow and no matter how, having, in that process, to maintain his ego regardlessly and at any price. This implies that his leading motivation is drive for self-preservation operating at the expense of all others: the secondary thread, graphically, is a centripetal movement tending to reduce the short forms to their least possible vertical extension, i.e., to a mere point or dot, representative of the ego, continuously fleeing rightward and avoiding commitments on its way.

This implies that commitments cannot be handled for lack of both emotional and psychomotor substance, a constellation which, especially if the middle zone is highly reduced in its relation to the peripheral ones, conjures up the picture of coarctation in Rorschach psychograms. Another, and more specific, facet of the psychological picture of the thread, however, and one which applies both to primary and secondary thread, is the easy availability to the person of all kinds of "attitudes," a trait which specifically seems to relate to the most basic inner conditioning of creative talents, especially the musical one. In primary thread, where the primate of "self-preservation" merely implies indifference toward social norms of morality, this ambivalence, this inner indetermination of the child and the emotionally never-quite-maturing may be of great and genuine elementary force, and be coupled with the highest form level and an exceptionally high degree of rhythmical integration combined, of course, with extreme irregularity, as in the handwritings of Beethoven and Napoleon; in the secondary thread, where the same characteristic only operates by way of hinting, in a flighty, superficial, and more or less unoriginal or even mechanical manner, angles, arcades, and garlands, the mere implications of pathological lying and of a hysterical mimicry of emotions suggest themselves. The former can essentially always be assumed; the latter more especially where peripheral hypertrophies, instead of bearing down upon the middle zone in a manner of "pressing it together" rather tend to absorb centrifugal movement impulses abruptly alternating with centripetal tendencies of the thread itself. This absorption can show the form of blown-up or in other ways disproportionately enhanced extremities, particularly of the upper zone (the lower zone, in handwritings of the hysterics, is usually "crippled" but may likewise show significant abruptnesses of fluctuation); whether, in such cases, only a mild tendency toward hysterical "'exaggeration" or more serious conclusions are suggested again depends on qualitative attributes of this sign itself as well as on the global picture.

A special version of the thread is the double arch, which combines some essential elements of the general expressive quality of the thread with the greater allowance for vertical impulses of movement as well as with greater positive consistency of form. In the systematology of the forms of binding, it is important as the obviously most direct counter-pole, graphically as well as psychologically, to the angle; practically, it is rather infrequent. Its interpretation can be determined from its polarity with the angle: in the sense of the above statement it is the "winding line" per se, the gestural crystallization of a character which, while lacking in self-identification and actually avoiding commitments, has nevertheless a need to "approach" available values, even though at the actual moment of approach he avoids the obligations which values tend to impose. Behaving "as though" he were a moral and emotional entity and subjectively quite sincere in this attitude, it is not his self-interpretation but the possible scope of meaning of "sincerity" itself in his case which is subject to doubt: the double arch writer is "balanced" at the price of a constant external balancing, an inveterate diplomacy without ultimate aim or purpose, i.e., an all-out compromise both of his inner experiences and of his external behavior, which, positively, implies a special degree of social adaptability, negatively, the ivy-like "creeping" of the social parasite (fig. 69).

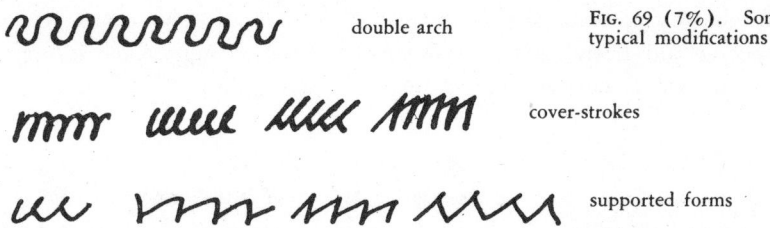

double arch

FIG. 69 (7%). Some typical modifications

cover-strokes

supported forms

FIGS. 68-86 (7%). Forms of binding (Cont'd)

Finally, one specific possible attribute of all forms of binding may briefly be discussed: the cover-stroke, either in the form of upstrokes following, to a certain point of their movement, the paths of the preceding downstrokes, or, vice-versa, of the latter following the paths of the preceding upstrokes, depending on the nature of the specific binding form; in the case of angular writing, it is clear that this movement is possible only at the price of the highly calculated and self-coerced appearance of a "third angle" in the interior of the middle zone in its vertical aspect. The sign combines the essential characteristics of narrowness, i.e., impediment of impulse externalization, with the more specific gestural quality of "hiding," "covering-up," "hands under the table," i.e., of *concealment;* further specific indications for the latter trait of character from other particles of handwriting will be taken up in a following section. While the full weight of the interpretation of this movement of over-control and an all-out craving for security as one of actual *mendacity* presupposes the presence of other signs indicating an unsincerity of motivations on the writer's part, and while it is restricted to a more extensive mutual coverage of the two strokes, the gravity of the sign as an indicator of concealment is lessened in the direction of mere "opportunism" where the extent of that coverage is reduced to a more limited section of the path of the first stroke. This modification of the movement necessitates a greater articulation of one of the graphic consequences of the cover-stroke in general which in the case of angular handwriting has already been hinted: a change in the direction of the second stroke at the point of departure from the path of the first one. In the graphological nomenclature, this modification of the movement, on account of its appearance, is referred to as "supported form," and is being considered as an approximation of the "worn-off" quality of secondary thread. Both its reduction in actual stroke-coverage and accentuated inconsistency of direction suggest the indicated specific modification of its psychological meaning (figs. 70-86).

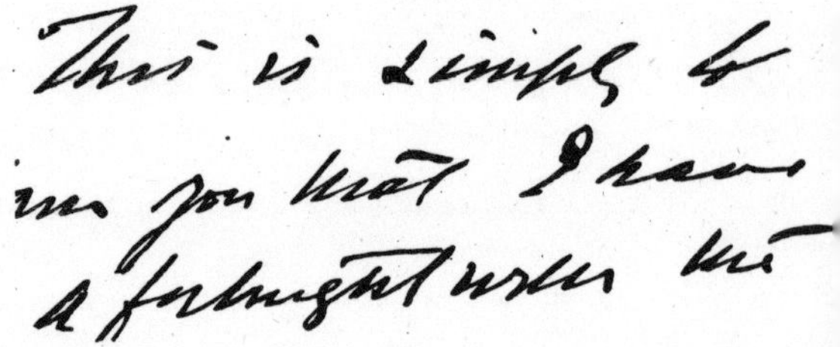

FIG. 70 (26%). Angles

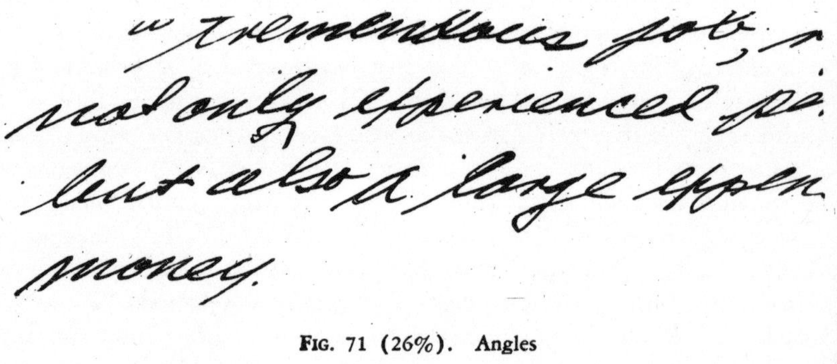

FIG. 71 (26%). Angles

FIGS. 68-86 (7%). Forms of binding (Cont'd)

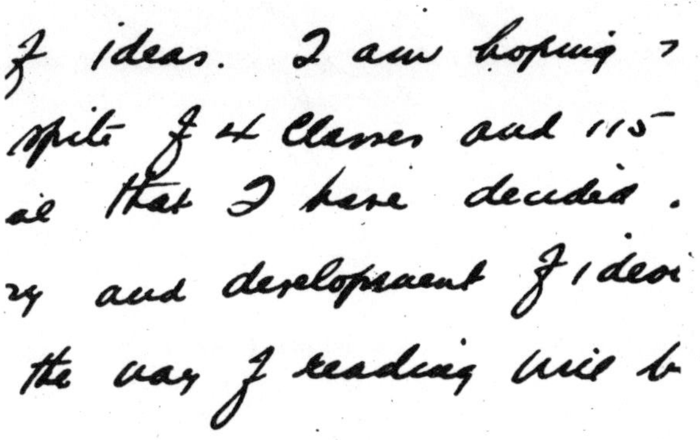

DIMENSIONS OF RATING

[handwriting sample]

FIG. 72 (7%). Garlands

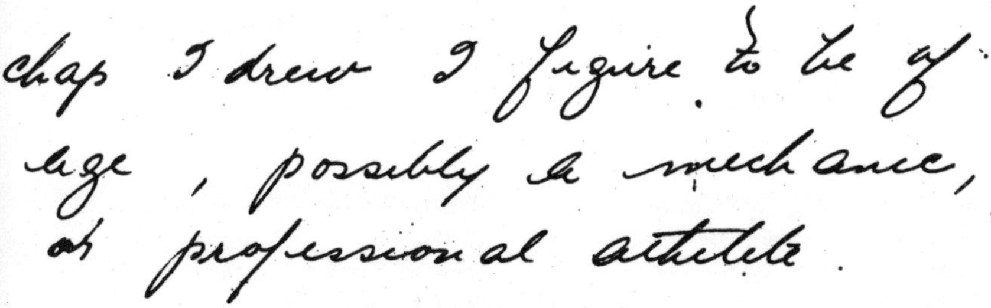

[handwriting sample]

FIG. 73 (7%). Garlands

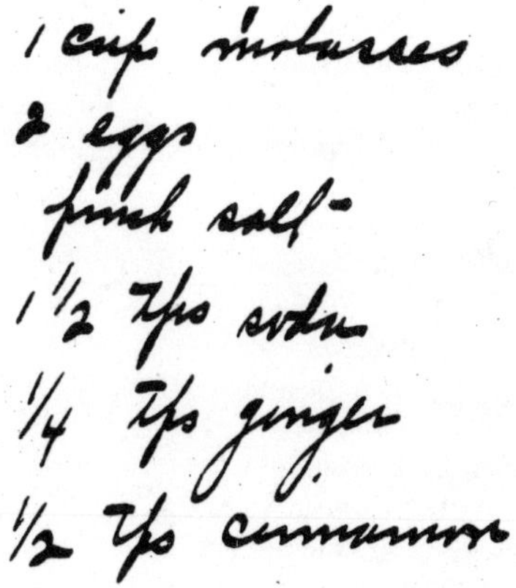

FIG. 74 (7%). Arcades

[handwriting sample: recipe]

FIGS. 68-86 (7%). Forms of binding (Cont'd)

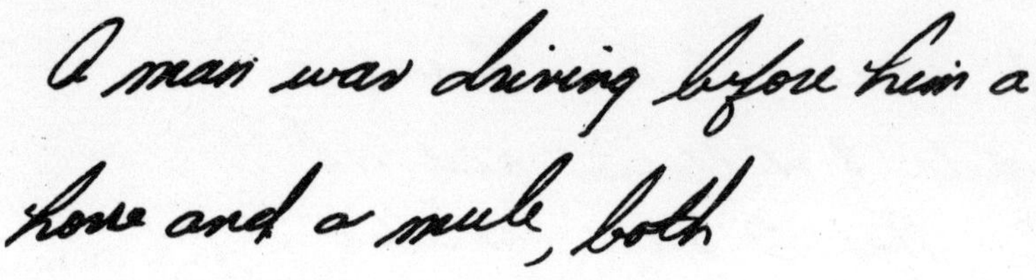

A man was driving before him a horse and a mule, both

FIG. 75 (7%). Arcades

FIGS. 68-86 (7%). Forms of binding (Cont'd)

TABLE IX

Forms of Binding

Angle		Arcade	
Orientation to goal image		Orientation to ego	
+	−	+	−
Purposefulness	Rigidity	Restraint	Insincerity
Stability	Obstinacy	Reserve	Mendacity
Resistance	"Hardened"	Distinction	Artificiality
Energy	Coldness	Sense of distance	Affectation
Firmness	Stubbornness	Sense of form and style	Pretention
Planfulness	Intransigeance		Egotism
Direction	Indifference	Sense of tradition	"Emptiness"
Determination	Vengefulness	Sense of stable values	Distrustfulness
Steadfastness	Pitilessness		Suspiciousness
Imperviousness	Negativism	Consistency of attitudes	Mannerism
"Uncompromising"	Irreconcilability		"Shut-off"
Sincerity	Inadaptability	Skepticism	(Lust for power)
Sense of obligation	Argumentativeness	Caution	(Loss of reality)
Responsibility	Quarrelsomeness	"Noblesse oblige"	
"Critical-minded"	"Disharmony"		
Self-criticism	Self-conflict		
Dutifulness	Aggressiveness		
Moralism	Self-aggressiveness		
Inclination toward ethical problems	Irritability		
	Excitability		
Manliness (in men)	(Temper tantrums)		
Creativeness in thinking	Masculinity (in women)		
	Abstruseness in thinking		

DIMENSIONS OF RATING

	Garland		Thread	
	Orientation to environment		Orientation to self-preservation	
			Primary thread	
				Decadence of values
	+	−	+	−
	Confidence	Indetermination	Immediateness and intensity of inner experience	Lack of sense of social obligation
	Goodness	Dependency	Originality	Lack of conscience
	Sincerity	"Easily influenced"	Readiness for any situation	Ruthlessness
	Frankness	Distractability from own course	Creativeness	Immoralism
	Tolerance	Over-confidence	Spontaneous "understanding" of others and of cultural and historic complexities	"Demoniac" qualities
	Elasticity	Lack of firm attitudes		Destructiveness
	Reconciliability	Changeability		"Evil genius"
	Adaptability	Fickleness	Prophetic foresight	
	Mildness	"Weakness of will"	Genius	
	Warmth (Naturalness)	Lack of discipline	Richness of inner resources	
	Empathy	Sloppiness		
	Ease of social contact	Emotionality		
	Readiness to recognize others	Affective swings		
	Readiness to help others	Femininity (in men)		
	Desire to give			
	Devotion			
	Womanliness (in women)			

Secondary thread

+	−
Versatility	Ambiguity
Prolificness	Insincerity
Dexterity	"Lack of character"
Elasticity	Resentment
Intuition	Envy
Adaptability	Femininity (in men)
Multiplicity of "talents"	"Cunning"
Actor's talent	Deceitfulness
Political sense	Mimicry
Diplomacy	Manipulation of affects
Ability to "survive"	Pathological susceptibility for "suggestions"
	"Mediumistic qualities"
	Hysteria
	Poverty of inner resources

(Musical talent)

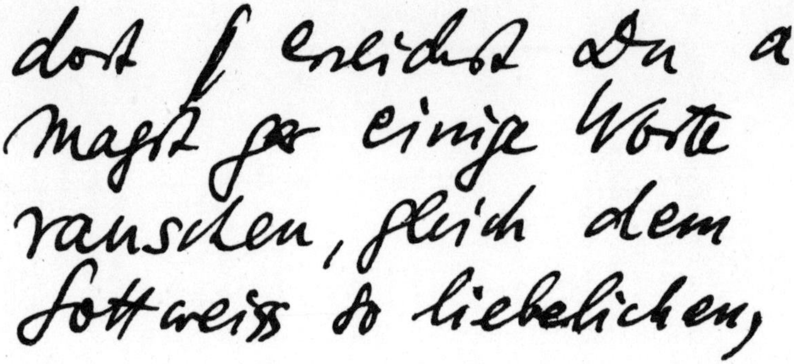

FIG. 76 (7%).   Primary thread

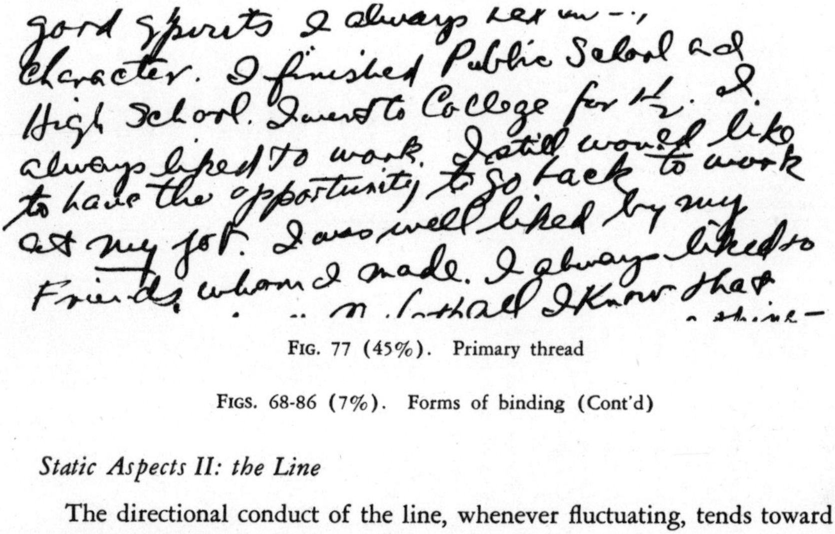

FIG. 77 (45%).   Primary thread

FIGS. 68-86 (7%).   Forms of binding (Cont'd)

Static Aspects II: the Line

The directional conduct of the line, whenever fluctuating, tends toward a greater amplitude of the visible results of fluctuation than any other graphic quality does. This suggests its particular closeness to the momentary emotional conditions experienced by the writer. A realization of the motoric processes underlying line-directional changes supports this view. The line "falls" whenever the arm of the person, due to a decrease in muscular extension in the movements of release, gradually sinks back toward the body. After the writing activity has covered a few pages, a slight degree of such decrease simply is the common consequence of

DIMENSIONS OF RATING

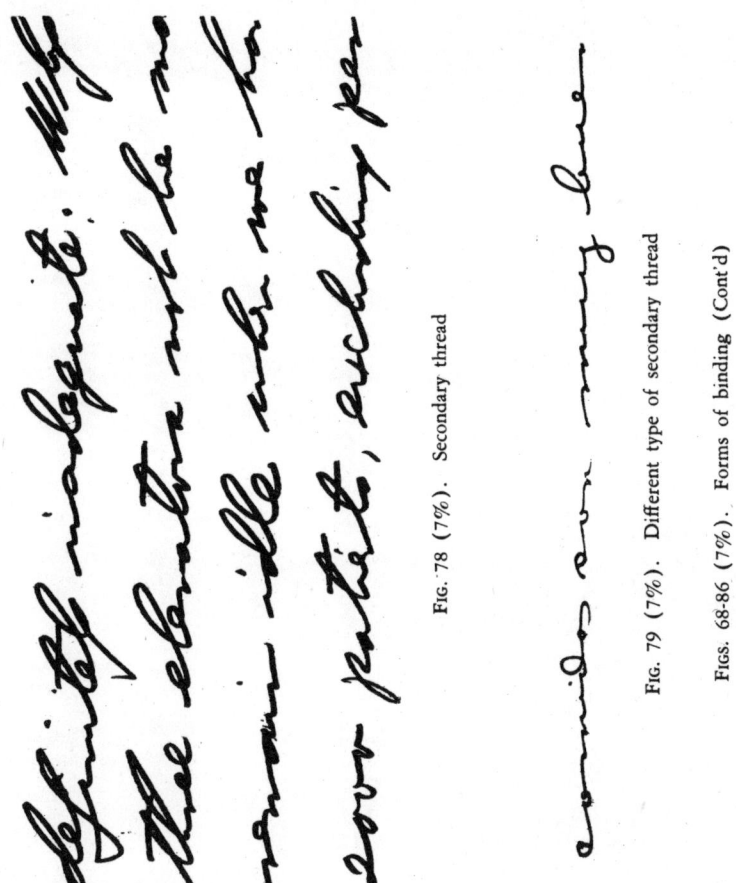

Fig. 78 (7%). Secondary thread

Fig. 79 (7%). Different type of secondary thread

Figs. 68-86 (7%). Forms of binding (Cont'd)

normal muscular fatigue. An unduly early decrease in muscular extensivity can be due to an originally present state of physical fatigue of a more acute nature, and the latter will be assumed if indicators from other dimensions do not point in the direction of a more chronic condition. A more chronic condition, on the other hand, will seem present, and its psychological correlate, discouragement or depression, will suggest itself, wherever specific indicators from other dimensions, like low-saddled and anergic, "drooping" garlands, tend to confirm it in a way which links the acute graphic appearance of depression with the graphic expression

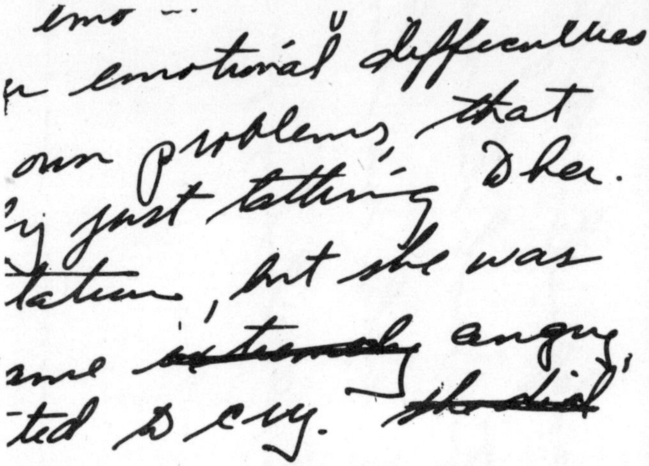

FIG. 80 (7%).
Different type
of secondary
thread

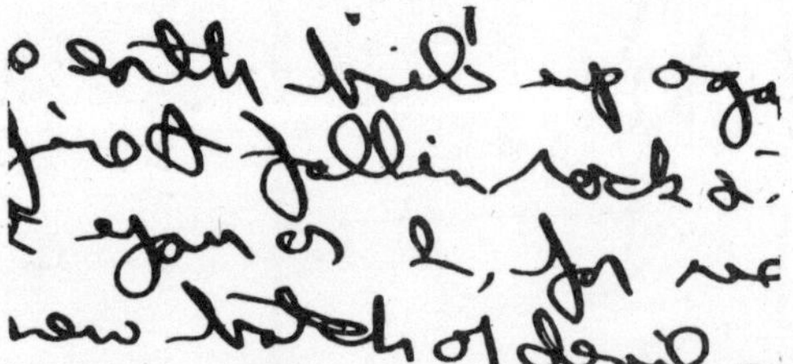

FIG. 81 (7%). Different type of secondary thread

FIGS. 68-86 (7%). Forms of binding (Cont'd)

of prevalent emotionality in the writer's character. The corresponding indications of a feeling of optimism, zeal, "elevation" suggest themselves for rising lines both on account of their gestural implications in terms of symbolic quasi-spatial experience and, as far as the more direct effectiveness of the paralleling muscular processes is concerned, of the increase,

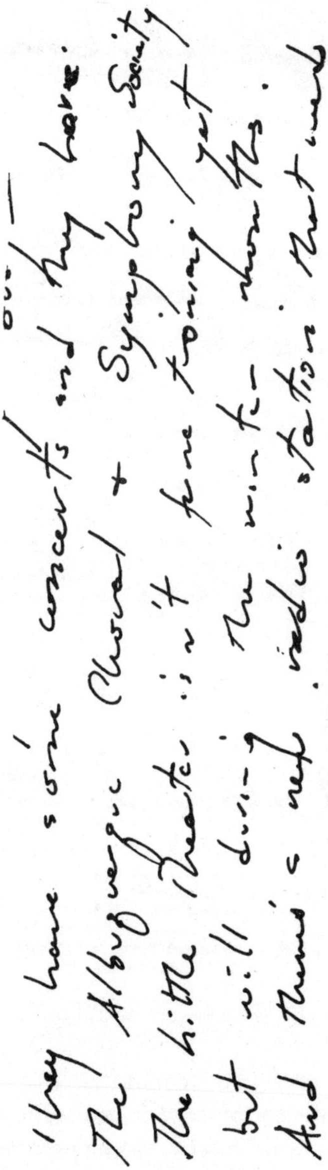

DIMENSIONS OF RATING

[Handwriting sample rotated 90°:]

"They have some concerts and they have
The Albuquerque Chorval + Symphony Society
The Little Theater isn't fine towns. Just
but will during the winter months.
And there is not radio stations that work"

FIG. 82 (7%). Different type of secondary thread

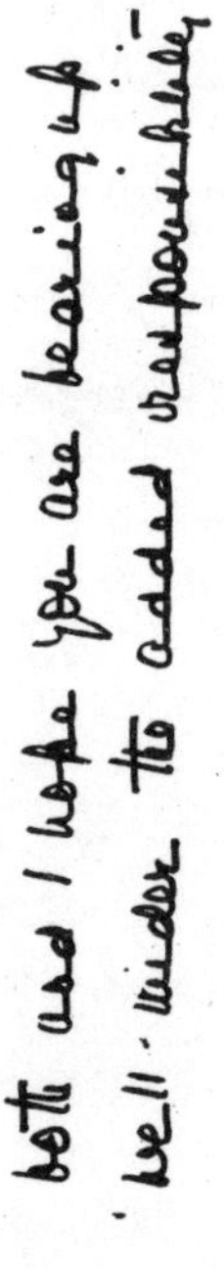

[Handwriting sample rotated 90°:]

"both uns I hope you are bearing up
well under the added responsibility"

FIG. 83 (26%). Cover-strokes

FIGS. 68-86 (7%). Forms of binding (Cont'd)

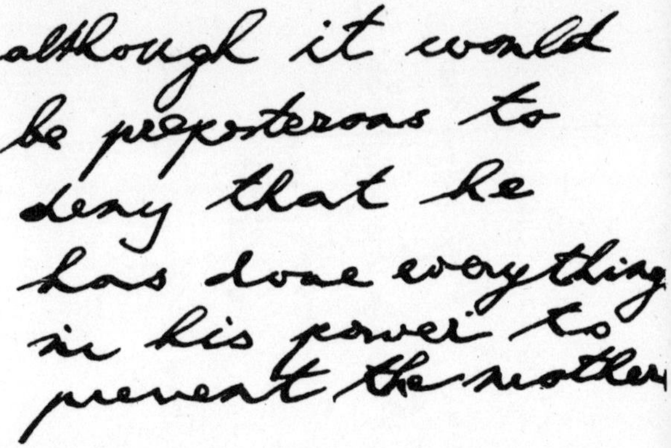

Fig. 84 (7%). Supported forms

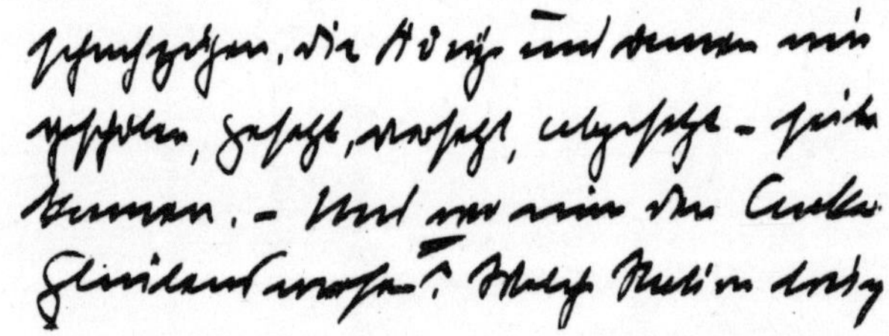

Fig. 85 (26%). Angles with an arcadic tendency in the writing of an ambulatory schizophrenic

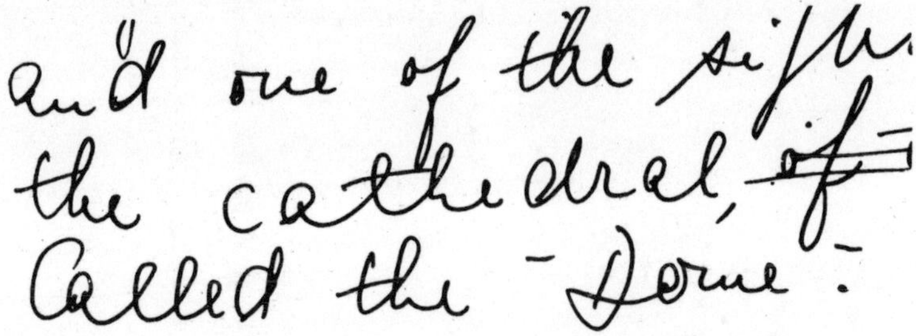

Fig. 86 (26%). Drooping garlands of a patient with depressions

Figs. 68-86 (7%). Forms of binding (Cont'd)

necessary for this quality to come about, in motoric extensivity of the movements of release. The steadily horizontal line, accordingly, is the product of attitudes not significantly influenced by the swerving effect of uncontrolled emotion.

The particularly close psychological relation of the falling line to a total preponderance of contraction, of the rising line to a total preponderance of release, suggests their appearance in handwriting samples in corroborative conjunction with related signs. This is an important differential criterion for the recognition of "genuine" falling or rising, in distinction from instances of lines simulating these qualities and actually owing their "rising" and "falling" to an oblique position of the writing paper.

Extreme fluctuation of emotion accordingly would be indicated by a more or less pronounced alteration of rising and falling lines, and other constellations of the ego-affect relationship are indicated by an expressive analysis of the various graphic constellations occurring. While, like in any of the rating dimensions, not all characteristics conditioned by conceivable fluctuations of line direction can be elaborated upon, five main types of a greater complexity are differentiated.

The wavering line is understood as a manipulation not so much obeying any particular upsurge of affect as trying to hold emotions in check. Its relation to diplomatic talent which already the old graphology of signs claimed, is herefrom understandable and also is suggested by its expressive relation to—and frequent actual concomitance with—the binding form of the thread, and in particular again to its sub-species, the double arch.

The caved-in line follows an original impulse of "theoretical" pessimism which in the course of action gives way to the generating of more self-confident and increasingly hopeful impulses. Its predominance in the manuscripts of philosophers of pessimism whose lives were productive, socially successful, and long, has been noted.

Lines of upward convexity demonstrate impulses of relative over-optimism soon exhausting themselves in action and giving way to the generating of impulses of resignation, depressiveness, and, potentially, despair.

The roof-tile arrangement, upward version, is the trail of an operation trying to hold consistently optimistic impulses in check.

The roof-tile arrangement, downward version, is the trail of an operation trying to hold consistently pessimistic impulses in check.

The roof-tile arrangements, moreover, appear to have a specific and empirically frequently confirmed relationship to the person's sense of responsibility, not so much in terms of degree as of specific structure. The

*Uhm? Oh — the —
Dinah; someone's with Dinah, strumming; someone's in the kitchen — "Fee,
someone's in his old banjo. — singing;
ming on his old banjo. Fiddle-di-i-o,
Fee, fiddle-di-i-o; fee, fie, strumming on his
O, O, e fiddle-di-i-o,*

FIG. 87 (7%). Elation

FIGS. 87-92. Line directions

the kitchen' after you have eaten you can help a little with the work that has to be done or if you do not feel like doing it if you do not have too

Fig. 88 (7%). Despondency

Figs. 87-92. Line directions (cont'd)

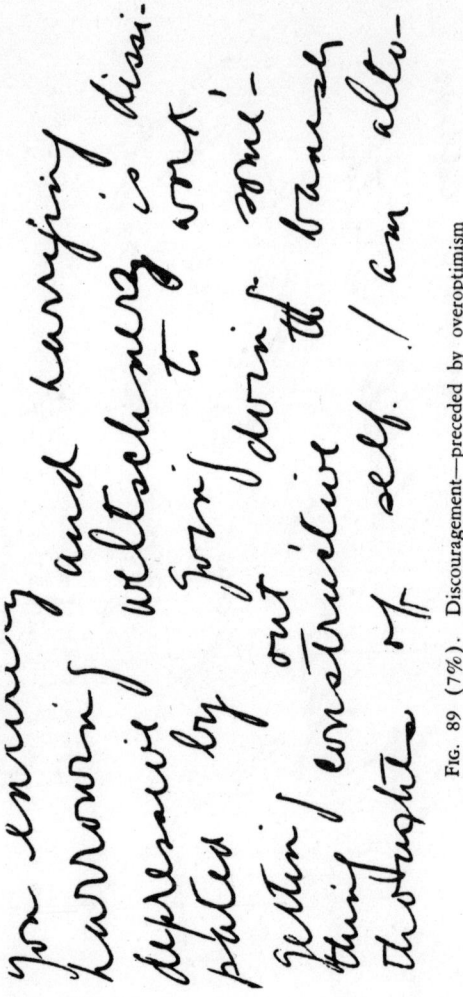

Fig. 89 (7%). Discouragement—preceded by overoptimism

Figs. 87-92. Line directions (cont'd)

expressive quality of having-to-return-to-the-ground in the upward version implies shades of meaning pointed out in our previous discussion of the vertical dimension. The interpretation here would tend towards an attribution of the personal sense of responsibility to the "material," i.e., the reality of object and instincts, social and family bounds, etc., combined with an escaping from the obligation of self-account in the face of spiritual values. Vice-versa, the expressive quality of having-to-return

DIMENSIONS OF RATING

The little girl is 5 yrs old. She has blonde hair, blue eyes and is a very gay and friendly child.

FIG. 90 (18%). Skepticism and growing self-confidence

FIGS. 87-92. Line directions (Cont'd)

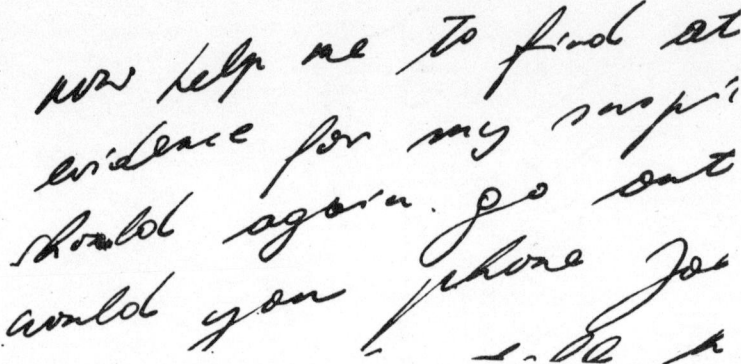

FIG. 91 (7%). Upward version (with rising of lines): realistic controls trying to rein in feelings of elation

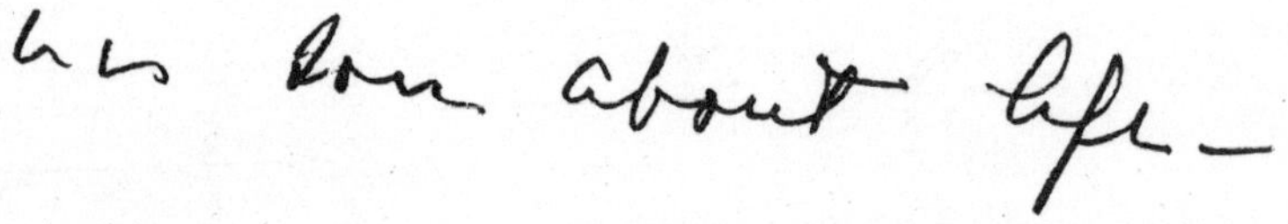

FIG. 92 (26%). Downward version (with falling of line): an affirmative philosophy of life, struggling with depressions (handwriting of a patient with early multiple sclerosis)

FIGS. 91-92. Rooftile arrangements

to an elevated position would emphasize responsibility toward superpersonal standards, combined with a shunning of responsibility toward the "given," i.e., objective, social, and instinctual demands.

Concerning more specifically the affect-indicative facets of expressiveness of all of these various arrangements, their further differentiation, in terms of even more complex directional qualities of the line, would follow the trend of the above discussion (figs. 87-92).

THE DIMENSION OF BACKGROUND INVOLVEMENT
Fullness and Meagerness

In an earlier chapter, emphasis was laid upon the person's quasi-spatial experience of his writing in relation to the writing field, or background. In experience processes, "background" is the undifferentiated and indistinct, yet, for reasons of these very qualities, indispensable counter-pole to the articulateness of the experience object. In direct symbolic experience, "background" is the "neutral chaos" of the dead and the unborn, the already dissolved and the yet unmaterialized, i.e., of the unreal, negatively formulated. In positive formulation, the unreal is the potentially real, i.e., the *imaginary*.

Accesses to the "background" have been presented before in this book. In discussing the psychological implications of "doughiness," the dispersion of organismic energy implied in that sign was defined as a state of decentralized sensorial and sensual readiness for environmental contacts "laterally" offering themselves to the life course. While one of its facets was seen to be "intensity of imagery," the characteristic per se was definitely placed on the side of "realism," and the modality just mentioned is in no way psychologically contradictory to this, as imagery functions and reality functions complement one another: the livelier and more intense the sensorial, the less articulate the structural aspect of reality images, the "fuller," i.e., more intense, but also the less subject to selective discrimination, the experience of reality also. How, then, does this emphasis on reality, indicated by "doughiness" as *one* means of background involvement, conform with the general significance of this tendency as an indicator not of the *intensity* of images but of imaginativeness per se, i.e., of ideomotor rather than sensorial emphasis on personality functions extending into the *unreal?*

The contradiction is a seeming rather than actual one. The degree to which "background" is experienced as such depends on the articulation of the figure-foreground; the degree to which the indeterminedness of the blank space in writing is experienced as "polar" to the writing person, i.e., as unreal, would then depend on the graphic relationship between the stroke and its blank space embankments, i.e., on the degree to which this relationship itself is "polarized." In ductual dispersion, or doughiness, everything is attempted to reduce that polarity, to lessen the peremptoriness of the embankments, to disperse oneself into the "background." That implies that the latter is perceived as lending itself to such "lateral" transition, i.e., as real environment rather than as representative of any non-reality principle. Thus, in "doughiness," the contrast between figure and background is reduced only in terms of the distinctness of the figure per se, and only at the price of an enhancement of its contact with the remaining background in terms of their dark-bright relationship which the "chiaroscuro" effect of this quality brings forth. This relates to an inner situation of the writer in which the functions of imagery and of reality experience, both being saturated with sensual and sensorial stimulation, tend to become congruent: therefrom the "realistic images" but also the "imaginative approach" of the externally and instinctually overengaged. The tendencies toward "background involvement" here and in what will be taken up in this sub-chapter do not by any means represent mutually exclusive and not even opposite principles of system action but simply relate to different functions of the personality; both can be combined in the actual person but neither of them implies the presence or absence of the other.

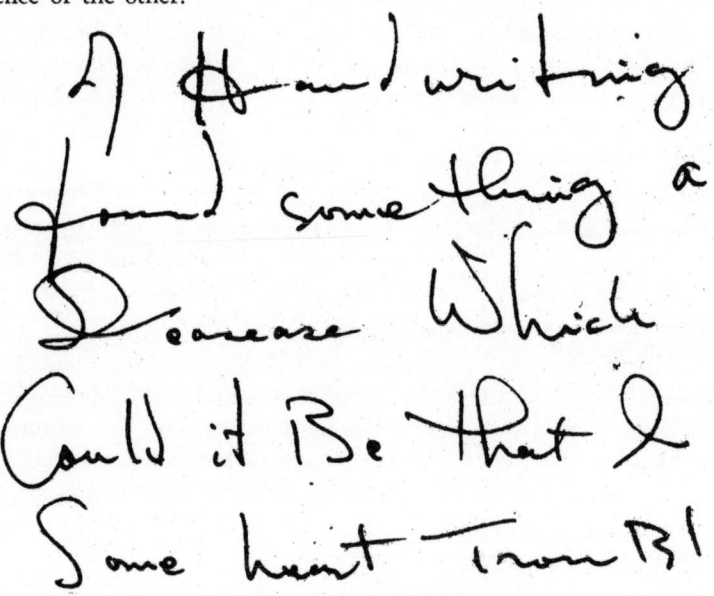

Fig. 93 (7%). Artificial fullness

Figs. 93-97. Background involvement

But imaginativeness as such, with its processes of ideation articulated, as psychomotor actions, by temporal succession only, can then in any case be expected not to be revealed by any qualities of the ductus but by a *linear* type of background involvement only, which presupposes an accentuated, "polarized" experience of dichotomy between the real and unreal and engulfs the "indefinite" by way of well-rounded curves, rather than penetrating into it by lateral ductual dispersion. The accentuation of this dichotomy is essential for true imaginativeness as much as the resulting graphic characteristic, genuine "fullness" itself, is essential for its graphological representation. This is, in one of its aspects, the reason why the handwritings at least of the paranoid type—catatonia following different lines of experience as well as of expressiveness—of schizophrenic patients are never genuinely "full" despite their accentuated "fantasy-life" which is essentially the preponderance of unreality in their inner order of experiences rather than, as in true imaginativeness, the conscious conversion of unreality into reality images which follow more or less "realistic" lines of concept-building and are ultimately serving realistic purposes; what represents genuine, what artificial fullness, will be shown in the following. The richness of inner living which, as one of its necessary attributes, is implied in our concept of a full-blooded personality inevitably expresses itself in the graphic quality of *fullness*.

In order now to distinguish between the genuine and artificial versions of this quality the observation is essential that the impression of fullness as one of the essential properties of the writing structure depends on the presence of it primarily in the *middle zone* which again is consistent with the results of our previous analysis of the psychological functions of this zone as representative of "living" per se in the discussion of the vertical dimension; "artificial fullness" however tends to either "blow up" or linearly enrich (often without even effecting an impression of actual fullness anywhere and in any sense) the peripheral forms, while the middle zone and thereby the whole structure appears "meager"; the more developed and differentiated, on a basis of "genuine fullness," the person's spiritual and instinctual life, the fuller will, of course, be the forms of the peripheral zones also (fig. 93).

Regarding artificial fullness, its relation to certain signs of hysteria, which were mentioned in the discussion of the thread, suggests itself from this analysis; its relation to schizophrenia which, in terms of more specific graphic characteristics, is marked quite differently, will later be shown. A further discussion of "artificial fullness" would already involve "elaboration," the topic of the following sub-chapter. The table for fullness and meagerness, as here presented, can be given without a separate discussion of "meagerness," since its overall psychological implications will already be evident from the foregoing. The "negative" potential tendency toward an over-expansiveness of concepts and therefore toward disclarification of the thought processes also embodied in "fullness" may be stated at this point.

TABLE X
Amplitude

Fullness		Meagerness	
+	−	+	−
Imaginativeness	Lack of clarity in thinking	Acuity of intellect (in terms of relative capacity)	Lack of imagination
Richness of inner life			Dearth of imagery
	Lack of external and self-criticism		Dryness
Wealth of emotional resources		Relative strength of theoretical thinking	Asceticism
	Indulgence in daydreaming		Philistinism
Good memory			Thinking in clichés
	"Fantasticalness"	Critical sense	Quality of being "boring"
		Acumen	
		Clarity of concepts	Stereotypy
		Intellectual soberness	Poverty of inner resources
			Weakness of memory

Elaboration and Simplification; Ornamentation and Neglect

The tendencies either to elaborate the school pattern by particles of movement not prescribed in it, or else to simplify it in the direction of its essential structure spring from motivations completely different from those underlying fullness and meagerness; yet, "enrichment" as an unsuccessful attempt to make up for a "meagerness" born from a lack of inner resources which the ego cannot tolerate has been mentioned already, and the propensity of both criteria—a handwriting can be extremely simplified and yet extremely full, as well as extremely elaborated and yet extremely meager—to become confounded by students of the method furthermore suggests the discussion of elaboration-simplification at this point despite its only indirect relation to the functions of background involvement.

Elaboration is being defined as an enrichment of graphic form which does not conflict with the essential structural qualities of letters according to the school patterns; simplification is being defined as a reduction of graphic form which is applied to the school pattern of letters though not to the essential form qualities which this procedure rather tends to make more articulate. This implies that enrichments and reductions affecting the legibility of letters in either direction (ornamentation and neglect), although related to the characteristics here discussed, are nevertheless beyond their scope in its exact sense: while representing extreme degrees of the tendencies of elaboration and simplication, ornamentation and neglect also involve impulses foreign to these tendencies proper.

Simplifying the situation, one could say that the urge for elaboration points toward a higher development of the sense of "form," the urge for simplification toward a higher development of the sense of the "essential." This view, however, does not seem sufficiently clarified; it conflicts with the realization that form and essence are complementary attributes and that the specific determination of the mentioned personality trends is dependent upon the individual level of form quality, i.e., on a third criterion outside of the polarity of elaboration-simplification. Concerning the latter objection, it seems hardly necessary to state that the cultural and intellectual level on which a certain "emphasis" is operating, is of course not implied in it as a mere attitude; neither, then, does this affect the presence of the attitude as such. Regarding the interpretative problem posed by the complementariness of "form" and "essence," we can make observations of tendencies closely related to those here discussed by looking at the history of art. It shows us periods stressing "stylization," "the great line," alternating with others stressing a more or less baroque, more or less naturalistic multiplicity of form development. The latter imitates the tendency of *life* itself to "fill space" by producing its shapes in never-ending variations, the former the tendency of *thought* to create separating distances by reducing shape to its symbolic core. Regardless of the specific social, religious, and cultural incentives which were operative in this periodicity (yet themselves were subject to it), its great consistency and the consideration that whatever influences were at work in it must have functioned through the medium of the artist's own inner experiences, allow us to use the general trends of thought and culture historically connected with the observed phenomena in art development as directives for an understanding of individual attitudes following the directions of these trends. Thus, in working out the broadest categories possible to cover elaboration and simplification as expressive tendencies in handwriting, we can conclude that they relate to an intrapersonal preponderance of basic cultural needs: elaboration, to one of the imitative or creative or both, simplification, to one of the intellectual or spiritual or both. This preponderance in turn is to be understood, as it is in the realm of art itself which was chosen as reference, as one in terms of the person's inner identification and *not* of the strength of the available forces of either creativeness or thought: an elaborate movement can be more expressive as well as intelligent than a simplified one; a simplified one can have more beauty as well as pattern-adequacy than an elaborate one. While, in our present state of civilization, it is true that a person's intellectual development usually coincides with the rate at which a graphic trend towards simplication is materialized in his handwriting, intelligence per se is not indicated by either trend but, in the case of "elaboration," by the relative ease with which additional particles of movement within one letter lend themselves to the transitional movement producing the next one; in the case of "simplification," by the relative distinctness with which essential form is safeguarded and brought out. It is clear that considerations of this kind already enter into the larger realm of the level of form quality, but also, that in combination with the latter criterion, and with that of the speed of writing, the degree, for example, of simplification indeed allows important conclusions in respect to the person's intelligence itself.

The table of personality traits as developed for the two types of expressive quality results, as always, from a realization of the order of inner experience and outer behavior by which the corresponding attitudes can be determined. As already indicated, the farther-reaching trends toward ornamentation and neglect are tabulated separately; evident are the additional implications of vanity but also, potentially, of bluffing, pretentions, and false pretenses for the former, and of sloppiness but also, potentially, of a need to "hush over," i.e., conceal, for the latter, especially when in combination with threading. For systematic rather than practical reasons, one exemption from the graphological criteria here applied to "ornamentation" may be stated explicitly. In documents from past centuries, where ornamentation is an integral emergence from a yet unbroken collective sense of style inherent in living traditions of penmanship, the decorative-

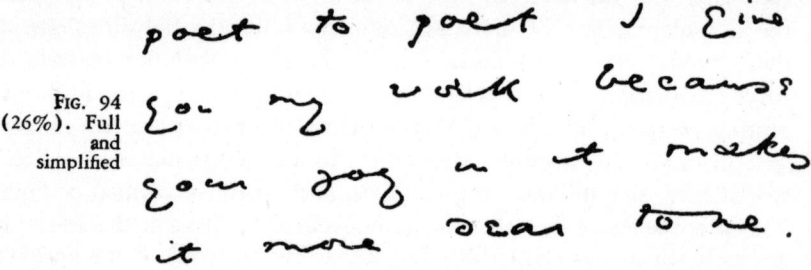

FIG. 94 (26%). Full and simplified

FIGS. 93-97. Background involvement (Cont'd)

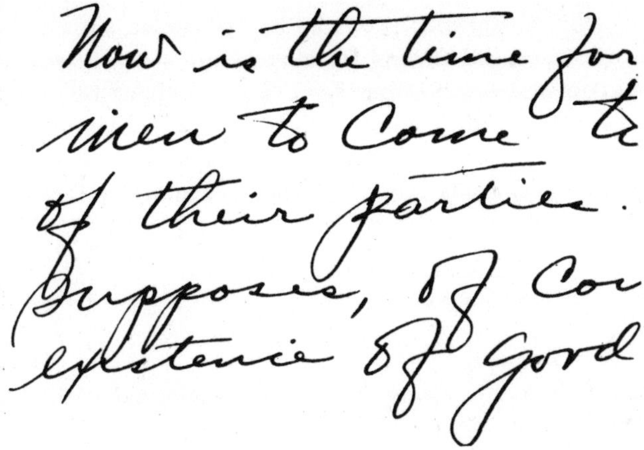

DIMENSIONS OF RATING

[handwritten sample:] Now is the time for men to come to of their parties. Supposes, of Co existence of God

FIG. 95 (26%).
Full and elaborated

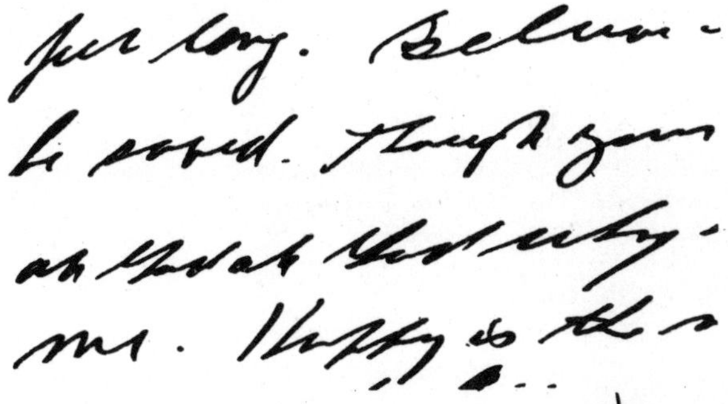

FIG. 96 (7%).
Meager and simplified

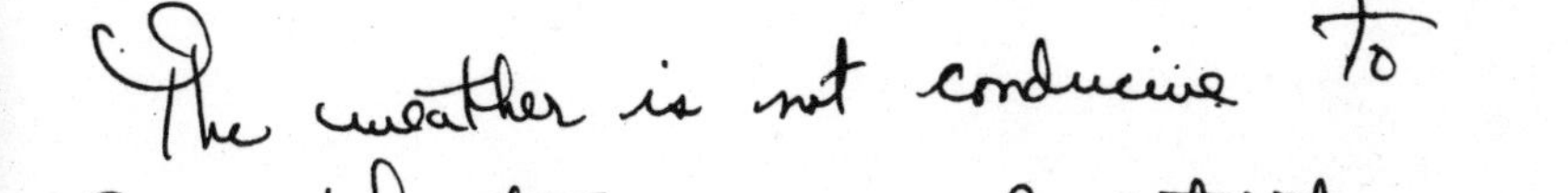

[handwritten sample]

[handwritten sample:] The weather is not conducive to lively thoughts, or normal activities. Actually, it stinks! Respectfully Yours,

FIG. 97 (26%). Meager and enriched (degree of elaboration approximating ornamentation)

FIGS. 93-97. Background involvement (Cont'd)

ness of enlarged and richly ornamented majuscles has, of course, little to do with the pompous make-up and craving for effect which seems bound to characterize graphic ornamentation in our age. The likelihood of encountering in present-day handwriting formations of similar intricacy but also of similar aesthetic quality and inner consistency of stroke-conduct as we find in handwritten documents of the centuries preceding the nineteenth is virtually nil (figs. 94-97).

TABLE XI
Degree of Enrichment

Elaboration		Simplification	
+	**−**	**+**	**−**
Desire to form, build, organize, develop	Lack of simplicity	Simplicity	Lack of social form
Sense of representation	Over-emphasis on formality	Purposefulness	Lack of culture in daily living
Sense of social form	Ceremoniousness	Sense of order	Utilitarianism
Sense of arrangement	Pedantry	Objectiveness	"Ends justifying the means"
Cultivation of the pleasant details in daily living	"Hair-splitting"	Grasp of the essential	Abruptness in interpersonal relations
Urge for the creation of a "personal atmosphere"	Circumstantiality	Determination of judgment	Tactlessness
Ability to reconcile and smooth out (in interpersonal relations)	Verbosity	Good taste	Lack of sense of tradition
Sense of tradition	Lack of objectiveness		
	Lack of good taste		
	Eccentricity		

Ornamentation	Neglect
(1)	(1)
Vanity	Sloppiness
Pompousness	Inexactness
Conceit	Disorderliness
Boastfulness	Lack of punctuality
Craving for originality	Flightiness
Craving to please	Unreliability
(2)	(2)
Deceptiveness	Ambiguity
Bluffing	Insincerity
Pretentiousness	"Cunning"
False pretenses	Mendacity

Distances and Margins

A previous chapter, in discussing the overall arrangement, had focused on the wider aspects of the sample but had not yet systematized it in terms of figure and background, the relationship of which is obviously involved in the manner in which the text is dense or dispersed on the paper, spreading towards its edges or keeping itself within margins. The general graphic consequences of *distinctness* for dispersed and of *crowding* for dense handwriting already in themselves suggest certain psychological types which in our previous discussion were briefly stated. Evidently now, while the need for articulateness in communicating is guiding the producer of dispersed writing trails as well as of accentuated margins, the latter quality—emphasis on margins—does not necessarily follow from that need; the additional assumption of a sense of aesthetic effectiveness—which, in turn, implies a higher awareness of values, of personal "distinction"— is required to explain such emphasis, wherever it appears. Furthermore, the particularly close relationship of crowding and dispersing, respectively, to the functions of saving and spending, i.e., to the personal sense of economy, is obvious. Regarding word distances, the impulses bringing about their various possible degrees appear essentially identical with those governing the degree of width within the word; yet, the particular symbolic role played in our order of experiences by the "word" as the smallest ultimate unit of communication, i.e., as criterion of verbalization per se, suggests an operation of the same principle on a different functional level, namely, that of articulateness of thinking and communication; this also makes it understandable why distances between words may show proportions relatively quite different from those of the inner horizontal extension of the word itself.

Distances between lines, in view of total "spatial" considerations and of the interruption of the flow of writing caused by the necessity for the pen to travel back to the left-hand side, are subject in particular to the personal time economy: since the more accentuated experience of "interruption" here implies a brief moment of conscious re-orientation, which allows the writer to take or not to take the time to begin the new line in a certain distance from the previous one, this distance will be the lesser the less time the writer has or believes he has, the larger, the more of it he can dispose of. Either condition, of course, can in any specific case simply be explicable on the basis of momentary zeal, optimism, passion, absorption by one's topic of writing (or, respectively, of their absence), and these interpretations suggest themselves in those cases where high speed for interlinear narrowness—low speed for interlinear wideness—tend to support them; in terms of the resulting expressive qualities, the physiognomic unity between interlinearly crowded and generally "animated," interlinearly dispersed and generally "listless" handwritings (drooping garland of the depressive) is quite distinct. However, the more these acutely corroborating marks are lacking, the more can line distances be regarded as indicative of the overall time economy displayed by the writer. In symbolic experience, the writing space, as a field of action to be traversed by one's total movement in producing a text, is a time equivalent; a general need for "saving" or else for "spending" time hence is indicated the more the survey over the field and awareness of its total extent is disclosed by a degree of interlinear distance not proportionate, in the above sense, to the speed of the writing movement. The fast writer who, staying aware of the overall dimensions of the field, takes time to start his new line in a relatively considerable distance from the previous one, thus reveals a more general habit of spending time leisurely. The slow writer who chooses to start his new line in a closer distance from the previous one than his slow pace of movement (in itself rather suggesting a leisurely movement downward) seems to necessitate, is *generally* likely to price his time highly; and corresponding conclusions of an inconsistent and disorderly time disposition with alternate wanting and wasting can be drawn, to the extent of their conspicuousness, from changes in interlinear distances.

The lack of verbal and conceptual articulateness generally disclosed by "crowding" will of course be found accentuated where lines get entangled, a characteristic which usually results from high psychomotor pressure and an absorption by momentary thought and communication so complete that survey over its own total trail becomes lost, a manifestation which implies the possibility of a verbal and conceptual self-contraditoriness of particularly high grade. The old graphologists' interpretation of widely separated lines as a sign of the need to venerate greatness or submit to authority may be mentioned here; while possibly too specific to quite cover this graphic trend, the above-named interpretation is implied as one of its potentialities in the combination of the sense of order and distinction generally conveyed by spaciousness with the specific self-restraint necessary to "observe," in terms of symbolic experience, accentuated distances and "subordinate" one's movements to them; the implication, on the other pole of this dimension, of an anxious obtrusiveness in the overcrowding of lines as well as in neglecting to keep margins was mentioned earlier in this book. Absence of the upper margin has clearly a clumsy, "obtrusive," disfiguring influence upon the whole appearance of a text, while its over-emphasizing, particularly in a letter, immediately conveys the impression of a submissive exaggeration of respectfulness. Concerning the remainder of the margins, the lower one, graphically, plays a comparatively minor role. Its absence is generally due to an absorption by the writing process leaving the person unaware of the approaching arrival of the end of the page; its presence, to the extent of its spaciousness, is subject to the above defined criterion of a sense of aesthetic distinction generally applying to margin-emphasis. This criterion, granted that an evenly wide distance permitting an effect of aesthetic unity is provided for the whole of a text, also applies for the right-hand and left-hand margins but does not apply for their following variations.

The left-hand margin, as the writing proceeds downward, may show a gradual widening or narrowing; in some cases, this change is so consistent that the resulting left-hand edge of the text runs in an oblique yet remarkably straight direction. From the viewpoint of paper absorption, the "economic" implications of these tendencies are again quite clear but their expressive qualities are so articulate that the saving and spending of paper, of space, of money, of time, appear but as the more specific facets of character trends embracing more than the personal sense of economy in the material meaning of the term only; at least it can be said that "economy" here would necessarily involve similar shades of meaning as we have found in the case of relatively increased total right-and-left-wardness among the general dynamic qualities of the horizontal dimension. Two principles of analysis can be applied to the growth and shrinking of left-hand margins, and, as always in the study of expressive movements, the resulting interpretations converge toward identical characterological concepts. The person allowing his left-hand margin to broaden, on the one hand, appears so much inwardly inclined toward his subject matter or partner of communication, so much absorbed by his activity, that he experiences the necessity of returning to the left-hand side as a more and more unwelcome disturbance. The person who allows his left-hand margin to shrink, vice versa, in the advanced stage of externalization represented by the right-hand edge of his text—and the more so the farther he advances in that process as a whole or the more, in other words, he has to expose himself—seems to welcome an opportunity to return to the security of the self. The directional identity of the self with the left-hand side generally we remember from the analysis of the left-rightward phaseology of the word. The person allowing his left-hand margin to broaden, on the other hand, can also be said to experience a "demand for space" on the part of the self which increases at the rate of the increase in his conscious goal absorption, an observation which in turn is consistent with the generally affect-generating nature of all cognitive and volitional processes in which the focus of consciousness is *outward;* this tendency, of course, can then also be said to imply personal "expansion" stimulated by communicative processes and its general economic consequence of "spending," but we also understand better now why this characteristic is so frequent in the handwritings of creative artists, writers, and thinkers. Correspondingly, the person allowing his left-hand margin to shrink appears to experience a contractive impulse on the part of his self which resists an all-out identification of his with the goal image; thus, a gesture of allaying and reassuring of the self must be performed, a "price" be paid at the beginning of the new line, before externalization can again get under way; the "economic" aspect of this gesture, of course, like that of increased total leftwardness also, is one of "putting things behind one," i.e., of a saving accumulation of riches, and while this trend may be articulated towards the emphasis on money, it can, of course, as in increased total leftwardness likewise, obey other differentiating impulses also. A study of fluctuations of the left-hand margins, finally, together with the related studies of the horizontal extension of the word, shows the manner and degree in which the basic trends of the total intrapersonal economy are affected by the functions of control as well as by counter-impulses of their own general order and will frequently allow of specific conclusions in respect to the person's actual social behavior.

Right-hand margins, finally, apart from their more infrequent conditioning by a conscious attention to aesthetic effects, are not in the natural line of writing which generally tends to become faster, more impulsive, and more space-absorbing as the line proceeds towards the right. Appearance of frequent but quantitatively inconsistent right-hand marginal distances can therefore at least be said to represent an amount of caution warranted less by objective external necessities than by personal contact-shyness. The more neurotic tendencies of this in the writer, the more space is left on the right-hand side; moreover, obsessional traits of the character may specifically be demonstrated either by additional narrowing of the last word or its ending or, as sometimes is seen, by a horizontal stroke emanating from the ending and reaching out towards the right-hand edge of the paper. The quality of a "magic" conjuration of threats can well be said to be obvious in such gestures of "avoiding" or "touching the wall"; of course, the operation of impulses of that order as unconscious motivations in the more manipulated aestheticized versions of the right-hand margin must also be considered in those cases where supporting symptoms from other dimensions are at hand (figs. 98-102).

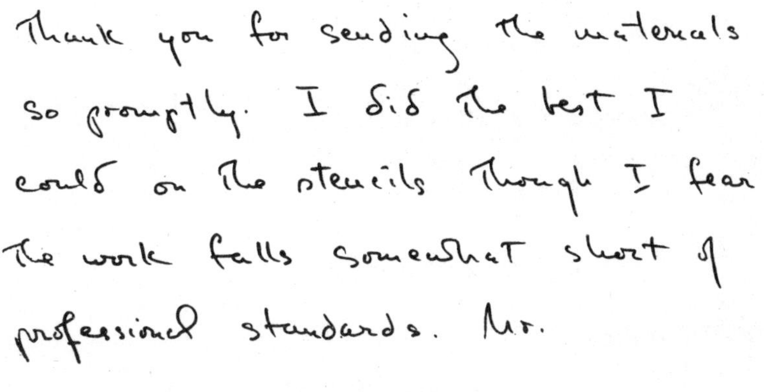

FIG. 98. Dispersion

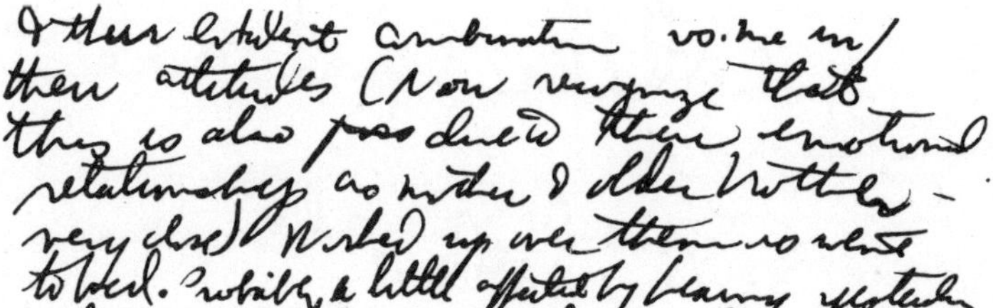

FIG. 99. Crowding

FIGS. 98-99 (20%). Distances

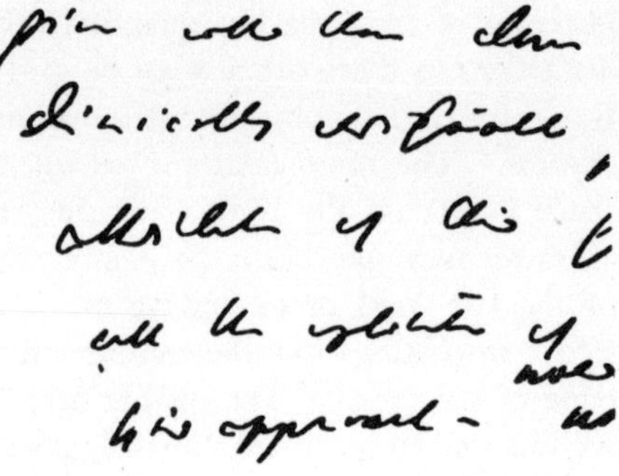

FIG. 100. Broad and growing left-hand margin

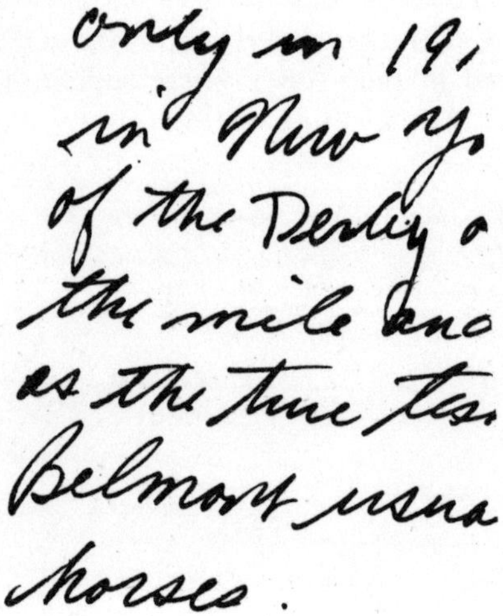

FIG. 101. Narrow and shrinking left-hand margin

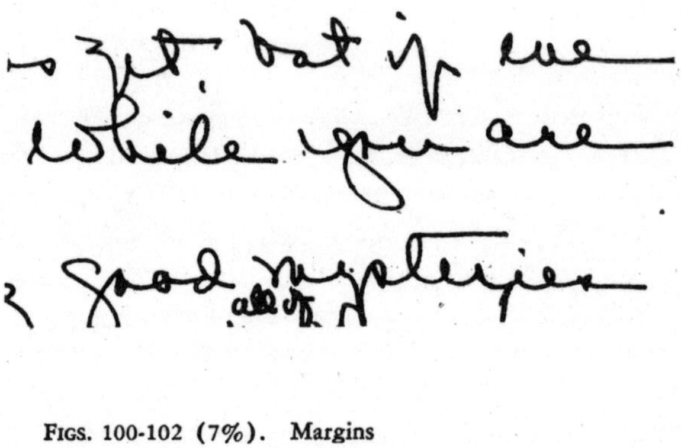

FIG. 102. Right-hand margin "touching the wall."

FIGS. 100-102 (7%). Margins

General Qualities of Curve

The physiognomy of graphic movement was previously said to find its most expressive crystallization in the personal forms of binding, the possible range of which was outlined in the discussion of their prototypes. More diffuse qualitative nuances, while tending to escape systematization, yet play an important role in the analyst's perception. The ductus, for example, is not simply governed by the sharpness-doughiness dichotomy but, apart from cruder characteristics like tremor, by many more subtle qualities like "shivering," "glassiness," etc., which will occupy us farther along in this study. Likewise, beyond being "angular," a handwriting may have the specific qualities of "prickliness," "thorniness," suggesting of course a particularly militant sensitivity of the writer's ego, and similar examples could be given for "curvedness" and for many other graphic qualities allowing of a practically endless subdivision of shades.

Motorically as well as symbolically, the general qualities of curve are equally dependent on all three dimensions and in our present context are therefore independently dealt with. Despite the enormous scale of their possible make-ups and their diffuse distribution in the writing trail, at least two main types can be distinguished; in order to allow a clearer picture of them, it is advisable for us to focus on movements permitting them to appear in extenso: on the long forms. We can then observe that many handwritings show a more or less accentuated deviation from the straight line implied in the direction of the letters, i.e., apart from movements conditioned by the necessity either to form curves immanent to the shape of letters or to bind them together. Movements thus conditioned are therefore not being considered here. The less angular and less fast a handwriting happens to be, the less it tends toward an exactly straight course of its up- and downstrokes, which in consequence may show a generalized convexity, either toward the right- or left-hand side, and most frequently and normally the choice of the sides of convexity is a different one for the up- as for the downstrokes. The gestural properties of both types are particularly articulate and therefore easily defined. In the upstroke, it is the appearance of rightward *concavity* which immediately conveys the notion of ebullience, of "appetite," of an emotionally and instinctually well-sustained movement of acquisition or environmental engagement; it looks as though an angler's line was swung through the air. Rightward convexity in the upstroke suggests a counter-impulse of shying back from the environment generated in the very course of obeying the action impulse by which the environment is being approached; its interpretation as an indicator of traumatically conditioned feelings of frustration and lack of confidence thereby becomes understandable. In the downstrokes, conditions are found reversed: the rightward-concave movement here is clearly a gesture of withdrawal from the environment, the rightward-convex one with equal clearness one of personal protrusion into its sphere.

The dichotomy becomes of particular clinical importance in view of the lesser degree of consciousness present in movements of release than in movements of contraction, i.e., of the lesser degree of it in down- than in upstrokes. As the qualities of movement here investigated primarily follow the vertical, and as they tend to involve background, an analysis of them could also, as already hinted, derive from other criteria of observation than the one applying to their horizontal aspect, and considering the unity of the laws of expression, which we so frequently have now found confirmed, it could still be expected to result in concepts psychologically convergent with those here evolved; for the limited purposes of this book, however, the foregoing discussion of the general qualities of curve will most likely be sufficient (figs. 103-105).

The Signature, Special Signs, and Miscellaneous

While the system of rating dimensions represents the necessary skeleton without which an analysis of handwriting would be in danger of falling apart, many significant observations lie outside of that system. The expressive importance of the signature, for example, which suggests itself from its function as a social representative of the ego, can on the whole not be defined in terms of dimensional analysis but only of that function. An exception from this is presented by the criterion of size. While its general psychological implications are valid for the signature as they are for the rest of the writing, it is clear that an application of the size criterion to the signature is of exceptional relevance in view of its particular conscious role. Thus, it tends to reveal better than the text the person's true self-esteem, and differences between the scope of the latter and the scope of self-esteem generally displayed in everyday behavior are reflected by

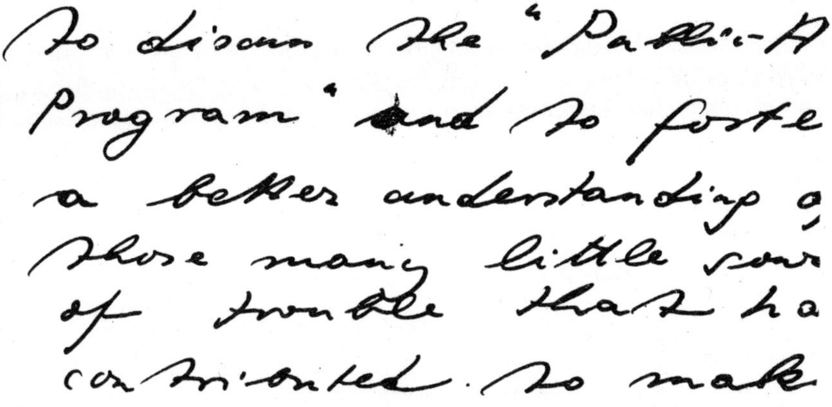

[handwritten sample]

FIG. 103. Rightward concavity of upstrokes, rightward convexity of downstrokes

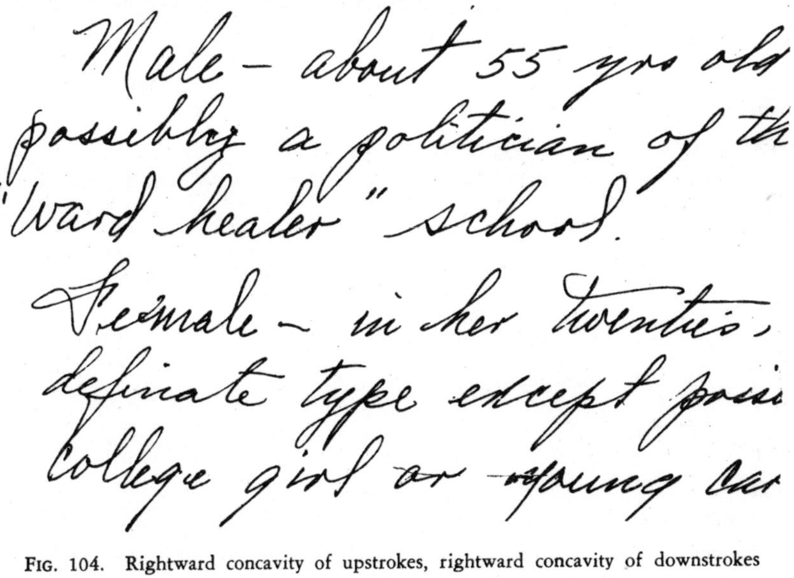

[handwritten sample]

FIG. 104. Rightward concavity of upstrokes, rightward concavity of downstrokes

FIGS. 103-104 (31%). General qualities of curve

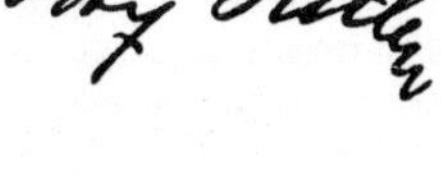

FIG. 105 (7%). Signature I. Signature of Hitler. Note affect-laden relationship to own public role in high pressure of family name, and anticipation of doom in its tumbling.

differences of size between the signature and the text (figs. 106, 107). Likewise, differences of size between the given and family names can be very revealing in respect to the person's prevailing self-identification with either his private or official roles, and, in accordance with this, tend to be considerable at the expense of their new family names in the signatures of women unsatisfactorily adjusted to their marriage.

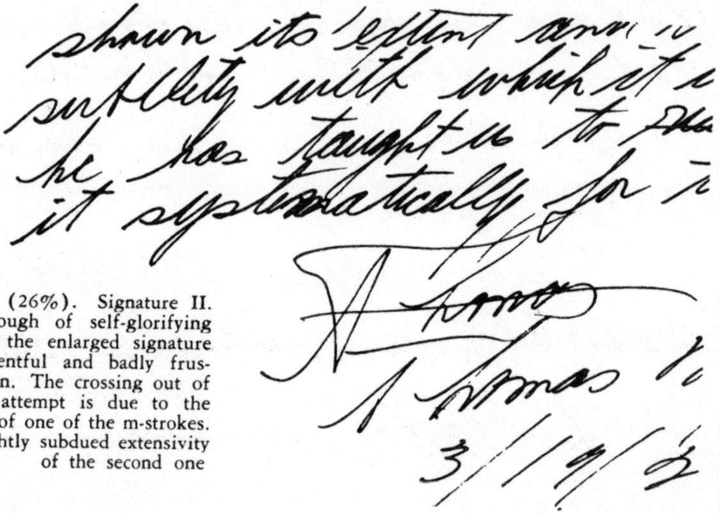

FIG. 106 (26%). Signature II. Break-through of self-glorifying needs in the enlarged signature of a resentful and badly frustrated man. The crossing out of the first attempt is due to the omission of one of the m-strokes. Note slightly subdued extensivity of the second one

FIG. 107 (7%). Signature III. Disproportion between majuscle of family name and the rest of the signature of a person with feelings of inferiority and despondency, "escaping" into his official life role

A sign of demonstrative self-esteem is, of course, the habit of underlining the signature ("paraphe"); its more specific psychological evaluation will depend both on the quantitative emphasis placed on its execution and on aesthetic criteria determining the degree of originality or triviality of the movement. The same generally holds true for any of the signature's more conspicuous symbolic qualities and particles of form, among which only the majuscular beginnings may be mentioned at this point, since their significance as symbolizations of the ego-image is bound to be accentuated by the signature's particularly ego-representative role. Apart from the self-evident quantitative criteria governing this accentuation, the majuscular beginnings of the signature lend themselves to qualitative representations of personal roles which in specific instances appear as actual "stylized" symbols, sometimes of stupefying distinctness, of the person in his preferred type of activity, particularly if this activity itself, as for example in the dancers' profession, is of a kind which naturally relates it to the activity of writing in its quality as a rhythmically articulated species of movement (fig. 108).

FIG. 108 (7%). Signature IV. Self-symbolization of a stylized dancing pose in the first letter of the first name in the signature of a professional dancer

Apart from the signature, certain elements of the left-rightward phaseology of the word may merit an ampler discussion. Emphasis or disemphasis on initial upstrokes, i.e., of upstrokes preceding the first downstroke of the first letter and thus starting the entire movement of the word, can be said to be of the greatest significance for what in the person's inner order of experiences lies to the left of the first letter, i.e., the self as the sum total of the personal past. The laws of expression here applying are related to those governing the widening or narrowing of the left-hand margin of the text but are not identical with them since no element of leftward movement proper is involved in the prolongation of the initial upstroke which, in consequence, must be assessed on the basis of the symbolic significance of the first downstroke as a more or less articulate representative of the ego-image. Prolonged initial upstrokes thus indicate that the person, before going into action, has to traverse a certain margin of accumulated inner resistance, which accentuates his activities as experiences of personal effort rather than of service to the goal, while inner absorption by the objective headed for, correspondingly, would tend to disemphasize the initial upstroke in the direction of its total omission. This implication of fixation upon the personal past in the prolonged initial upstroke can be accentuated, positively, by a rightward-concave movement expressing, in accordance with our analysis of the general qualities of curve, a feeling of confidence in one's actions rooted in the emotional effect of past achievement, negatively, by a leftward-concave movement which in a more specific manner, owing to the initial upstroke's particular relation to the personal past, would accentuate the general "traumatic" indicativeness of this quality which was pointed out before. Regardless of these more specific differences, the person letting himself be guided by past experience and generally by his memories can be expected to emphasize the initial upstroke, while absence of it can be said to indicate a freer, more unbiased attitude towards the future and the task ahead (fig. 109).

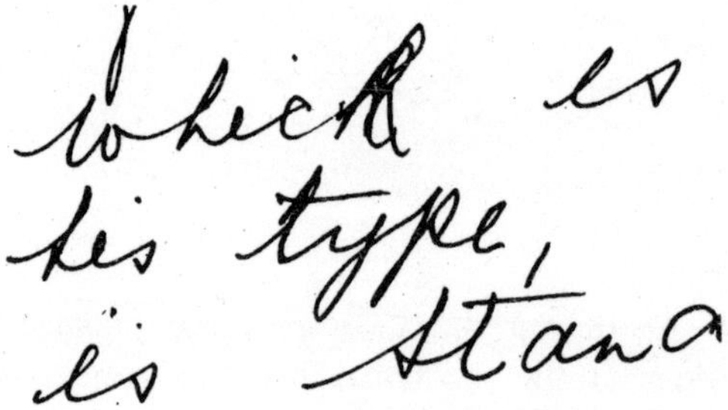

FIG. 109 (7%). Prolonged initial upstrokes of leftward concavity

Mention may be made here also of the "dark point" at the beginning of the initial upstroke which the old French graphologists took for a "dark spot" on the person's past, an interpretation of great plausibility both on account of the intense and immediate conveyance of meaning in the expressive quality of the sign and of the ample empiric confirmation it has received, like many of Michon's original assumptions, in many decades of graphological practice. Initial upstrokes of straight and pointed course, finally, disclose a basic attitude of aggressiveness, a readiness to attack or criticize which waits for its objects to come up rather than needing their presence to be aroused. Its presence, together with aggressive "dashes" rightwardly emanating from the word endings, in the handwritings of certain paranoid subtypes and of persons perpetually occupying themselves with civil law suits can be understood on this basis (fig. 110).

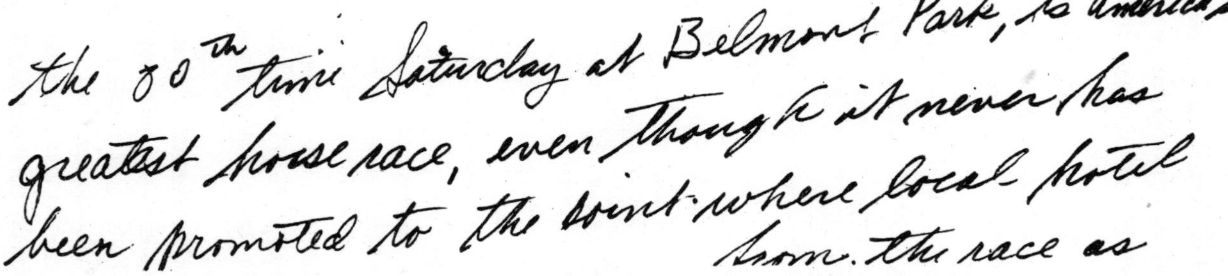

DIMENSIONS OF RATING 123

*The 00 to mi Saturday at Belmont Park, to insure
greatest horse race, even though it never has
been permitted to the trent where local hotel
from the race as*

Fig. 110 (14%). Prolonged initial upstrokes combining "dark point" formation with an alternation between rightward concavity and aggressive straightness

Fig. 111 (7%). Temper tantrums

Fig. 112 (7%). T-bars: gestures of ideational self-protection in the writing of an opinionated individual

Concerning now the contact-representative *ending* of the word, it more than any other component of handwriting can be taken as a key to an assessment of the person's "manners" in the word's literal sense, i.e., his manner of social and interpersonal approach which, like the endings themselves, may be abrupt or conciliatory, cautious or confident, distant or obtrusive, closing off or opening up, depending on an application of the previously-developed multiplicity of criteria to this particular section of the word. The critical, aggressive implications of the pointed dash have just been mentioned; if this movement follows an upward rather than horizontal course, if it is bigger, faster, and betraying higher pressure than the word itself from which it emanates, temper-tantrums rather than controlled aggression can be assumed (fig. 111).

Rightward dashes can be present also in the form of prolonged t-bars and other movements of over-stroking but here, in consideration of their placement in the upper zone, would be attributable to a type of aggressiveness accentuating a theoretical and dialectic mode of attack. Generally speaking, the t-bars, as well as graphically less warranted and therefore especially significant overstrokes, are media of graphic expressiveness allowing of a multitude of articulate gestures, among which only the "power stroke," the "ambition stroke," the "protection stroke," and the "sense of humor stroke" (affixing a previously omitted upper sign by a leftward movement emanating from a subsequent part of the word, with following rightward return of the trail) may be mentioned, all of which, of course, again exist in an infinite number of individual subtypes, requiring an astute spontaneous understanding of visual qualities for their correct interpretation (fig. 112). I-dots should likewise not be excluded from our discussion. Their placement close to the upper part of the letter discloses a degree of care and orderliness which is likely to make its bearer a minute observer of detail; the psychological implications of the i-dot placed at some distance from the letter require a realization of the different dimensional criteria entering here. If the sign "flies forward," the only possible interpretation of its distance from the upper end of the letter, in as far as this distance is due to the rightward impulse of movement, is that the person is absorbed by his goal images to a degree fostering his spontaneous processes of externalization and revealing itself in a manner related to the corresponding indicators within the dimensions of width and of slant. If the handwriting, on the other hand, shows rightward advances of the i-dot together with little general speed and inclination, distance of the dot from the letter can only be one in the vertical dimension, and since the above explanation would not apply to it, the interpretation here would safely be the opposite of the one given the close dot, which means that the writer would have to be thought of as a poor and inaccurate observer. The i-dot flying backwards, finally, would involve a movement of momentary withdrawal towards the self which, since, in English, for reasons of linguistic structure, it is unlikely to occur at the ends of words, would point toward impulses of generalized withdrawal reaching beyond the mere implications of social caution and reserve which otherwise could be thought to exhaust its scope of significance; its appearance in the handwritings of pathological liars but also of withdrawn schizophrenics without overt accentuation of the mentioned trait can thus be understood. The conversion of i-dots into circular movements, finally, like all graphic movements of "rolling" but in a more articulate manner than is true of most of them, is a gesture of self-enclosure and circularity of impulses moving around in their own "rings" without external outlets; it is therefore one of the most specific gestures of pathological narcissism, and we not only would expect to find it, but find it in many instances in the handwritings of schizophrenics, particularly of the hebephrenic sub-variety. At this point, the related role played by this sign in the interpretations attached to the Bender-Gestalt Test may only be mentioned.

An almost inexhaustible number of "special" signs, of which the limited framework of this book can admit only a relatively few, still seem to offer themselves for our discussion. Many of them are signs originally defined and interpreted by Michon, the interpretations of which as given by him have sometimes been found too narrow and specific but on the whole, owing to their articulate expressiveness and relative graphic independence of dimensional criteria, have survived the holistic revisions of his system. Most of them, on the basis of the general principles of expression with which the reader has become familiar and which in the graphological practice sometimes involve more motoric, sometimes more symbolic criteria will already be found self-explanatory. Of the few dozens of Michon's and his followers' several hundred original "signs" which empirically as well as systematically have proved themselves, this handful may be presented: 1) loops: the appearance of expanded "bags" in the lower zone can relate to money-emphasis but also to all other accentuations of power which might find their expressive representation in this symbol (fig. 113). As the loop is perfected by a movement of

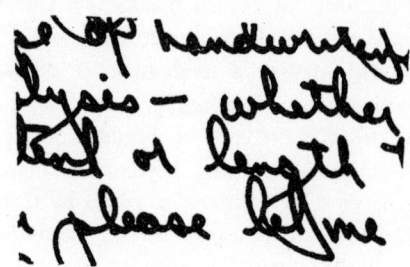

FIG. 113 (7%). "Bags" in the lower zone

crossing a previous downstroke, the tendency to shift the point of crossing away, in a downward direction, from the middle zone, relates to an impulse of hiding the need for, and exercise of, power: it is therefore found in persons of a domineering character seeking the form of domestic tyranny rather than exposing itself to the light of the broader social relationships (fig. 114). Difficulties to perfect the crossing correspondingly relate to specific inhibitory difficulties in more intimate life situations. The movement of paralleling the previous downstroke for a certain stretch of its way and to the left of it, before crossing, is a gesture of cunning

FIG. 114 (7%). Combination of "obstinate" triangularization, pressure displacement, and downward displacement of point of crossing in the *y* of an hysteric tormenting his family with constant criticisms and demands

preparation for unexpected action. The relation of the lower zone to the symbolic realm of the "maternal" has previously been stressed, and it is clear that combined emphasis on it and on leftwardness with its implications of inclination towards the self as the accumulated personal past will accentuate this relation. Correspondingly, a broad, open, leftward-swinging lower loop is a gesture of lyrical introspection tending to embrace the very roots of life, and has frequently been found in the handwritings of poets of power and profundity; the corresponding contemplative gesture of the broad and open leftward curve of the small *d* ("lyrical *d"*) of the upper zone may also be mentioned (figs. 115, 116).

FIG. 115

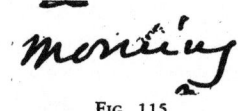

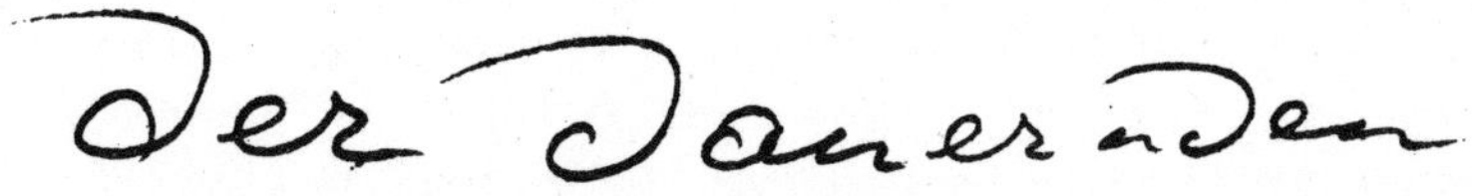

FIGS. 115-116 (7%). "Lyrical" *g*'s and *d*'s

2) Growing upper forms have reliably been found to express ambition. 3) "Cracking," particularly of the long forms, invariably discloses more or less far-reaching traumatic disruptions of the writer's emotional life; a particularly emphatic expression of touchiness is the bending-sideward or splitting-off of minor uppermost components of long forms. 4) Self-aggressiveness, for reasons no longer needing elaboration, can be expected to appear in the form of sharp leftward dashes, particularly of the lower zone; in the upper zone, it rather tends to reveal a personal emphasis on the more articulate functions of self-criticism; its appearance in the middle zone, finally, is of the gravest significance: the leftward movement of crossing-out the word, emanating from its ending, is one of the most characteristic signs of suicidal tendencies thus far defined. 5) A more passive demonstration of anticipation of doom are word endings falling below the line; both this sign and the one last mentioned already enter the realm of clinical manifestations to be taken up later (fig. 117).

FIG. 117 (7%). "Self-aggressiveness" (see lower peripheral movements), "touchiness" (see first *f*), and their consistency with the plobal form character of the specimen

Regarding the rightward endings of words only two versions may be singled out from their multitude: the tendency to shift this movement downward toward or beneath the line can be found in persons pursuing their interpersonal contacts by way of psychological speculation, i.e., of "guessing" their partners' motivations; the opposite tendency, correspondingly, derives from a more theoretically accentuated consciousness of *mission*—it "faces" arguments in the broad daylight of conscious ideational intercourse with the environment and implies a recognition of the partner's personal and spiritual integrity, as much as the maintenance of one's own; the latter, of course, is likewise, in an ultimate sense, given up in the first mentioned (shifted-downward) version of this movement, the close relation of which to the *thread* cannot escape us (fig. 118). A

FIG. 118 (7%). An attempt at "tripping" the partner by identification with his motives

graphically related movement of slyness, furthermore, dictated by the feeling that one has better chances of successful environmental contact being "small" than being "large," is the progressive decrease in size of words as they approach their endings, as though in order to "slip through" somehow; to find the opposite tendency (an increase in size of the word in its left-rightward phaseology) in the handwritings of the stubborn in general, and the paranoid in specific, will not surprise us.

In one sense, of course, all handwriting consists of "special signs," i.e., of individual coinages of gesture none of which is ever congruent with any standard form or graphic prototype, which it more or less approaches, more or less deviates from, requiring corresponding interpretative modifications on the psychological side; in cases where no known "prototype" seems close, it is clear that such coinages require to be subjected to the fundamental motoric and symbolic principles governing all expressive movements. One group of "special signs," on account of its considerable practical importance, however, may still be presented. Specific gestures of *dishonesty,* due to their articulate expressiveness and relative independence of other criteria—which make their empirically proven validity understandable—exist in a certain number. According to our general dichotomy of prevailingly curved and prevailingly angular handwritings, we can expect, in curved handwritings of the dishonest, to find the movement of "rolling," in angular ones to find the movement of "hooking" predominant. Both will be understood from their direct visual conveyance of concealment and secretiveness, which in the first case appears as the mendacious aspect of narcissistic introversion, in the second one, especially if combined with movements of controlled aggression, like brief and pointed "daggers," as the semi-conscious trickery of a hardened, coldly planning, extremely self-coercive negativism, ready to trap its antagonists in cabals and intrigues; both types of gesture are of the greater significance the more they tend to be found in leftward movements, especially if the latter are enhancements and graphically unwarranted additions rather than parts of the school pattern. A further general mark of real or potential lack of honesty is the tendency, approaching the quality of rolling or hooking movements, to close the tops of letters when, according to the school pattern, they should be open, and it is doubly significant if the same letters are found open at their bottom, i.e., if their normal structure is reversed in a way implying the expression both of concealment towards the "daylight" and of corresponding ostensible increases in self-intimacy (fig. 119). More pathological forms of lying, finally, also tend to "mend"

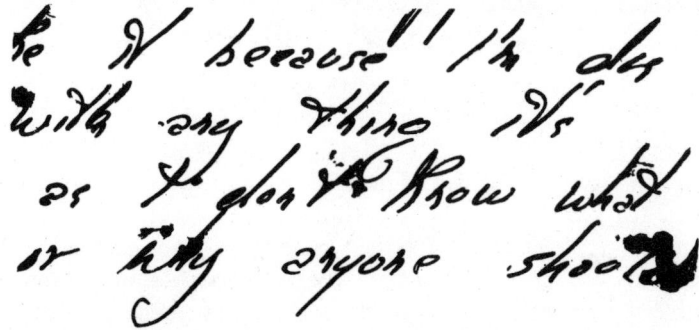

FIG. 119 (7%). Tendency toward "closed" tops and open "bottoms" of letters in the handwriting of a pathological liar. Note relation of this characteristic to the arcadic forms of the trail and to the occurrences of centripetal rolling.

their already produced words and letters by either tying originally disconnected parts together or by subsequent improvement of the aesthetic quality of other parts; here the implication of a hysteric manipulation of the normally spontaneous emotional basis of forms of behavior is the more ostentatious the less an instance of mending appears governed by the exclusive purpose to correct a writing slip or increase legibility. As mending in the first sense—that of tying together originally disconnected parts—also is frequently present in the handwritings of stutterers, where the element of graphic disjointedness, in distinction from its overall implications, appears specifically related to their oral behavior, a series of questions arises regarding the types of psychologic trauma tending to condition juvenile speech impediments; at least in one case of a stuttering child which has come to the author's attention, it was found that both stuttering and "mending" disappeared (as did lying), and that graphic connectedness grew after a complex of guilt concerning previous instances of lying to the parents, of which the child had been convicted, had been dissolved in the treatment (figs. 120-121).

FIG. 120 (7%). Graphic motor inhibitions of a patient with speech difficulties

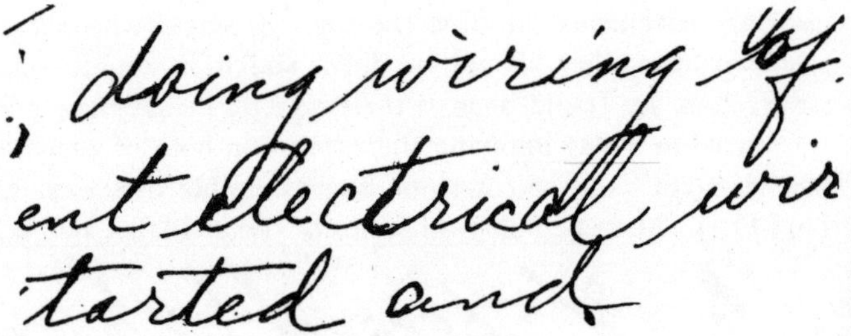

FIGS. 120-121 (7%). Mending

Having arrived at the end of our discussion of the dimensions of rating and related specific areas of investigation, a more exhaustive picture of the graphic representation of certain guiding analytic concepts can finally be drawn. While clinging to the view that no section of the trail of expressive movement is ever representative of any single stratum of personality structure without the participation of all others, a dominance of different ones of the diverse strata over specific phases of the contraction-release cycle is nevertheless implied in the dynamic and symbolic make-up of that cycle, a fact which allows a limited allocation of stratum-representation to components of movement, primarily in terms of the *directional* impulses underlying them. Several principles demand their combination: 1) the height of the middle zone, relative to the peripheral ones, was found to shrink and expand at the rate at which superego pressure in-

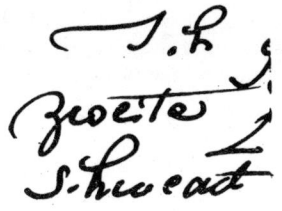

Fig. 121 (7%). "Embellishment" of upper particles of *h*'s in the lines of a writer with an inveterate idealistic *pose*

Figs. 120-121 (7%). Mending

creases and diminishes; 2) in the person's system of inner orientation in the realm of available values, the upper zone was found to express not consciousness per se, the lower zone not unconsciousness per se; instead, the symbolic place of either in the person's inner order of experiences was found to be represented by the corresponding "zone." These two positions are mutually consistent in view of the fact that the concept of the superego simply implies the presence of unabsorbed inner demands of whatever derivation and that the intensity of its consciously experienced impact on the ego and of the unconsciously exercised demands of repressed libidinous urges are the two correlated theoretical side-aspects of what in the person's realm of direct experience is the intensity of feelings of anxiety. 3) Regarding a lessening of conscious articulation of impulses of whatever derivation and direction, the movements of release and the interiors of words were found to give the investigator a better chance to observe the writer unwatched by his own ego control than was found true for

Fig. 122 (26%). Quarrelsomeness in handwriting

Figs. 122-125. Various "special signs"

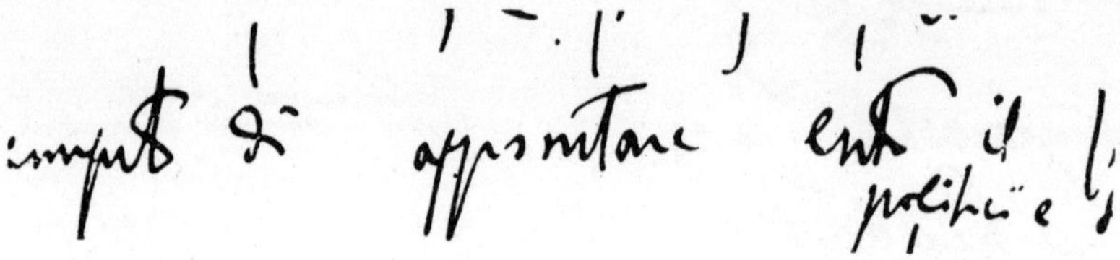

FIG. 123 (26%). "Power strokes" in the handwriting of Mussolini

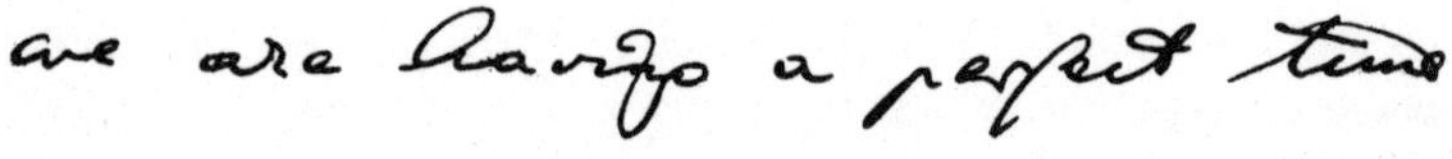

FIG. 124 (26%). "Sense of humor" strokes

the movements of contraction and the beginnings and endings of words. 4) Finally, combining the results of our analysis of the dynamic aspects of both the vertical and horizontal zones, graphic representatives of impulses arising from the person's organismic needs and tending toward articulation and externalization can be said to follow a general direction from the lower left towards the upper right; graphic representatives of impulses of repression, vice-versa, from the upper right towards the lower left, with the placement of specific components of movements within the zones and the phaseology of the word deciding their specific character in terms of degrees of conscious articulation and of closeness to either the self or the environment of the impulses expressed (figs. 122-125).

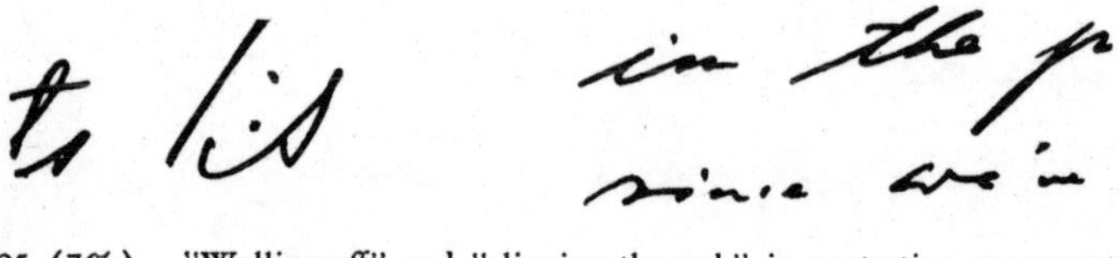

FIG. 125 (7%). "Walling-off" and "slipping through" in contacting movements

FIGS. 122-125. Various "special signs" (Cont'd)

As apparent from this analysis, a graphological "translation" of the "superego" (respectively, "id") concept is at least not meaningfully possible without restricting its dynamic application to states of a relative disintegration of the personality structure in which the ego as the organizing principle is opposed by repressive counter-claims to intra-personal dominance arising from the periphery of the realm of inner experience. Beyond such states, its application can still be useful for the assessment of some *static* aspects of personality organization—and in this sense has been used in our overall analysis of one of the interzonal proportions of the vertical dimension of handwriting—but cannot be expected adequately to account for normal personality *dynamics* which, instead, require the qualitative structure of the ego (graphically, of movement impulses arising in and from the middle zone) as the primary object of focus.

THE INTERPRETATIVE SYNOPSIS
Age, Sex, Handedness, and the Cultural Background

While the special conditions applying to children's handwritings cannot here be discussed in any detail, a general hint, basic to all graphological work in that particular realm, may be given in regard to the most fundamental differences between the inner situations of the writing child and the writing adult. As the command of the writing system is still less automatized in the child than it is in the adult, it does not "lend" itself to the purposive goal of the movement with any such facility as it does in the adult: in consequence, writing still being a task, the writing system itself will share in the purposive goal. While this does not alter the accessibility of the movement to impulses escaping consciousness, it alters the range of the writer's inner focus upon the *expressive* goal of his movement and thereby the way in which impulses escaping consciousness can manifest themselves. This becomes most clearly visible in the dimensions representing temperamental qualities. Articulation of writing as a task presents the child with an obstacle experience which tends to slow down the speed and to increase the pressure of his writing; at the same time, however, the range of focus on reality, implied in the criterion of extensiveness of the movement and represented by the size of the trail, does not diminish with this increase in "absolute" nearness of the obstacle but on the contrary tends to be found enlarged, the reason being that in the child's inner order of experiences writing not only figures as a relative difficulty of accordingly considerable importance as an obstacle, but as an even more important, i.e., "distant," goal, a realization which is necessary to account for the fact that a considerably larger size than is found in the average adult handwriting tends to persist in children's handwritings for years after its attribution to relative difficulties of motor-coordination has ceased to be justified.

Aging generally betrays itself by a renewed increase in most of the contractive qualities, of which the tendency toward greater disconnectedness was previously mentioned and of which the one toward an increase in sharpness suggests itself from the previous analysis of the lateral ductual qualities; apart from the latter, a tendency toward meagerness is the most significant one among the more generalized symptoms of aging, and it may or may not be joined by more or less accentuated qualities of the ductus, such as traces of tremor, apart from the overall dichotomy of doughiness and sharpness.

Conclusions in respect to the relative masculinity and femininity of expressive traits can easily be drawn, on the basis of their general psychological significance, from the results of our dimensional analyses, and should be guided by the overall realization of the generally masculine tendency toward greater contractiveness and of the generally feminine one toward a greater accentuation of the impulses of release.

Both the calendaric age and the biologic sex can, of course, be decisive for the establishment of a proper frame of reference for the ultimate psychologic evaluation of graphic traits pertaining to such qualities as "immaturity" or "aging," "masculinity" or "femininity," for which different specific data of the above orders present totally different interpretative premises. The age and sex of the writer, therefore, are the only data generally held indispensable for all handwriting analysis, "blind" graphological diagnoses included.

The psychological relationship between entire group attitudes, as connected with differences of the cultural pattern, and the various national school patterns of writing, has previously been mentioned, and the tendency towards a relative individual abandonment of the school pattern has been discussed; some reasonable degree of acquaintance with the overall styles of the principal school patterns at least of the western world, in order to dispose of adequate points of reference in the assessment of educational backgrounds and their relative abandonments, is thereby suggested. For example, the greater angularity of the German, the greater curvedness of the Western European and American school patterns, the prevalence of the garland over all other binding forms in American handwriting—these and some other "collective" characteristics of national and supernational handwriting patterns the graphology student not only should know but should understand in their psychological connections with trends of the culture. This is more important for the purpose of widening his graphological knowledge and deepening his psychological understanding both of personality development and of super-individual entities than it is for the purpose of graphoanalytic procedure per se. Knowing the writer's original national school pattern, his social background and specific type as well as total level of education, will always be desirable but cannot be considered an absolutely indispensable datum. All three groups of criteria are significant only in as far as the "backgrounds" implied in them have become effective in the individual development; in as far as they have, however, they merely partake in the total system of personality functioning and hence themselves are subject, along with this system, to the motoric and symbolic principles governing expressive movements.

A few comments on handwritings of the left-handed may here be added. The constitutional and characterological conditions of handedness have not been sufficiently clarified to allow the extension of the discussion beyond a more technical consideration. One clue to the left-handed writer's situation is given us in the fact that the identification of the rightward direction as that of externalization per se does, as a basic one, not hold true for the left-handed person writing with his left hand: as left-hand movements swinging away from the body in a natural and unstrained manner will of necessity follow a leftward direction, the psychological criteria for the dynamic properties of graphic movement in its horizontal dimension primarily do not apply to him. While interpretative errors from this source are always possible, qualifying distinctions appearing in the writing trail itself should narrow their margin down considerably: without considering here the quality of artificial wideness, which is a particularly accentuated degree of inconsistency between the rightward extension of letters and of letter connections, it can be stated that all truly wide handwriting shows a tendency to broaden, all truly narrow handwriting to tighten its letter forms *relative to their connections,* though to a lesser extent than implied in the mentioned special characteristic. This latter tendency now is missing in the otherwise "narrow" handwritings of left-handed individuals externalizing their impulses in an unimpeded manner, and a reasonable basis of differentiation is thereby offered; yet, information concerning the writer's handedness as a third "necessary datum," in addition to his age and sex, while not utterly indispensable to the trained observer and generally not requested by graphologists now, may well have to be considered as a future standard requirement in the graphological practice.

As far as the use of their *right* hand by the originally left-handed is concerned, the problem posing itself, apart from the possible implications of lack of dexterity in the writing movement, is one of the presence of inner conflict due to an external adjustment inconsistent with the writer's inner structure of motor-coordinative orientation. Empirically, this inconsistency can be said to be only one aspect of a broader conflict of adjustment; and whether or not it is basic to it in a causative sense, its graphic representation in any case enters into the realm of whatever, in expressive movements, signifies the presence of an interdependent complex of adjustment difficulties on the one hand, self-conflict on the other. In the left-handed child being forced or forcing himself to act a right-handed one, however, a conflict-causative role on the part of this situation is likely to be present in all instances where the graphic manifestations of the conflict directly relate to the motor-coordinative disturbance; thus, in situations of this type which are marked by a particular acuity of the conflict, the symptom of sporadic *mirror-writing*—of right-leftward reversals of letter forms—is often observed. Since, at the same time, it is interpreted as a narcissistic symptom, and as such is of some prominence in the handwritings of certain subtypes of the hebephrenic variety, the relations between left-handedness and narcissism seem to offer themselves for a more ample general investigation, quite apart from that of their graphological aspects. An ability of the left-handed using his left hand to produce an entire *trail* of leftward mirror-writing is most probably abnormal at least in adults, but the problem remains what, objectively, this abnormality implies; its relation—as that of certain well-integrated and continuously creative adult forms of "infantile" narcissism generally—to rarer cases of *genius* appears, apart from less prominent yet characterologically similar instances, from Leonardo da Vinci's reported mastery of this feat. Closer studies of the ways in which conflicts revolving around handedness in children are reflected in their writing habits tend to accentuate the general symbolic significance of the two horizontal directions, as previously pointed out in this book, in a sometimes very drastic manner. Thus, is a case which has come to the author's attention, a normal girl of eleven, who had never been observed to be left-handed in either writing or any other activity, was observed to use her left hand in writing a "letter" to her mother who had died a short while before. Subsequently, under closer observation she still did not exhibit any signs of handedness conflict; yet, in addressing herself to the past, she quite spontaneously and naively had experienced her left hand as the more proper means of communication for this purpose.

The use of script or "print," finally, while making the graphoanalytic attack more difficult, does not render it altogether impossible: sufficient individual characteristics, of which the person is unaware, usually make their way into this manipulation which should nevertheless be outruled for the ad hoc production of graphological samples. Preference for it is in itself psychologically revealing, indicating, as it does, an inner order of experiences in which distinctness of communication appears possible only to the degree to which the self of the writer is being hidden behind a facade of non-committal "correctness."

The Arrayal of Indicators on the Contraction-Release Scale and According to their Accessibility to Conscious Modification

In the introductory part of this book, the three main dimensions of personality functioning were related to the criteria of consistency of effort and direction (the relative graphic regularity) for the dimension of progression, the degree of impulse release for the dimension of depth, and that of rhythmical integration for the transverse or coordinative dimension. Since conflict between the person's orientation in the first-mentioned dimension and his organismic needs, as constituting the second one, affects the smoothness of coordination as apparent in the third one, the respective degrees of rhythmical integration and disintegration can be assessed as representatives of the person's mental health per se.

Yet we have seen that the available *direct* criterion for the degree of rhythmical integration is not easily defined. While this is of little importance in the more clear-cut cases plainly falling, on account of their particularly even or particularly uneven manners of distribution of the particles of movement, on either side of this dimensional polarity, eye-training, especially in beginners, may not be sufficient to assess reliably the diagnostically most important states either of inadequate yet, in its inadequacy, not too obvious *static* integration, or of processes of disintegration in their opening phases. The investigator's orientation in the face of the multitude of data gathered in the graphological process therefore needs support from the part of the following consideration.

Since all well-integrated states of personality structure can graphologically be defined as states of an approximate consistency of the expressive profile throughout the various layers of the structure, the more subliminal ones among the disintegrative conditions, while tending to escape a more immediate visual grasp, would still show up by way of an inconsistent distribution of emphases on either contraction or release within those areas of rating allowing of the appearance of impulses tending to escape the writer's conscious control both in terms of his self-perception and volitional processes. We might, in clinical cases, thus find a one-sided cluster of highly contractive qualities in the first group, of "released" ones in the second, or vice-versa. In order now to allow ourselves a total picture of the system of graphic qualities from the viewpoint of their relative closeness to, or remoteness from, conscious control, we shall first have to clarify them according to the criteria of contraction and release themselves; secondly, we shall have to investigate the relative accessibility of each of these qualities to deliberate attempts by the writer to alter them in his writing performance.

Conclusive experimental work in this area has been conducted by Klages in his seminars for the study of expression. The table (p. 140) of accessibility of qualities to conscious modification, and the one, preceding it, which clarifies them according to their overall positions on the sides of either contraction or release, are essentially based on his experimental work; omitted from the former one, in accordance with the stated differences in concepts, were only some listings for rhythmical qualities of insufficiently clarified definition; in terms of the psychological necessities which these tables reflect, they will easily be understood on the basis of our foregoing discussions.

The Work of Determining, Eliminating, Combining: Evolving the Finished Analysis

The student of handwriting analysis now disposes of a considerable mass of criteria for gathering, assessing, arranging, and evaluating his data. Beyond the point which we have reached in our discussion, however, he necessarily, as in all other methods of personality inspection also, is left alone with his personal talents of combination and interpretation. Visualizing his situation, we recognize a number of main difficulties which present themselves in the following most frequent objections to graphology on the part of laymen and students verbalizing their disbeliefs: 1) "I can write as I want"; 2) "My handwriting has changed so much"; 3) "It is in constant flux"; 4) "Applying the dimensional system, I arrived at the mutually most contradictory findings." Regarding the first one of these objections, there is no reason not to grant that one indeed is free to write as one wants; what matters is that one is not free to want but what one

TABLE XII

Global Classification of Graphic Qualities

I Motor Tendencies		II Accessibility to Intentional Changes (in order of decreasing accessibility to change)
Contraction	*Release*	*Easy to produce*
Regularity	Fluctuation	Smallness, slowness, pressure
Smallness	Largeness	Largeness, fastness, lack of pressure
Slowness	Fastness	Perpendicularity
Pressure	Lack of pressure	Regularity
Sharpness	Doughiness	Doughiness
Disconnectedness	Connectedness	Lower zone exceeds upper zone
Disemphasis on middle zone	Emphasis on middle zone	Narrowness
Lower zone exceeds upper zone	Upper zone exceeds lower zone	Disconnectedness
Narrowness	Wideness	Rightward slant
Perpendicularity	Rightward slant	Sharpness
Leftward slant	Increased total rightwardness	Wideness
Increased total leftwardness	Garland	Disemphasis on middle zone
Angle	Double arch	Connectedness
Arcade	Rising line	Angle
Falling line	Fullness	Upper zone exceeds lower zone
Meagerness	Elaboration	Arcade
Simplification	Crowding	Garland
Emphasis on distances	Broadening of lefthand margin	Thread
Narrowing of lefthand margin	Righward concavity of upstroke	Emphasis on middle zone
Rightward convexity of upstroke	Rightward convexity of downstroke	Irregularity
Rightward concavity of downstroke		*Difficult to produce*

does; even the limited scope of individually "possible" handwritings thus left—which not in a single one of its internal positions coincides with a single internal position of the scope of "possible" handwritings of any other person—the writer can render visible only by conscious focus on his "freedom of choice"; usually, his choice of "position" even within the scope is determined by spontaneous preferences which definitely escape his awareness, even though they themselves may change. Ad (2), in this case, as in all other "changes" of handwriting, nothing is reflected but a more or less superficial, more or less deep-reaching change of the personality structure itself; corresponding conclusions, in terms of mood changes, etc., suggest themselves for (3) the phenomenon of constant flux; the latter, of course, does not, or at least hardly, affect those qualities of handwriting which tend to escape the attention of the laymen, while being the most important ones to the graphologist. In as far as personality is a functional unit extended in the dimension of time, holistic principles apply to its processual aspects as they do to its static ones. This means that no phase of the life course repeats itself and that, in terms of the writing movement, no graphic trail, or any part of it, is ever produced more than once in an exactly identical manner. Ad (4), "self-contradictory" traits within a personality picture graphologically derived can be due to a misunderstood, i.e., too narrow, application of dimensional criteria; in other cases they are mutually contradictory tendencies in the personality system itself; if both possibilities apply at once, the graphologist's findings will of course tend to appear disparate rather than to shed light on the imminent self-contradictoriness of the character.

In order to facilitate the student's approach, the following over-all procedure is recommended: he or she should first determine what appears most incontestable in a handwriting graphically and accordingly most "generally valid" psychologically. On the basis of this first phase of combined recordings, a number of specific assumptions potentially suggested by one or the other of them will already eliminate themselves; in the light of the newly-won, and already narrower, hypothesis thus gained, more specific observations, which the student should note down as he makes them, will acquire more meaning; weighing them against one another and against his assessments of the level of form quality, the rhythmical qualities, and the over-all arrangement of the sample, he can take a new step by entering, under the continuous guidance of the principles of ambivalence and of interdependence, into the second phase of elimination of potential traits suggested by these more specific characteristics, and can then combine all of his preliminary findings of these first two phases into a tentative assessment of the personality structure as a whole which will serve him as a frame of reference for all further and more differential stages of the investigation. He will then find these further stages already much easier to traverse, but in order to beware of sweeping judgments, halo-effects, etc., he should essentially keep up for them the same general order of steps as before, i.e., a repetition of cycles of determining, eliminating and combining processes of perception and reasoning.

A worksheet, such as proposed by some for this purpose, would restrict him unduly in one respect of central importance: the way in which a perceptual field organizes itself, the order of turns in which its "unity" and its "multiplicity" prevail under his focus and acquire more and more specific meaning varies from observer to observer, and this variability exists quite independently of the interconsistency among the rounded-out concepts at the end of the investigation—the finished products of graphological analysis conducted by different workers; neither do individual differences in approaching the sample interfere with this interconsistency, nor is this interconsistency ever achieved at the cost of sacrificing that necessary variability of procedure. To a certain extent, of course, the same already holds true for the overall approach just recommended. It is meant to facilitate the student's first practical contacts with samples of handwriting, but once he becomes more spontaneous in his investigation and begins to experience the "over-all" procedure as an impediment rather than an aid, he should disregard it and entirely follow his own way; for the more facility he develops in his graphological training, the more will he be able to perceive and understand the complexities he deals with "at once," i.e., in a synoptic rather than syllogistic manner—even though, in verbalizing his findings, he again will have to resort to the discursive approach necessitated by the task of "describing" his subjects. Against the new background of his own "synoptic" experiences, the concrete and lively precision which graphological studies of personality can have (and which his own may acquire before long) will no longer astound him then either, for already he will have ceased merely to line up trait names in his analyses. He will have understood personality as the functional unit which it is and which does not allow for mutually inconsistent and arbitrarily aggregated properties but only of specific and definite ones which are determined by the system principle. This means that the recognition of the system principle itself is implied in that of any sector of the configuration. The more of the latter, by way of either direct of "supplementary" perception, becomes visible, the more limited, from the observer's viewpoint, becomes the scope of possible properties of those parts of the system still out of his immediate perceptual reach. Graphological analysis, therefore, could be defined as a succession of multiple effects of closure, each of them setting the background for the following one and all together tending toward greater and ever greater specificity of the characterological percepts (fig. 126).

FIG. 126 (7%). On first glance graphological analysis, the writer was diagnosed as a passive homosexual whose personality organization is centered in his need for locomotor action. According to the clinical diagnostician's statement, he is a passive homosexual who has taken up a career in physical education. Note the low middle zone, the fluctuating upper lengths, the narrowness of the rounded forms, the pressure displacements, and the coincidence of stiffness and impulsivity, inhibition and aggression, in his writing

III. GENERAL AND CLINICAL APPLICATIONS

TWELVE LINES FROM JOAN

A Demonstration of the Graphological Method

Reasonably prepared for his first direct experience in applied graphology, the reader is invited to accompany the author in his analysis of the handwriting of a thirty-years old right-handed woman—Joan (fig. 127).

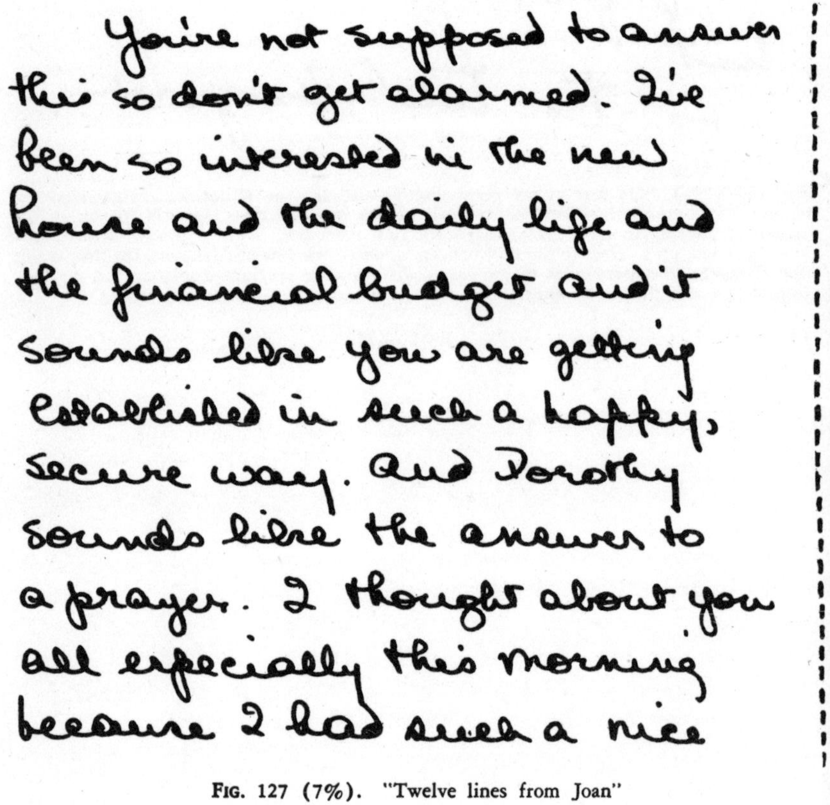

Fig. 127 (7%). "Twelve lines from Joan"

From our first glance at the sample, we receive the impression of an orderly, steady, spontaneously well-organized and effortlessly self-consistent pattern—the outstanding qualitative characteristics of which seem to be its fullness and roundness and the warmth of its ductual tone. The uncontested reign of "womanliness" in the subject thus speaks to us at the first sight of her handwriting, and these qualities are joined by a few others which likewise seem constituent to our first total perception: the over-all arrangement displays an impressive degree of good spatial disposition, characterized by both evenness of form quality and by leisure; the letter direction is consistently perpendicular, with a slight slant towards the left, denoting a type of personality organization which is articulated toward self-reliance, self-control, and some degree of self-denial. The subject, evidently, does not depend on environmental stimulation and communication, and her momentary impulses are unlikely to get the better of her often. Furthermore, we are not surprised to find the total aesthetic aspect of a pattern possessing such qualities to be inambiguously satisfactory: the "harmony" of this trail is not a superimposed smoothness or windy elegance of the surface but is the result of a natural balance in its smaller as well as in its larger proportions: it seems to caress and cultivate rather than neglect the letter forms, yet it never gets stuck either in superfluous or arbitrary detail or in mutually conflicting particles of the overall movement of writing. The consequence, to our eyes, seems to be an originality which is the more genuine as it refrains from loud utterances of unconventionality, from anything bizarre, yet almost always succeeds in an unobtrusive uniqueness of form coinage. This, in turn, not only implies that we are dealing with an excellent form level representative of superior intelligence and a high degree of personal culture, but that the handwriting, on the whole, and despite the "uncommunicative" letter direction, is half way between release and regulation; and a brief check readily confirms this conclusion. Assessing the pertinent quantitative aspects of the middle zone, we find a constant substantial flux in width, length, and specific stroke direction and a more subtle one in pressure. Considering also the already-stated indications of "womanliness," the intense capacity of affection displayed by the first-mentioned characteristics of the trail, the subject can be thought of as an impulsive and straightforward and at the same time creative person—notwithstanding the self-reliance and behavioral control conveyed by the slightly leftward-slanting perpendicularity of the letters: with the massing of indicators of wholesomeness, of inner integration, of consistency between emotion and intellect which we already have found, those potential interpretations of leftward perpendicularity which lie more in the direction of calculating coldness, stand-offishness, insincerity, etc., very obviously do not apply.

But at this point we already find ourselves in the midst of closer dimensional discernments; and in order to go on with them safely, a more global consideration of the rhythmical properties of the trail is suggested. Except for the—inambiguously "regulated"—letter-directional aspect, as we have found, we are dealing with a semi-released, semi-regulated handwriting, but we do not know as yet how well-rhythmicized it is in a positive sense, i.e., how well the subject's personality formation is supported by all strata of her psycho-biological functioning. Our first impressions regarding this question are somewhat conflicting. The excellency of form integration which we have perceived, as it involves a primarily aesthetic criterion, does not answer it conclusively. The directional impulses and the manner of pressure distribution of the writing vary, and so do many of the peripheral lengths as well as of the short forms in the middle zone. At the same time, we find a swelling of pressure particularly in rounded strokes and in straight ones of short linear extension, and both tendencies betray a contractive quality in strata of functioning which, as we know, are fairly remote from the subject's "conscious"— i.e., from those layers of experience on which ego-ideals and identifications with a chosen life role become articulate.

Still, these variations never seem to lead to any "clashes"; and the reason for this is not only that the combining movements "negotiating" between them are *formed* with intelligent graciousness and that their freely flowing roundness seems to attain a particularly high degree of background involvement, but that the stroke itself seems to adapt itself to their conflicts: highly doughy—and thus "compensating" for the stated contractive qualities on an even deeper stratum of functioning—its doughiness never has the quality of "formless" sensual indulgence but is consistently modulated, consistently "plastic"—weaving, as it does, even the most impetuous pressure impulses into an imaginatively enlivened tissue of darker and lighter shades which intricately, almost playfully, seem to interact with the background-involving formal qualities of this handwriting. And thus, while our initial impressions which favored a high rating of the sample in respect to its degree of rhythmical integration are confirmed by a more scrutinous discernment, the way in which this integration comes about *graphically* already allows of a more specific conclusion *characterologically*: in order to operate as a well-concerted being, in order to turn her inner conflicts into sources of strength, the subject must engage in a persistent activation of her imaginative potentials; and these potentials, in turn, according to the overall type of aesthetic properties we have found, can safely be assumed to lie in the direction of visual rather than auditory experience, visually rather than auditorialy oriented creativity: doughiness of such extent and at the same time of such degree of modulation, combined, moreover, with such articulateness and compactness of form, is an almost exclusive writing characteristic of painters, draughtsmen, designers, and sculptors.

The more minute dimensional observations now to follow seem to corroborate these findings from a great many different angles. The quantitative extension of the movements is well-measured; it never gets involved in "crippling" over-scrupulous detail, it lends solid and consistent support to the architecture of the whole, yet while paying full respect to the form potential of each letter the way it does this is marked by a painstaking affectionateness which seems to cherish the intimate and the idyllic and which we find most of all in those letters—like *a*'s and *o*'s—the very make-up of which invites such movements of a tender caressing. The speed is good without being hurried, the pressure cycle strong even in this medium of a "modulated" doughiness: the subject, apparently, has plenty of vitality. No major displacements of pressure occur, the goal-directedness of the energy applied persists throughout the sample, but the accentuation of the pressure in rounded movements exhibiting, at the same time, a "rolling" tendency will still occupy us later. What about the degree of connectedness? The handwriting is almost totally free of interruptions of the ductus, a remarkable feat in view of the articulate coinage of each letter form and of the relative shortness of their mutual connections and a sign that the subject is able to combine her enjoyment and cultivation of the present with a steady planfulness and consistency of purpose in moving toward future goals.

While this conclusion is reinforced by the vigorous—yet never disproportionate—vertical extension of the middle zone of the trail, taken in its total proportion to the peripheral movements, the individual extensions within the middle zone show a variability large enough to suggest marked variations in the subject's self-confidence, a finding which the corresponding variations of long-form initials as well as of the majuscular movements tend to confirm. The proportion between the peripheral zones themselves shows an overall preponderance of the upper, and, in view of all the indications already encountered for an active, creative spirituality, the dominant accentuation of some of the upper peripheral movements—movements of introspective search as in the final sections of most of the small *d*'s, movements of a spirited self-account as in the *h* in *house*, and movements of "protection" as in the small *t*'s and their bars—appears as a very express manifestation of idealism. The "searching" trend, however, is strong also in the many straight-downward vertical movements of the lower zone which, pressure-accentuated as they are, lend themselves to an interpretation on multiple strata of psychological significance. The subject is likely to detest the superficial, the easy, the conventionally pleasant, the shortcuts, and is likely to cherish the profound, to be full of devotion to whatever cause or task may inspire her work and personal undertakings, and to be loyal and dependable in her personal relations; at the same time, however, she is also likely to engage in some self-repression, some curtailment and disciplining of needs—a trend already suggested, as we recall, by the slight leftwardness of the letter-direction. In order not to miss out on its natural proportions, the latter finding we must view against its given characterological background. In a person of such élan, such emotional intensity, and such aspiring imaginativeness, some "self-repression," especially if not stirring up disrhythmicizing counter-impulses on the part of the movements of release—which counter-impulses here are missing entirely—is an obvious necessity of the intra-personal psychic economy, in the order of which such hierarchic control comes to play an integrant rather than disturbing or devitalizing part.

Carefulness, consideration, a contemplative tendency, and an attitude of "screening," "selecting" reserve towards social and interpersonal engagements are indicated by multiple signs which we encounter within the horizontal dimension. The handwriting not only is perpendicular (with a slight leftward-slanting inclination), but total leftwardness is distinctly increased, and the final movements of words, while never engaging in gestures of secretiveness or concealment, are characterized by a conciseness which often amounts to determined "briefness" and which at frequent points alternates with movements of a semi-hesitant, semi-affectionate "searching" (see the final swing in the several occurrences of *you*). What about the width of the trail? We are entering upon one of the most interesting aspects of this specimen: the order of accentuations upon horizontal extension which we remember from our discussion of "artificial wideness" we here find reversed, the letters rather than their connections being wide. The subject's antipathy to an artificial, mechanized, soulless sociability which we already could conclude from several others of our findings, thus expresses itself very directly, and at the same time—as the sign here under discussion has a very immediate and very positive bearing upon the sample's high degree of background involvement—we are faced also with a new facet of the full, "spacious," imaginative richness of the subject's inner life. Moreover, we also begin to understand *why* this person is bound to be discriminating in her external relationships which are only too likely to crowd in on her unless safeguards in this respect are provided.

The line directions are fairly straight. In their relative straightness, nevertheless, we encounter a first phase of slight downwardness, followed by a slight upward movement and a subsequent tendency to maintain the line on that level. We can conclude that the subject approaches her objectives with some timidity and even pessimism yet warms up in action and then follows an increasingly steady emotional course. The form of binding—very manifestly the garland—will not surprise us in view of the many other indications of an all-out womanliness; considering especially here the even and harmonious distribution of the particles of movement with which we were faced already when assessing the rhythmical properties of the writing, its broad middle zone, the "personal" rather than "social" type of impulse externalization denoted by the wideness of letters rather than of connections, the generalized roundness, and, last but not least, the peculiarly oscillating warmth with which the stroke seems saturated throughout, no doubt can remain that the subject has an excellent capacity for sincere friendship as well as for faithful and affectionate love in those selected relations which she admits to her inner sphere of life.

In terms of the general qualities of curve, the slight rightward concavity of the downstroke which we encounter in the long forms can only be interpreted as a sign of sensivity for emotional injury, a conclusion which is consistent with the rest of the picture; farther reaching conclusions regarding a possible positive trauma of disturbing effects cannot be drawn as corroborating indications in the areas of rhythmization, peripheral extension, and width are missing entirely. Along the polarity of simplification-elaboration the writing holds a medium position, never missing a chance either to accentuate essential structure or to elaborate gestures of particular emotional appeal. Neither ornamentation nor neglect are anywhere encountered. In view of the high degree of background involvement, the distinctness and orderliness of the whole—which is neither "crowded" nor "dispersed"—gain an especially positive significance, since the value of articulateness naturally rises with the wealth of inner experiences which—as in this case—enter into it, while in so many other instances, as we know, the psychological factors represented by "background involvement" rather tend to exercise a disclarifying influence on the person's thought processes and verbal presentation.

While this mark of the writing also implies good economic qualities, and while the shortness of the letter connections, the relative briefness of the word finales, and the increased total leftwardness are likewise in support of this finding, the personal sense of economy is more likely to focus on saving per se than on "saving time," a conclusion which is implied in the fascination which single letter forms seem to hold for the subject: her emotional and volitional engagements in the task, the experience, the situation at hand so intensely absorb her attention and "carry her away" that she is likely often to "forget herself," i.e., to "forget time"—and the reduced dispersiveness of the interlinear distances of the sample, which we remember, on the contrary, as an indicator of the trend toward *time-saving,* thus is likely to find its explanation on the basis of a compensatory attempt on her part to catch up with this weakness. The formation of the margins, finally—and of the leftward margin especially—follows the general trend, so predominant here, toward an aesthetically accentuated display of personal culture and distinction. The slight "waverings" of the left-hand margin we remember as traces of alternations between "spending" and "economizing" impulses. The right-hand margin at least shows a tendency toward an aestheticized consistency of formation. Its interpretation as an obsessional sign—which otherwise might have been indicated—here fails to apply not only for the above reason but also because of the interesting fact that, following the establishment of the marginal direction in the second line of the sample, the only word stepping out of the text and into the marginal area happens to be the impulsive, personally engaging, quite uninhibited *you* at the end of the tenth line.

Our personality picture now is almost complete, yet a few of those marks of the handwriting which seem to attain to the highest degree of uniqueness our interpretation still does not seem to have covered quite fully. The coincidence of high pressure with a slight rolling tendency which we had saved for a more ample discussion we can now safely take up. Scrutinizing this movement, which we encounter especially in *a*'s and *d*'s, we are in need of the following realization: the secretiveness, the "concealing" quality of the "rolling" gesture evidently demands its centripetal, inward direction; "rolling" here, however, takes place in the opposite direction, from an interior point outward. In the "interior point," moreover, the movement seems anchored also from the point of view of pressure: the pen, rather than "acknowledging" the two-dimensionality of the writing paper—i.e., of the surface of reality—seems to defy it, seeking to penetrate into the "ground"; the movement "takes roots" before getting into action, and this action then becomes one of externalization, of circular growth-around-a-nucleus, comparable to the "annual rings" observable in tree trunks. Viewed against the personality background in its already formulated outlines, the symbolic character of this gesture, as a whole and in all its significant phases, thus qualifies it as a particularly well-coined mark of the subject's specific and exclusive form of creativity —which, rather than "copying" nature, is likely to proceed in nature's own way. And no doubt can now remain, after so many indications for it have supplemented one another, that the subject either is or should be an artist.

Remembering here our earlier statement regarding her needs for a continuous activation of her creative capacity in order to be able to turn her inner conflicts into sources of strength, remembering, furthermore, the close relationship between the outwardly "rolling" gesture just discussed and the inward "narcissistic" rolling which we find in graphic patterns of many forms of mental imbalance, we will comprehend not only the intricate and well-known relations between "creative" and "disturbed" personality pictures but, more effortlessly and in the concrete, we will also comprehend now the particular inner situation of our subject: in order to live her life and keep it as straight and well-ordered as she is used to, she must "create"—but in doing so, the resources, both inside and outside of the creative processes proper, at her disposal seem indeed substantial. With all her imaginativeness, her stand in reality is solid enough, as her economy, her practical sense, and her dexterity inform us—traits, all of them, which we can easily infer from the excellency of the spatial disposition of these lines, from the express, "pictographic" physiognomy of the letter-forms, from the ease in connecting them and from the "plastic" modulation of the pressure throughout. Nor are even these qualities the most characteristic ones which are likely to distinguish her life conduct and social appearance. The many minute waverings of the line, the leftward reinforcements within the upper zone, the tiny but contrastful "hooks" (see lower ends of small *y*'s and small *g*'s) and other "briefnesses" in this otherwise softly and leisurely woven pattern of movements, and the self-mockery of a word-gesture such as we find it in the nonchalantly-handled adversities of *established*: all these indicators clearly point toward a sense of humor original and forceful enough not only to facilitate her handling of social relations but, in all probability, greatly to enrich and enliven also the creative workings of her fantasy.

That the "conflicts" on which our discussion has touched have left the inner integration of this personality unaffected we have seen in the beginning and have found corroborated by a great many signs which came into our focus in the course of the analysis. A more specific definition of the nature of these difficulties may, however, not be useless. The coincidence of an emphatically *garlandic* type of movement with a preference on the part of the impulses of rightward extensivity for letter-forms rather than letter-connections can serve us here as the best and most direct clue. The former, as we know, denotes the subjct's need for motional tie-ups with the environment, the latter, her need to cultivate her inner life at the expense of these tie-ups—from which its experiences and creative images must be, and are being constantly, "protected." The never quite satiable need to do full justice to both divergent trends at once is likely to show up in mild periodic depressions which, graphically, are directly suggested by the heavier distribution of pressure in the lower (downward) peripheral movements and by the occasionally noticeable tendency toward deep-saddled garlands. This interpretation, moreover, also is supported by many of the previously considered final movements of words denoting hesitation-in-contacting. A global view of the character picture as yielded by our analysis likewise seems to bear it out. More than that, it almost seems to make difficulties of this kind a self-evident necessity for her life as, more or less, for that of any truly creative personality—the inevitable yet in itself by no means disquieting condition for an effective operation of all her other qualities and strengths.

A PROBLEM IN PERSONNEL SELECTION

There is a vacant position at the N— Company, a firm which handles the import and wholesale and retail sale of children's toys. At the present moment, the company is in need of a chief buyer. The required qualifications involve not only the applicant's educational background and work experience but also character and personality. The firm wants for the position of chief buyer a man who is honest, intelligent, reliable, and energetic, has personal warmth and social poise and ease, a good sense of humor, a sound sense of discrimination for qualities, an understanding of parents' mentality, and a good intuitive sense for the psychology of children. We are called upon to assist the company in selecting the right man for the job according to these criteria and on the basis of handwriting samples of the four men whom the firm has already selected from the candidates as the comparatively best risks. All four are right-handed and between twenty-seven and forty-one years old.

How do we go about it? Remembering that specific traits of personality can only be diagnosed graphologically by inferring them from total personality pictures derived on the basis of handwriting, we avoid the mistake of organizing our handling of the task by taking each trait separately and looking at the four handwritings from the viewpoint of whether or not and to what extent that trait is indicated. Instead, we organize our work by taking each specimen separately, in order to let a full and distinct picture of each of the four persons emerge. This must not mean necessarily, as it would in clinical and other lines of graphological work, that we have to go into great detail in developing these personality pictures but it does mean that we have to advance their development to a point where their "contours" have become definite enough to enable us to make specific "trait" statements with a reasonable degree of certainty. Samples I and III (figs. 128 and 130) are sections from personal letters of the writers'; II and IV (figs. 129 and 131) are ad hoc copies from newspapers which were produced with the writers' full awareness of the graphoanalytic destination of their writing.

Sample I (fig. 128) combines a good level of form quality with some rhythmical disturbance. The handwriting is primarily released, it has a freedom of movement which implies a lively *need* for integration, a biological "attempt" at it, as we may say, but the disturbance is neverthe-

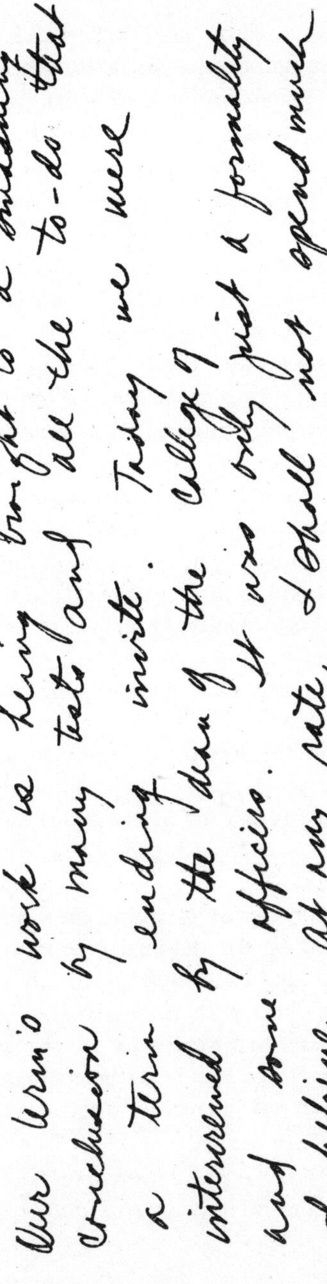

Our firm's work is being brought to a smashing conclusion by many tests and all the to-do that turn ending invite. Today we were interviewed by the dean of the college, and some officios. It was only just a formality I believe. At any rate, I shall not spend much

FIG. 128 (17%). Sample I. Male, age 27, right-handed

less substantial enough to cause such unmastered inner controversies as we find in the rather spastic formations of the words *brought* and *conclusion,* in the lack of a homogeneous directional organization as exhibited by *only just* and at other places. While the speed is fast—though likewise not very consistent—and the overall size well-proportioned, the pressure is both frail and unruly; at specific places, as the g-loops in *smashing* and *ending,* pressure displacement is tied up with a near-to ataxia (and with a failure to return to the writing basis) in a total movement which is rather contra-indicative of the writer's full emotional health and which other graphic trends tend to corroborate. Thus, in almost all proportions we not only detect a particularly high degree but also a disturbing abruptness of fluctuation. This holds true for the peripheral lengths, for the upper to lower zone proportion, for the extension of the middle zone, for the width—and the relative extent to which either letter forms or connections are wide—for the letter directions, the binding forms—some threading being evident—for the placement of i-dots, and for the interspacing of words. Additional signs for an inner conflict sufficiently strong to interfere with consistent goal formations and well-organized external pursuits are the "dissonant" doubling of the *b* in *brought* and the increasing narrowness and leftwardness, particularly of the lower lengths, as words approach their point of "contact" (see, for example, *formality* and, of particular significance in an otherwise "connected" trail, the highly disrhythmical breach in the interior of *brought,* a word altogether full of disquieting graphic physiognomy: in addition to the mark just mentioned and to the double formation of the *b*, the aimlessly lingering final movement of the small *g* is characteristic of an inner uncertainty of the writer which appears to confirm the general impression of a sensitive swaying perpetual *search* for consistent direction which these lines suggest and which is reinforced by the depressive final droop of lines as they approach or reach the right-hand edge of the paper). The form level, with emphasis on the emotional responsiveness and the readiness for integrant personal and spiritual experience which the coinage especially of very short words suggests, remains nevertheless highly promising, but the "promise" seems to lie in less "practical" directions than the vacancy to be filled has to offer.

Sample II (fig. 129) is of good form level and primarily regulated. Its warm, well-curved and well-modulated ductus immediately seems to

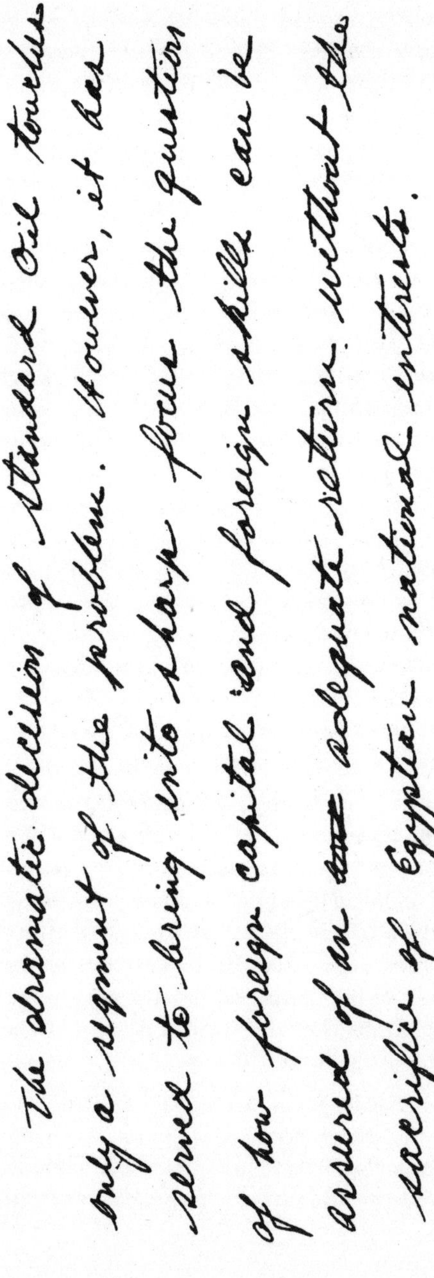

The dramatic decision of Standard Oil towards only a segment of the problem. However, it has served to bring into sharp focus the question of how foreign capital and foreign skills can be assured of an adequate return without the sacrifice of Egyptian national interests.

FIG. 129 (7%). Sample II. Male, age 32, right-handed

speak in favor of the writer, and there is a consistency and even relative independence of the form character despite the adherence to the school pattern of the forms of binding, i.e., despite a certain emphasis on "living by the rules" on the part of the writer's gestures of social adaptation. A somewhat self-coercive overemphasis on external adjustment, on "keeping steady," also is suggested by the straightness of the ductus and the fact that the system of regulation is not effortlessly absorbed by the movements of release, which are slow, hesitant, and often indecisive, and show a very slight tremulous touch (see the initial upstroke of *the* in the second line, the upstroke preceding the *r* in *assured,* the *b* in *bring,* and many others); evidently, as we can infer already at this point, the writer finds it difficult to relax. The "potential" hint at anxiety thus received is reinforced by the breaches in direction occurring, with varying sharpness, within identical letter forms as they enter the lower zone (see, for example, both the first and last *of* in the sample) and by the abrupt alternations in middle zone extension which indicate a rather excessive wavering in the writer's level of inner security. The increase in pressure of the final movements of words is likewise excessive at frequent points and together with the leftward hooks attached to the endings of *touches, capital, skills,* and *the* in the fifth line is a fairly definite indication of problems in interpersonal contact, for which an impeded externalization of impulses—the decrease in wideness as words approach their endings is very consistent—provides the basis and which should lead to experiences of greater insecurity on the part of the subject than his self-disciplined attitude is likely to convey.

Leftward angular gestures, implying a considerable amount of scrupulosity and of self-critical accentuation of control add to these findings. We encounter them at the very points of departure of a number of words (*served, sharp, return, national*), while in other word-initial upstrokes this movement is "abbreviated" in the appearance of a "traumatic" prolongation of the movement. In accordance with the tendency toward an interzonal inconsistency of the peripheral movements, the general qualities of curve in the long forms show leftward concavity of the upstrokes, leftward convexity of the downstrokes.

While anxiety thus is evidenced by a number of marks, the fact that the regulation system, even though not too successful is a rhythmical sense, is tenaciously kept up throughout these lines, makes it likely that the subject's ability to maintain his positions in the face of adverse circumstances, both within and without, is unimpaired, and that the only negative effect which his difficulties are likely to have on his life conduct and vocational achievements can be assumed to take the form of a certain hesitancy and occasional slowness. Otherwise, it is precisely the area of his intellectual aspirations and of those inner needs of his which culminate in the functions of self-account and of moral responsibility—graphically the upper zone—which shows not only a considerable quality of form but also a substantial amount of genuine, if somewhat subdued, spiritual élan: the speed, ease, and slenderness of his strokes are here at their best, and the striving for articulate concepts which we can infer is likely to compensate for his emotional stallings at a satisfactory rate. Characteristically, while words ending with middle zone movements show an increased perpendicularity of the letters, upper peripheral movements constituting word finales show an increase in rightward *slant*—a reliable sign for the fact that the writer, while generally over-cautious in his personal approach to the social environment, harbors a great amount of genuine empathy, of sincerity in selected interpersonal relations; and this need of his to communicate and to share in common experiences and ideas is only in accordance with the warmth of his ductus and with the search for harmony which, all its imperfections from the viewpoint of rhythmical integration nothwithstanding, characterizes the form coinage of his lines.

In view of these qualities as well as of the "self-maintaining" tenacity of his display of graphic regulation, he would seem to come into closer consideration for a great many tasks in life which imply a requirement for superior intelligence and for an accentuated sense of responsibility such as his. Considering all the observations which we have outlined and allowing them to merge, we see him as an excellent and loyal character, a person of superior abstracting ability and balanced judgment whose relative lack of emotional "steadiness" has stopped short of his moral integrity and intellectual effectiveness—and an industrious and reliable worker, if not a very fast one. Also, since the basis of his personality is undisrupted, chances for a gradual dissolution of his difficulties and a reduction in anxiety are good, and his general sense of quality, which is implied in several of the last-mentioned observations, would, in itself, probably likewise be adequate to the position at hand. Yet, since no indications for any specific interest or talent which would operate in the direction of the activity in question can be inferred from our analysis, not much real drive and zeal—all his sense of duty notwithstanding—can be expected from him in the service of any task—such as our "job"—which does not positively appeal to his intellectual interests and need for experiences of spiritual communication. Moreover, with his tendency toward regulation and connection, he is clearly the *deductive* thinker type and is likely to be somewhat lacking in realistic intuition—in that drive for aggression and for practical initiative which molds the environment rather than withstands it and which seems indispensable for any position in business life that implies a potential necessity for swift, bold, and frequently "unorthodox" decisions.

Turning now to Sample III (fig. 130), we are impressed at once with the particular originality of its form coinage. Together with the speed and ease of the movements and with the high degree of simplification, it points toward a brilliant intelligence and dependable sense of logical and qualitative discrimination; the writer's ability to perceive essentials appears at a glance. As the trail is steady without being regulated, a natural consistency of feeling, purpose, and direction can be assumed: the handwriting is markedly rhythmical in the double sense of being released and well-integrated, for whatever fluctuations we encounter—and we encounter them in a great many dimensions—follow a law of transition rather than of abrupt disparity. This holds true for the degree of connectedness, for the middle zone extensions, the degrees of width and of slant and a number of more subtle proportions. Concerning the temperamental qualities of the writer, the coincidence of high speed, fairly high pressure, and smallness conveys the general—and thus far tentative—concept of a modest and at the same time realistic yet vivacious individual who is persistent in his undertakings and forceful in his feelings and volitions.

What about the pressure? Owing to the peculiarities of his binding form which at this point of the investigation seems to weigh somewhat "against" him—a clear-cut thread—the existing cycle can better be deduced from the distribution of darker and lighter shade-contrasts over the whole sample than from an analysis of the skeletal movements. This distribution now, without ever being mechanically repetitious, follows an order of its own which is highly stimulating in an aesthetical sense; the pressure, by virtue of its dynamic qualities and without being in the least tremulous, vibrates like a violin cord, and it is enabled to do so because the medium

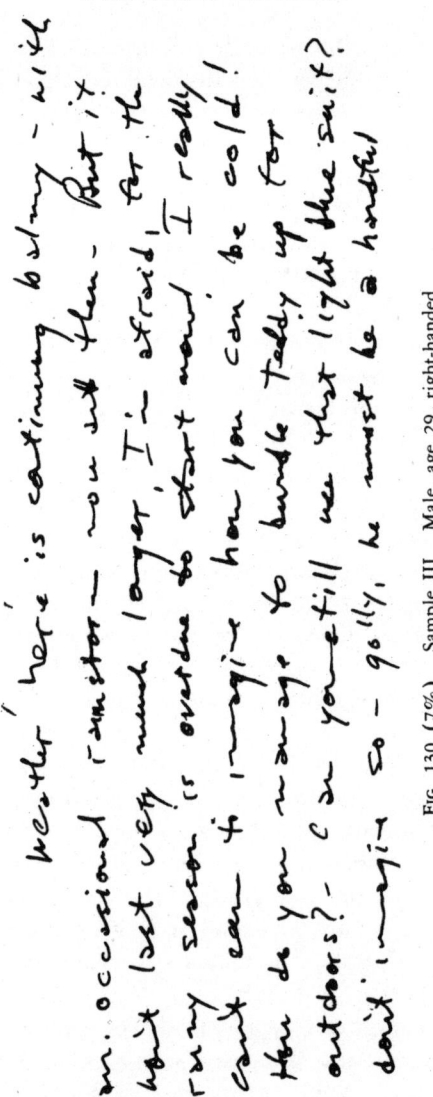

Fig. 130 (7%). Sample III. Male, age 29, right-handed.

in which it appears is a ductus of particular "lateral" constraint. At this point, we remember the implications of musical talent inherent in the thread and the relationship between auditory orientation in general and sharpness. The deduction at least of astute musical interests thus imposes itself, and the concept of a generally *artistic* type of personality which it implies is supported by the prevalent disconnectedness which, reorganizing, never fragmenting, the writing structure, converges with the oscillation of the pressure in indicating a person of empathy and intuition and also of considerable, if—considering the abstention from doughiness—subdued yet permeating personal warmth. The letters have a quality of both quiet determination and of "restrained imaginativeness" which is likely to be as refreshing in personal contact with the writer as it is in the trail of his writing.

What, then, can be said about his "threading" per se? That our interpretation will follow the "plus" rather than the "minus" line from a viewpoint of global personality value is implied already in our high assessment of the form level and in the many specific observations which followed it. Yet, in order to find out what specific trait statements can be inferred on this basis, a closer study of the type of thread at hand suggests itself. This, in turn, in the case under consideration, cannot be done without taking into account some other qualities of the writing with which the thread seems constantly interacting. Wherever we find threading movements clearly motivated by the avoidance of the vertical, the degree of connectedness is high; while, wherever we find vertical articulation and express form coinage in the middle zone, the handwriting is disconnected to a sometimes quite radical extent. The usual differentiation of "threads" into "primary" and "secondary" versions thus is of little help, or rather, it "helps" us only in a negative sense, by suggesting interpretative eliminations of certain trait names on the side of either version. Undoubtedly, much of the impression of an "excellent form coinage" derives from the particularly *rhythmical* oscillation of the pressure; for even though this oscillation is in itself not participant in the processes of linear formation, it supports the latter by creating a "third-dimensional" projection, a projection of depth which is a direct representation and indication of "depth" in the psychological sense—i.e., of emotional profundity—and accounts for the peculiarly "plastic" character of the writing. Yet, in the sense of the standard criteria for "primary thread"—which are criteria of the linear formation—the writing does at least not inambiguously belong into this category—relations to it, however, are shown by such forms as *that* in the seventh line—and not into that of secondary thread, either, as there is no opportunism in it, no superficial "smoothness," no all-out clamoring for self-preservation. The strokes defy the two-dimensionality of the paper, they seem hewn into it, they reject the shallow maxim of adaptation at any price: the "threading" of this spurting-fast handwriting is clearly a movement of impatience, and wherever it comes to a temporary end, connectedness does also.

This signifies that the writer knows *both* how to get along where his inner situation does not conflict with the "adaptive" demands of his outer and to contemplate, value, cherish, and enjoy wherever he gets a chance to do so. Notwithstanding the total prevalence of "release," his self-discipline in organizing his life and work cannot be doubted. The sparse and purposeful economy of the trail, the naturally "centripetal" accentuation of the movement impulses, the smallness, the good and consistent pressure, the harmonious proportion among the three zones—in those words where the threading impulse is lessened—and the movement of forethought, of gaining a distance of judgment, in the separation and setting apart from the rest of their words of most of the long form initials—all these characteristics combined indicate beyond doubt that we are dealing with a person who knows to subordinate his impulsivity and sensitivity and the manifold oscillations of his emotional life to goals freely and spontaneously conceived—a conclusion which is also suggested by the distinctness of the strokes and by the arrangement of the text on the paper (despite reduced legibility), by the impression of airiness and dispersion (despite actually rather small interlinear distances) and by the consistent formation of the left-hand margin. Our earlier attribution of modesty to the writer can now likewise be made more specific. Considering the observations just made as well as the combination of smallness and simplification which we find, we can assume the writer's attitudes and behavior to be marked by simplicity, naturalness, and good poise.

His particular *psychological* propensity and understanding appear from several of the trends already pointed out. In a combination of such qualities as intelligence, sensitivity, sense of quality, realism, "subdued yet permeating personal warmth," intuitiveness, knowing-how-to-get along, it is clearly implied, and the accentuation of the threading tendency in word finales with its gestural conveyance of *searching* confirms it in an even more specific manner.

The many subtle indications of an excellent sense of humor which the writing has to offer—a quality expressed very vividly by such playful yet simple movements as the *y* of *very* (third line), the *g* of *light* (seventh line), practically all *f*'s and *a*'s and several of the *o*'s—may finally be added to the character picture. More generally speaking, the handwriting's lack of regulation, of persistent connectedness, and of a "definite" binding form also implies that the writer has not lost a free and imaginative and quite spontaneous access to his own psychic resources, i.e., genetically speaking, to his boyhood—a fact which, among other things, should also make him a warm friend and effortlessly "understanding" observer of children.

Sample III, without question, is now leading in the race; but, far from allowing any bias against the last and yet unstudied sample to develop in us from this realization, we try to forget our observations and conclusions for a while and may even take a walk for that purpose before returning to our task and focusing, detachedly, on Sample IV (fig. 131). Our first impressions seem contradictory: the form level unquestionably is very good, yet it appears as the result of a painstaking laboring rather than of spontaneity—there is little flowing, little kinesthesia, the handwriting is regulated to an exceptional degree, and it is this regulation which seems to account for the aesthetic effect of the whole: one could not imagine these lines becoming more flowing and fluctuating without sacrificing in the process their somewhat fastidious refinement of form quality. While this does mean that the sample's "preciousness" is in a sense an artefact, that it is the effect of a continuous manipulation, "artificiality" here does not connote that the writer presents a "false front" to the world or that he pretends to roles and qualities not in accordance with his real nature: for that, the manipulation is far too consistent and far too successful, too well-integrated in an aesthetic sense and also, relatively speaking, too fast. What "artificiality" does connote in this case is that in the writer's own inner order of experiences an aestheticizing approach to life holds priority over all others and that everything is subordinated to the demand for "balance," for "self-harmonization," for feeling at peace with himself implied in this approach; and, in as far as a sample of such extreme reduction in release permits us to speak of "rhythmical qualities" at all, there can be no doubt that this claim for priority on the part of an "aestheticizing" system of self-coercion is met with obedience by the writer's psyche: throughout these ten lines there is no abruptness

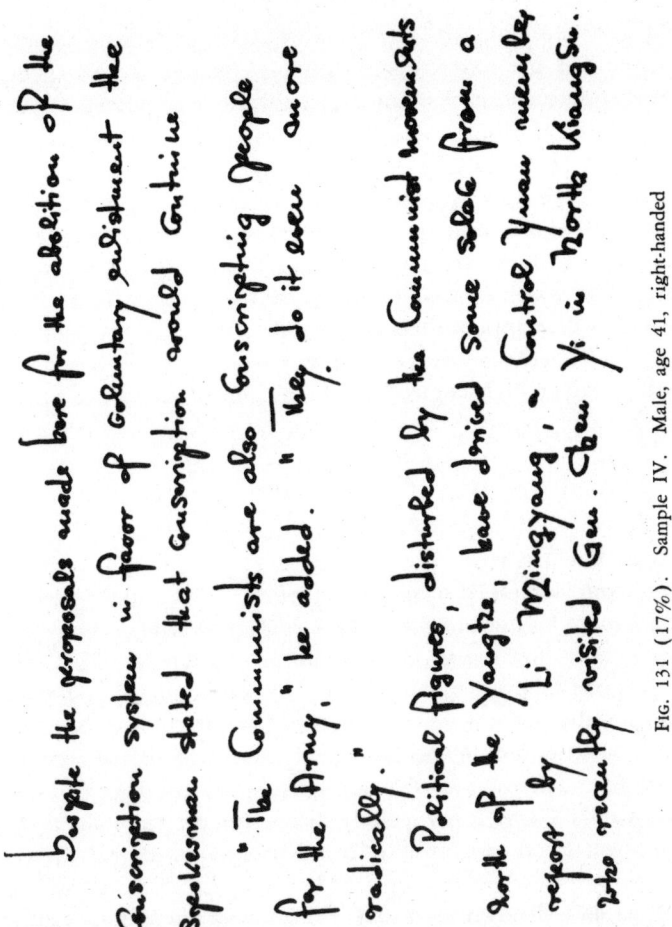

FIG. 131 (17%). Sample IV. Male, age 41, right-handed

of change or disparity of form and direction that would interfere with its successfulness.

Thus, while in Sample I were were faced with a released handwriting of disturbed rhythmical integration, in II with a regulated one, likewise of disturbed integration, and in III with a well-integrated released one, Sample IV can be called a well-integrated regulated one; and, undoubtedly, considering this its quality of harmony, it joins Sample III in coming into closer consideration than either I or II for the demands of this particular job. Many more specific traits speak likewise in the writer's favor. The total amount and the consistency of graphic pressure is quite good, and whatever displacements of it we find weighs little in comparison with these overall qualities of display and distribution. This points toward considerable—and considerably steady—working energy, and the fact that, in addition—as we learn from the almost overly tall long forms wherever they constitute world initials—the writer is an ambitious person also makes it likely that he will be energetically motivated in his vocational strivings. The smallness and precision of the writing, in at least one of its aspects which apply in this case, speak in favor of the writer's carefulness and conscientiousness, and together with the combination of good form with a rather high degree of fullness and of disconnectedness and with considerable originality in the specific variations of the latter quality, seem to suggest that the writer not only is of superior intelligence but that his personal *type* of intelligence involves a remarkable amount of imaginativeness and of independence in his judgments.

Yet, those qualities which previously were referred to as "preciousness," as "aestheticism," retain their disquieting effect as far as the writer's suitability for a more business-like activity is concerned; and this effect is not lessened by such dimensional observations as the narrowness of the sample, its perpendicularity, and its quality of increased total leftwardness which graphically not only results from the conjunction of the two last mentioned qualities within the horizontal dimension of the writing, but which shows an almost excessive accentuation in the ego-representative initials of words. This is particularly distinct in the *f*'s of the text, with their placement of an excessively leftward and, moreover, clearly walling-off kind of movement in the upper zone—a sign that the writer likes to be left alone with his own ideas and is hesitant in opening himself to the ideas of others; in connection with the accentuation of the personal past in this and in the related leftward movements observable in the initials of *conscription, more* (fifth line), *radically, political, north, report,* and in almost all words beginning with an *s,* this quality of the character also tends to suggest a lyrical type of contemplativeness. His *self-coerciveness,* certainly, as we have seen, is "successful"—but this successfulness is possible only on the basis of a primary introversion of his character, of an inveterate introspectiveness which not only demands that he repress a great amount of his instinctual longings (the leftward accentuation of the lower lengths of his *y*'s, the centripetal quality of all letter groups involving upper peripheral movements, and the fact—indicating a substantial amount of anxiety—that in most downward movements which begin in the upper zone the pressure is not generated in the course of the movements but tends to *impede* them at their upper points of start are characteristic in this respect) but which also seems to make him more interested in his own thoughts and emotional reactions and processes than in external reality. This is borne out by other marks of the handwriting also. Adding to the peculiarities of his long form initials, most of the *final* movements of words are either leftward or broken off or, if they are rightward extended at all, have an over-cautious, distrustful briefness and frailty which points towards an exaggeration of reserve in his personal contacts as well as, again, to feelings of anxiety.

Thus, we see him as a man of spirit whose talents, combining analytic and artistic qualities, seem to point in the direction of verbal articulation, i.e., of literary and possibly of certain scientific endeavors, or of a combination of several intellectual interests of these types; but we fail to see him as a primarily "practical" man. With all the articulateness and even imaginativeness of his lines, we are at a loss in trying to detect in them the naturalness and realistic simplicity and the "open" approach to things and people which the position in question seems to make imperative for its holder—and we can therefore now decide, and inform the company accordingly, that the job of chief buyer should go to the originator of Sample III. To the best of our judgment, and without a trace of doubt left in our mind as far as the comparative psychological position of each of the four samples is concerned, the writer of III not only is the smallest "risk" for the firm but a very good "bet" also.

GRAPHOLOGICAL AND PSYCHIATRIC CONCEPTS OF PERSONALITY

The fundamental difference between the objects of physical science and the subject matter of clinical and personality psychology, because of their different primary relationships to the investigator, was pointed out in an earlier chapter. In distinction from the distance and detachment implied in the "foreignness" of the physicist's objects of cognition, the "nearness" in personality psychology of the object as one *necessarily* involving the investigator's own sphere of existence was then shown only in terms of the impossibility of his using a frame of cognitive reference for his object other than that implied in the evaluations of human behavior conditioned by his own life as a human and in human society. There are, however, more ways for this "nearness" to manifest itself than this. One of its most perturbing effects on the psychologist's mind seems to derive from the fact that the functions of perception, symbolic experience, and thinking, which are among the most important ones in *constituting* his subject matter—personality—are at the same time the ones which he himself is exercising in investigating it; the behavior of the investigator and his object thus come to belong to the same general order of activities. Yet, instead of accepting the bounds of this common order as the necessary ones which they are, a tendency to assume an attitude "as if" one could break through them into a sphere of cognitive behavior which would be independent of the subject matter's own general principles of action and thus would allow it to be more properly a "subject" is as widespread among psychologists and psychiatrists as it is understandable. Where the psychological correlations of psychological processes and the somatic correlations of personality structures are under investigation, such an attitude of theoretical "sovereignty" may be entirely justified; in the face of the functions of perception, symbolic experience, and thinking themselves in their potential qualities as *objects* of cognition, however, such an attitude quite evidently is meaningless to the point of being misleading.

One of the most frequent minor consequences of this "maladjustment to the situation" are objections to symbolic interpretations deriving from a logical confounding by the critic of "object" and "subject" functions ("subject" here to be understood in its original meaning as the thinking agent in apposition to its object). Thus, the concept of "instinctual forces" may be opposed not on the legitimate ground of its underlying atomism (if, instead of being viewed as organismic needs encountered on a stratum of insufficient articulation, these forces are being viewed as "independent forces" in a literal sense) but "because there is nothing unconscious that cannot be made conscious" or "because it is a mystical concept"—implying that the critic feels uncomfortable in the face of a general order of part-objects on the side of his subject matter, acknowledgment of the presence of which in himself would question his integrity as a conscious being as conceived from the viewpoint of a rationalistic philosophy rather than of scientific experience. In the realm of expressive movement-analysis, a related type of reaction may occur, for example, when the symbolic meanings of the "zones" of handwriting are presented. Thus, the concepts embracing their polarity may be called "naive," "uncritical," or, again, "mystical," implying that human nature should be enlightened, critical, and rationalistic, and blaming the investigator for its failure to live up to these expectations.

Turning now to the more serious consequences of what this "nearness to the object" and the observer's natural disinclination to resign himself to it entails, we find more than ample reason to focus on the nature of the standard concepts of psychiatric nosology. As implied in their actual use for diagnostic purposes and their corresponding theoretical scope of application, the *practical* definitions of psychiatric nosology, which are of behavior-descriptive, symptom-classificatory derivation historically, are undergoing changes at the present time which threaten to jeopardize their logical consistency. Speaking only of the two main groups of psychogenic psychoses, the affective and the schizophrenic, their mutual average proportions, in terms of numbers of institutionally diagnosed cases, have during the last few decades undergone changes which, not having been adequately accounted for otherwise, are likely to find their explanation in a taciturn rather than articulate change in concept definitions. Thus, in the mental hospitals, the manic-depressive psychoses and, to a somewhat lesser extent, the hysterias have become a comparative rarity, while the applied concept of the schizophrenias appears to have been expanding. The situation is characterized, on the one hand, by the influx of speculative trends operating with a limited number of psychoanalytically derived standard "dynamic" concepts tending to mold the individual case interpretatively until it is ready to fit them, on the other hand by a corresponding disemphasis on attention for individual forms of behavior. This disemphasis, rather than involving a change in the formulations of diagnostic criteria, involves a change in the manner of applying them in practice: thus, "inadequacy," "flatness of affect," "poorness of judgment," etc., may mean widely different actual conditions from one diagnostician to the next. This situation results in an inevitable difficulty for the clinical psychologist, expected to verify clinical findings "objectively"; trained to organize his field of thinking in terms of constant versus variable factors, he will investigate the clinical scope of his techniques by testing them out on various diagnostic groups supplied by the psychiatrist and will, of course, assume the latter to be "invariables"; if they are, the better for him; if they are not, his own objectiveness, in the end result, becomes subject to questioning.

In the interest of a purposeful clarity ultimately required for successful therapeutic attacks in this realm also, no other solutions, then, would seem possible for both psychiatrist and psychologist than to return to the original basis of psychiatric nosology, the study of individual forms of behavior, or, in expression-analytic terms, of the individual gestural profile. At the Kraepelinian stage of psychiatry, the field of observation as a whole was still too new to allow of more than a comparatively rough classification of clinical behavioral types, the criteria for which, in addition, were still more articulated in terms of social norms than of morphological properties. Now the results, frozen into terminology, of the earlier undertakings in psychiatric classification somehow seem to block the way toward a strictly individualizing reorganization of the psycho-diagnostic field.

The research psychologist's dilemma in the face of diagnostic authority has already been stated. The psychiatrist himself, regardless how penetrating his actual awareness of the individual complexity of mental illnesses, or rather of disturbed personality systems, may be, still finds himself in the role of a diagnostician theoretically conceived along the lines of diagnostic concepts in somatic medicine, which entails an "either-or" situation where he has to decide between "labels"; if he dismisses them as such, the question by what they shall be replaced, due to the absence of a valid frame of reference generally agreed upon, still remains essentially unanswered; if he accepts, in "mixed" or borderline cases, the alternatives the "labels" imply, or else replaces them by too generalized and simplified "dynamic" concepts, he is bound to fail in the cognition of his object—the patient's individuality in its strict sense—to a larger or lesser degree. Still, the nosological concepts, simply by virtue of their being in existence, seem to retain their air of authority and corresponding actual influence. Doubtlessly also, this authority is still based on sufficiently good grounds to make it commendable to accept them as a starting basis for any undertaking to group and ultimately, in a however distant future, regroup the existing multitude of individual clinical cases. Beyond such provisional acceptance, however, it is clear that the investigator's focus must be upon individuality in its strict sense, i.e., on the individual patient's gestural profile.

The identification just made of "individuality" and "gestural profile" will undoubtedly meet with objections. One might even be inclined to grant a limited "indicative" significance to the personal forms of expression, but their *congruence* with the illness—i.e., with the patient's disturbed inner order of experiences—may not be found acceptable. Since this is likely to be so, it may be useful to investigate the concept instruments of nosological psychiatry itself, i.e., to concentrate on the logical nature of nosological definitions. The nature of his concept instruments normally tends to escape the awareness of the person who uses them. In situations where the object of cognition is "distant," as in physics, the satisfactory effectiveness of the concept instruments makes any special awareness of their nature unnecessary; in situations where the object of cognition is so "near" as it is in psychiatry, such awareness seems to become rather indispensable.

Thus investigating for example the definitions for such a prominent diagnostic concept as "schizophrenia" we find that whatever special definition of it found in the literature we may consider we inalterably encounter such—seemingly inevitable—terms as "shut-off," "split," "self-enclosed," "shallow," "flat," "withdrawn," and so forth. The clinical usages of these terms have become so inveterate, i.e., "concrete," that one is hardly any more aware of the fact that these usages—without a single exception in the above presented series—are purely figurative, and that they themselves—which are supposed to provide an independent, "objective" frame of reference for qualitative symptomatic observations—*rely totally on qualitative imagery analogously used.*

Thus, whatever genetic explanations may hypothetically be attached to psychiatric diagnostic concepts, these concepts themselves, very much in distinction from disease concepts in somatic medicine, are strictly phenomenal; and it is exactly the fact that this inevitable nature of the psychiatric disease concepts has long been overlooked that accounts for the speculative character which psychiatry has retained to our day. In the face of a subject-matter which by its very nature prohibits the investigation of "part-processes" assumed to account for the clinical phenomena, one chose to postulate these part-processes speculatively. The consequence has been a confounding of phenomenal data and genetic theories and a failure to follow the only road which promised a greater understanding of abnormal syndromes: a closer and ever closer observation and description of the phenomenal—of the patient's individuality in its irreducible uniqueness. It is clear that—along with the above-characterized epistemological error—the crudeness and vagueness of the phenomenal categories which early psychiatric symptomatology had evolved were bound to block that road; and this fact may be illuminated by a simple investigation of the logical make-up of the prominent diagnostic term that was cited. Of course the schizophrenic's emotions, in so far as they become articulate, are not "shallow" as a body of water might be but their form of articulation conveys the image of shallowness; of course the schizophrenic does not "withdraw" as an army might but his behavior seems to have the "gestural" implication of withdrawing; and so forth. As, according to the laws of logic, the definitions for a subordinate concept must specify but cannot extend beyond, those for the super-ordinate one, it follows that definitions of personality disorders in terms of qualities of gesture—either static ones as in the instance of "shallowness" or dynamic ones as in the instance of "withdrawal"—not only do not violate the general order of super-ordinate (nosological) concepts in psychiatry but are *directly required* by them for the purpose, set by the need to recognize as closely as possible the patient's individuality in its strict sense, of sub-specification.

MAIN TYPES OF PSYCHOPATHOLOGY AND THEIR GRAPHIC EXPRESSIONS

Affective Disorders

Considering the analysis of the rhythmical qualities of handwriting, mood disturbances can be expected primarily to affect the movements of release and thereby to bring about either a considerable increase in the total degree of fluctuation—involving, in consequence of this tendency, the qualitative consistency of the movements of contraction also—or else to show their impact on those more complex gestural characteristics of the writing trail which, like the garland, are "on the side of release" owing to their particular psychological articulation. The last named consequence, applying to states of depression, has already been hinted at on the occasion of the discussion of the forms of binding and has been made explicit when the directional qualities of the line were discussed; the former would ostensibly apply to states where impulses of emotional expansion not primarily conditioned by situational experiences but following a "law of their own" are powerful enough to cause sweeping changes of the quantitative and directional consistency of the total graphic organization.

Since, in *mania,* the disturbances in external and self-adjustment are due not, as in schizophrenia, to the upsurge of impulses in themselves disintegrative to the person's principle of system action, but to extreme temporal variations in the operations of this principle itself, the graphic picture of mania is primarily not one of conflict between impulses of contraction and release but of inconsistency in overall dimensions as well as overall directions of the trail of writing. Therefore, the degree of rhythmical integration as such will not only not be found affected but, in accordance with the manic's clinical traits of behavior, may be found particularly high; yet, the specific type of his graphic rhythm, owing to the enormous degree of fluctuation, is such that the resulting total distribution of the trail will appear exceedingly unsteady, although it may, in its own "dynamic" way, be aesthetically satisfactory like a work of art that accentuates contrast rather than harmony.

In manic-depressive personalities of considerable creativeness who are not clinically ill, this quality of the writing trail is usually found together with a high level of form quality, a high degree of fullness and curvedness of the writing, distinct single forms, and, except for their depressed phases, with a considerable size of the trail as well as, generally, an emphatic increase in most of the qualities arrayed on the release side of our previously presented table of characteristics listed according to the

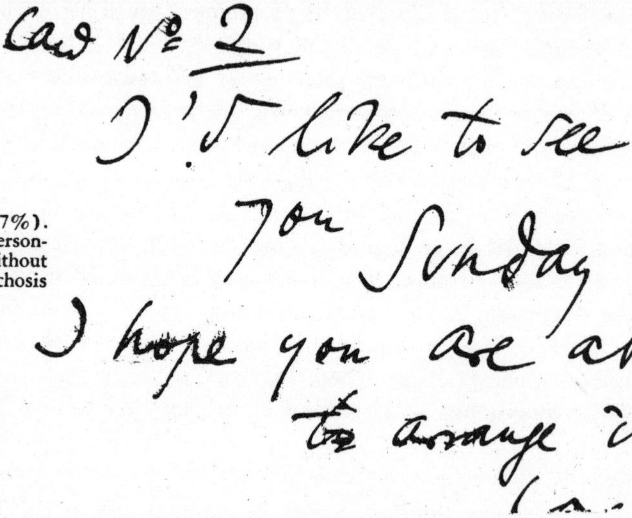

FIG. 132 (7%). Cyclothymic personality without psychosis

Case No 2

I'd like to see you Sunday. I hope you are ab to arrange it.

motor tendencies they involve (fig. 132). The clinically manic, however, tend to show the same features in conjunction with specific pathognomonic marks. The more psychomotor pressure increases, the more will the handwriting tend to "flee toward the right," with resulting increases in the dextrogyric tendency of the three general dynamic qualities of the horizontal dimension, with a flighty handling—despite their sometimes extreme fullness and sporadic aesthetic articulation—of single forms, with a tendency of lines to rise, and with other indications of a degree of "absorption by the present moment" which does not allow the writer to focus at all any more on the static organization of the writing trail, so that words "chase each other" and lines become entangled. In brief, except for the growth of such marks of spaciousness as result, like the broadening of the left-hand margin, from the elated accentuation of the rightward impulses themselves, the graphic expression of manic psychosis tends to show an unusually high degree, frequently greatly disclarifying,

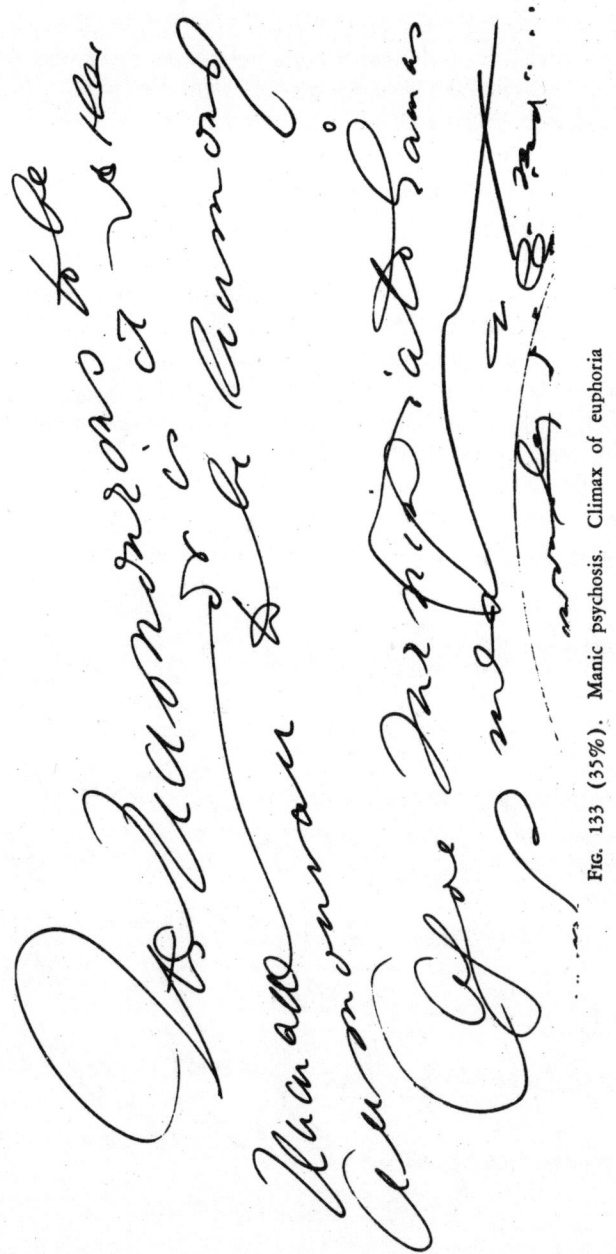

Fig. 133 (35%). Manic psychosis. Climax of euphoria

of background involvement. Only at the very height of the psychosis will the extensiveness of the movements become so great that the "conquest of the background" is being marked rather than carried out, i.e., that the "airiness" of the trail is again found increased, with corresponding euphoric increases in the size of the handwriting—a few words sometimes covering an entire page (fig. 133).

While more stationary conditions of *hypomania* may show all these marks in more reduced degrees, the picture sometimes is a rather different one for samples produced in hypomanic phases preceding the upsurge of euphoric agitation and experiencing its irresistible pressures. The layman, but also the graphologist, may be inclined to find the samples rather orderly, which is only in accordance with the facts, except that an impaired ability to keep line directions down and a disproportion between the reduced total height of the writing trail and its excessive wideness, in addition to continuous changes in degrees of the latter, will catch his attention. The patient's futile striving to resist his impulses, which thus is disclosed, can also manifest itself in an increased sharpness of the

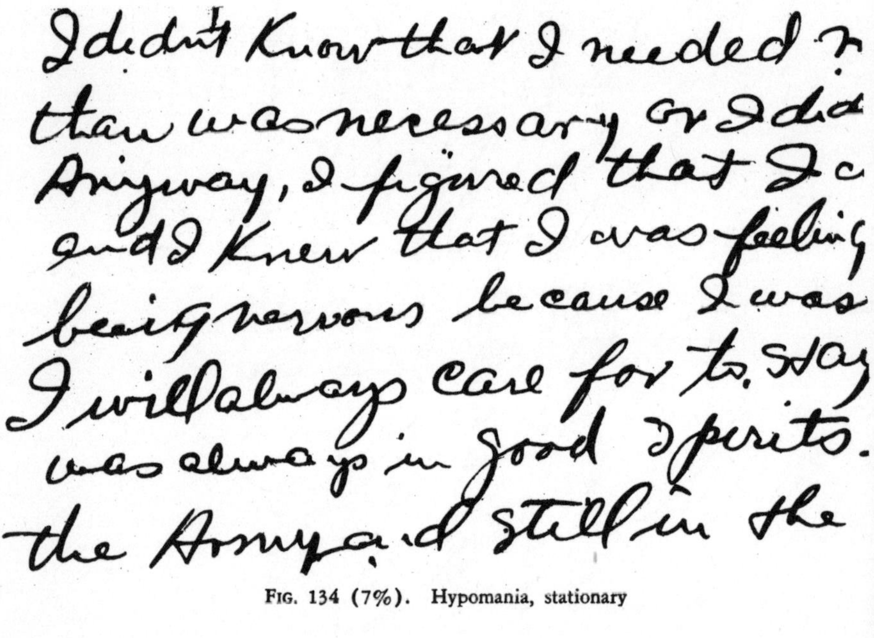

FIG. 134 (7%). Hypomania, stationary

Fig. 135 (17%). Hypomania, prepsychotic form

ductus and in an accentuation, appearing in this medium, of the pressure cycle, in brief, in attempts at *regulation,* and there may be no fancy curves at all: the impression conjured up in the observer is rather analagous to that which one might receive of a man on horseback who, seeing his animal go wild and anticipating a mad surge of uncertain direction and uncertain outcome, clings closely to his saddle, bending his head lower and tightening, along with the reins, every muscle in his body (fig. 134, 135).

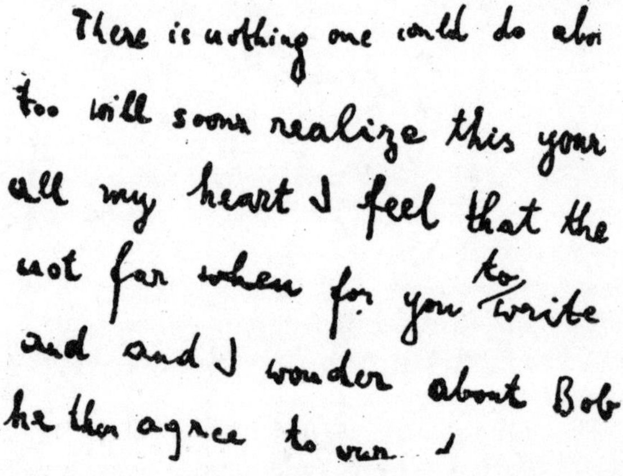

Fig. 136 (31%). Manic-depressive psychosis, depressive type

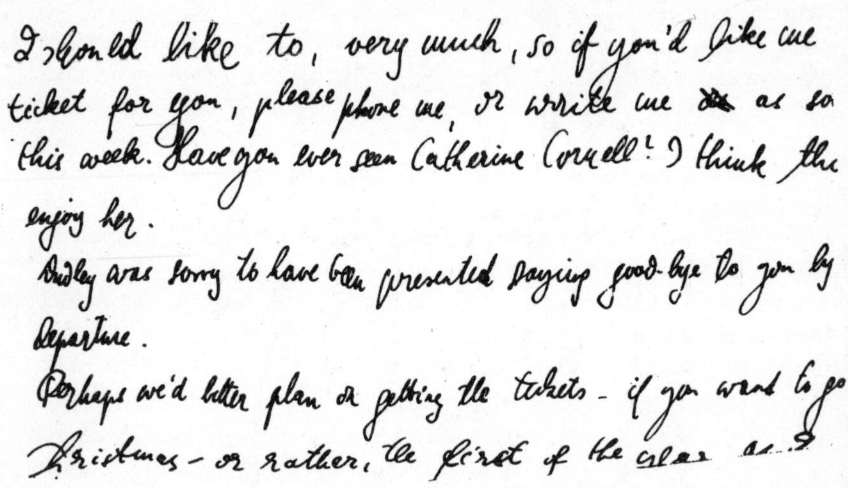

There is nothing one could do abo too will soon realize this your all my heart I feel that the not far when for you to write and and I wonder about Bob he then agree to run

I should like to, very much, so if you'd like me ticket for you, please phone me, or write me as so this week. Have you ever seen Catherine Cornell? I think the enjoy her.

Dudley was sorry to have been prevented saying good-bye to you by departure.

Perhaps we'd better plan on getting the tickets — if you want to go Christmas — or rather, the first of the year as I

Fig. 136b. Depressed state in the same patient in beginning remission

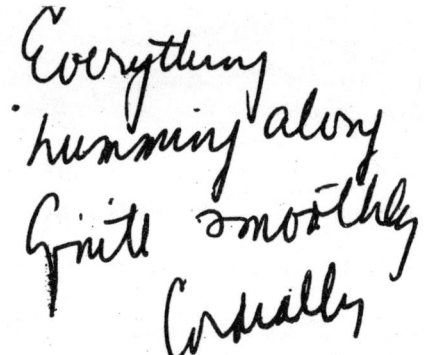

Fig. 137 (31%). Hypomania in a patient recovering from depressive psychosis

In cases of the latter type and in *pure cyclic depressions* marked by moralistic, self-deprecatory rigidity, we can expect a high degree of angularity sometimes appearing as the primary determinant of the specific individual form of binding, although even in these instances at least a garland *tendency* will be noticeable. The particular affinity existing between the garland and the affective psychoses generally suggests itself from the psychological conditionings of either; the low-saddled, "drooping" garland has been mentioned before as a mark of depression, as has the tendency of lines of the depressed to "fall" and of their inter-spaces to be spacious. "Downward" tendencies govern the picture of handwritings of the depressed, and it depends upon the nature of the depression itself which components of the trail will appear primarily affected by them; in pure cyclic depressions without a primary situational element, the tendency of letters to fall below the line will, as in the instance of the mentioned version of the garland, be a more generalized one, i.e., will be relatively independent of the left-rightward phaseology of the word, while *involutional* and *reactive depressions* are frequently characterized by a desperate attempt of the writer to resist a "falling" tendency of the word endings. Shrinking of the majuscular beginnings of words, in accordance with their overall interpretative positions, will be the move marked the more purely affective the condition at hand happens to be (figs. 136, 137).

Most general in depressions is a considerable increase in slowness, which becomes the more accentuated for those phases of the movement governed by obstacle experiences, i.e., for contractions: regardless of the absolute degree of the pressure which may or may not be high, pressure impulses

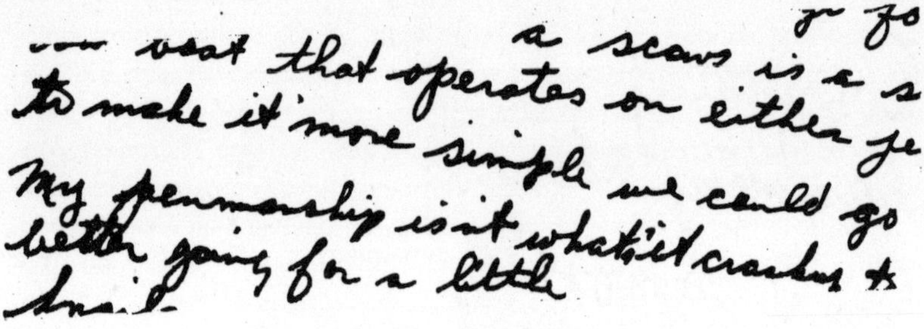

[Handwriting sample]

FIG. 138 (26%). Involutional melancholia

FIG. 139 (26%). Reactive depression, severe, with schizoid personality features

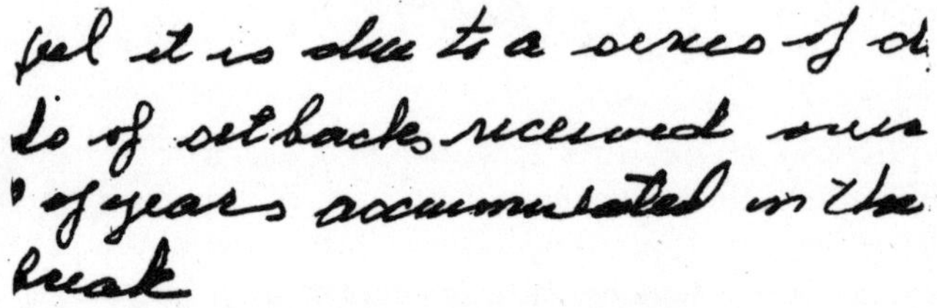

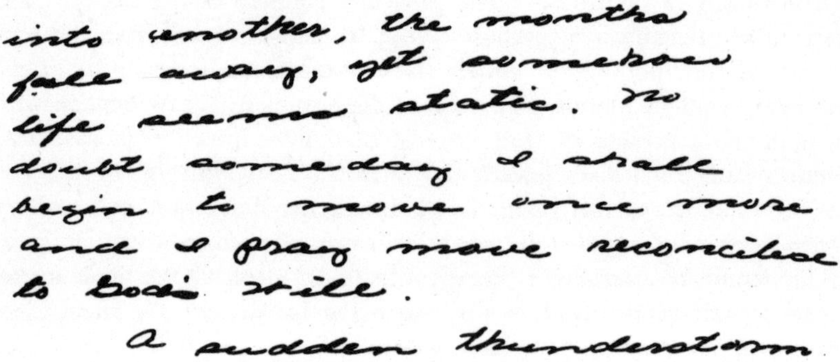

[Handwriting sample]

FIG. 140 (26%). Reactive depression, mild

in the trail tend to show the phenomenon of "lingering," i.e., an internal inconsistency of directions and width of the stroke and of darkness in those particles of movement in which swellings of pressure are predominant.

Involutional melancholia tends to show the specifically depressive signs in a way of far lesser consistency and generalization but far greater accentuation of their expressive character at specific points of the trail and tends to combine them with marks representative of physiological imbalance and instinctual conflict, as well as with signs of disrhythmization sometimes approaching a paroxysmal, sometimes a schizophrenic graphic syndrome. Thus, a marked inconsistency in the degree of doughiness, wavering between smeary excesses of that quality and extreme sharpness conditioned by abruptly upsurging impulses of ego-linear constraint, in addition to more or less advanced displacements of pressure into movements normally calling for release, and with crippled lower forms, possibly alternating with exaggerated ones, is very characteristic of the named condition and should make its differential diagnosis fairly easy; signs of a more paranoid character may enter its graphic syndrome as they may its clinical one. In addition to a more or less prominent appearance of the depressive signs proper and (depending on the genesis of the condition) of other traits of pathology, *agitated depression* is found marked by great inconsistencies in line or letter directions, while its overall wideness and slant may be exceedingly high (figs. 138-140).

In *reactive depressions,* as more or less in all neuroses, the width of the writing is found exceedingly decreased, practically all contractive qualities are in pre-eminence, and, while the height of the middle zone will depend on the clinical involvement of traits of hysteria, accentuation of the vertical peripheral impulses will be marked, yet, in a way characterized by specific disruptions of the peripheral forms, will conflict with "crippling" counter-impulses manifesting themselves at the extreme upper and lower points of their extensions. Involutional, agitated, and reactive depressions, finally, may all be more or less marked by cracked or "bumped-in" forms, inconsistencies in the directional physiognomy of lines, marks of self-aggression, and—as holds true for cyclic depressions also—by a prominent presence of those general qualities of curve which apply, in accordance with our previous analysis of them, more or less to all forms of psychogenic pathology, manic states and expansive phases of catatonia exempted (figs. 141-144).

Schizophrenic Disorders

Disintegration of graphic rhythm can be defined as the graphological criterion for the extent of personality disintegration. Unduly abrupt or unduly involved movement components, conflicting qualities of the contraction-release cycle, and a resulting sharply dissonant total distribution of the particles of movement within most sections of the trail are the

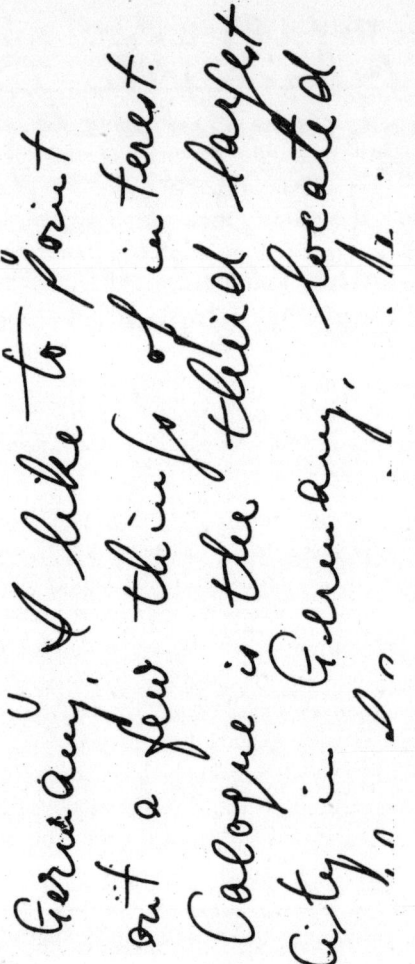

Fig. 141 (31%). Hypomanic patient with intermittent depressions

more specific forms of rhythmical disintegration to appear. In the more general terms of the underlying differences in experience structure between the schizothymic and the cyclothymic, the latter's propensity for curving and rounding, the former's for angularizing and splinting movements are embodied in the concepts of behavioral physiognomy applying to their social and clinical dichotomy and therefore, and in view of our previous discussions, do not seem to warrant further elaboration at this point.

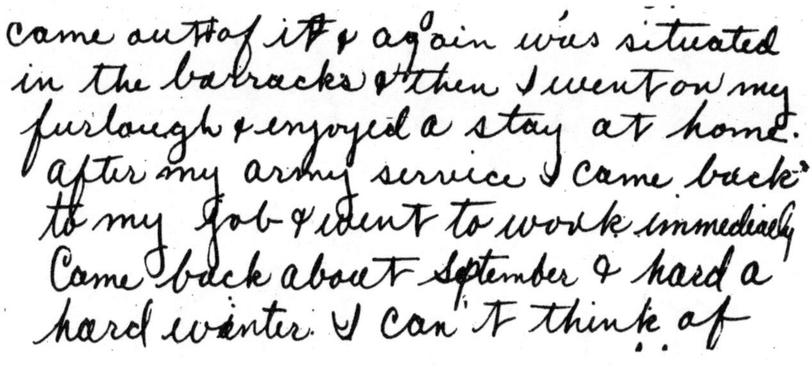

> *Came out of it & again was situated in the barracks & then I went on my furlough & enjoyed a stay at home. After my army service I came back to my job & went to work immediately. Came back about September & had a hard winter. I can't think of*

FIG. 142 (38%). Depressed schizophrenic

Aesthetically, the dissonant character of schizoid handwritings cannot be defined as a mere state of disharmony or self-contradictoriness of total qualities—as the graphic expression of the manic-depressives can—but rather as one of *disparateness,* i.e., of an absence of any principle, "contrast" and "contradictoriness" included, which would unite the writer's impulses of expression into super-ordinate wholes determining the specific function of each part of them. Therefore, while in terms of motor impulses contractive and more specifically centripetal movements are found at a maximum, aesthetically the trail rather appears "centrifugal," owing to the tendency of each of its sectors to follow qualitative principles of its own, without regard to the rest, and thereby to explode the whole structure of the writing (figs. 145, 146). In the handwriting of *schizoid personalities* not suffering from psychosis, this tendency is not marked by any paroxysms but by an empty, cold, and tedious stiffness of the ductus which dimensionally can be defined as genuine meagerness usually combined with sharpness, considerable increases in total leftwardness with frequent instances of closing-off or "rolling" reinforcements of the leftward particles of movement, narrowness, particularly of the letters, inconsistencies of pressure, and with more or less subtle losses in aesthetic proportions, in addition to which there may be a tendency of the pressure to become displaced and of the contraction-release cycle itself to lose its articulate character, while in other cases a particularly "artificial," i.e., self-coercive, regularity will be observed. The special propensities of the schizoid for the binding form of the *arcade* will be remembered here;

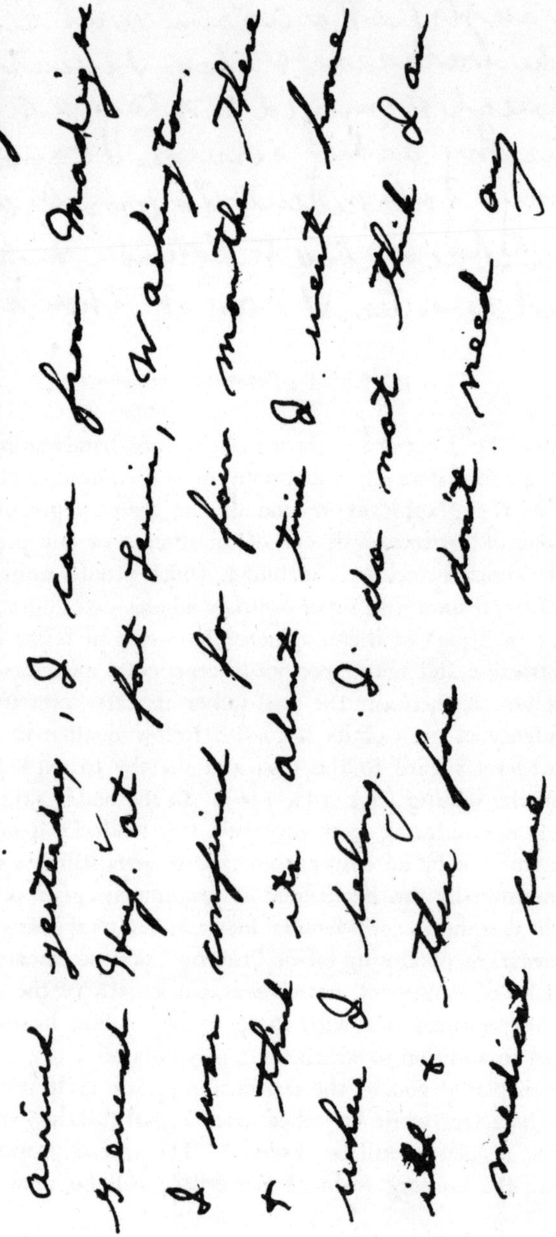

arrived from grammar school. I went to school yesterday. I came from Martigne I arrived today at Fort Lewis, Washington. I was confined for four months. I think it's about time I went where I belong. I do not think I am ill & therefore don't need any medical care

Fig. 143 (12%). Depressed schizophrenic

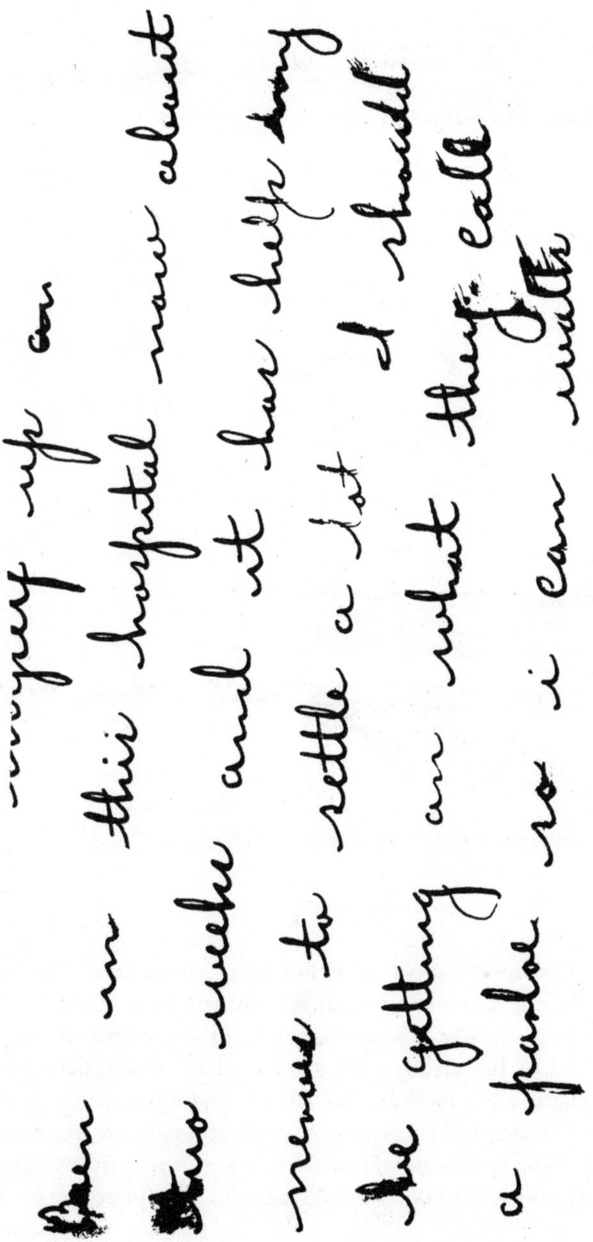

been in this hospital now about two weeks and it has helped my nerves to settle a lot I should be getting on what they call a puzzle no i can ....

Fig. 144 (21%). Depressed schizophrenic

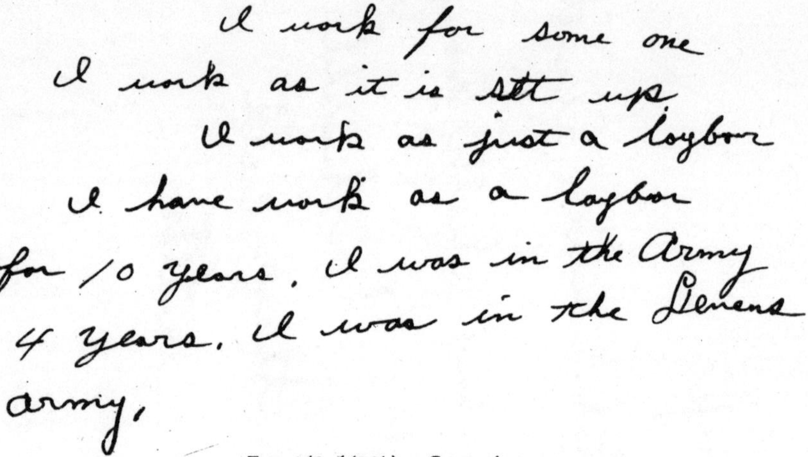

FIG. 145 (40%). Catatonic type

FIG. 146 (26%). Hebephrenia, with paranoid traits

FIGS. 145-146. Schizophrenic self-obstruction in handwriting

depending on the involvement of either more paroxysmal or else more paranoid trends, either threading or angularity will be in secondary prominence, but the specifically schizoid element in the realm of the forms of binding remains the arcade. Its specific place of emphasis is differentially important: the "final arcade" at the end of words is a distinct gesture of contact avoidance (also with implications of secretiveness and, potentially, of lying); the initial arcade is a gesture of introversive self-containment expressly indulged in; arcades in the interiors of words,

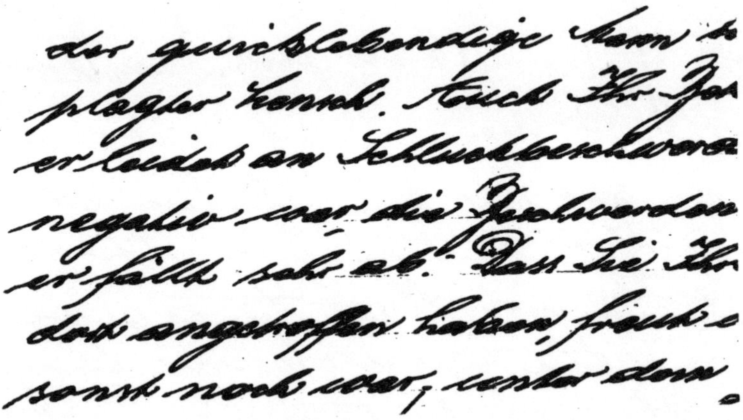

FIG. 147

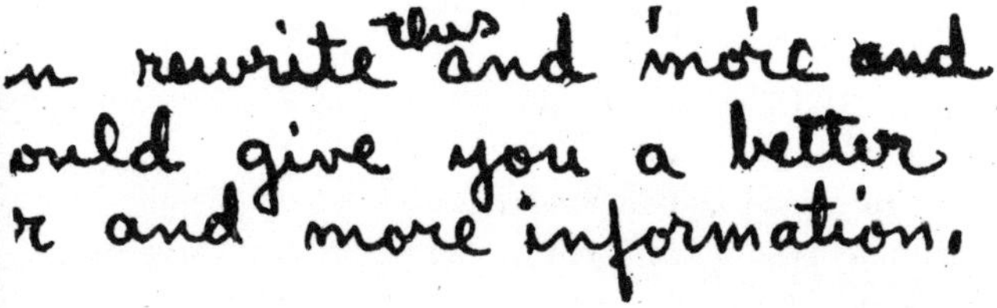

n rewrite thus and more and
ould give you a better
r and more information.

FIG. 148

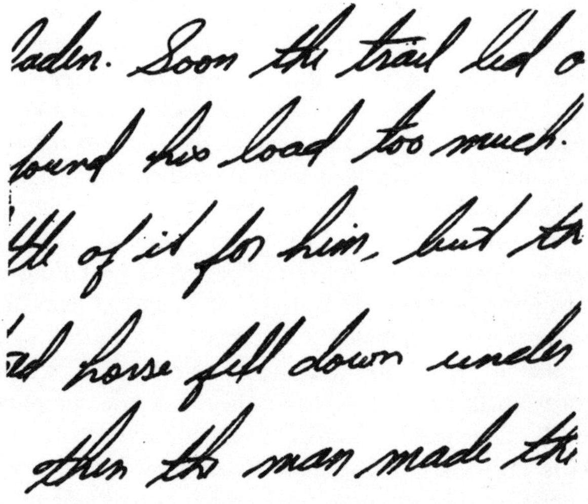

laden. Soon the trail led o
found his load too much.
tle of it for him, but th
ed horse fell down under
then the man made the

FIG. 149

FIGS. 147-149 (7%). Schizoid personalities without psychosis

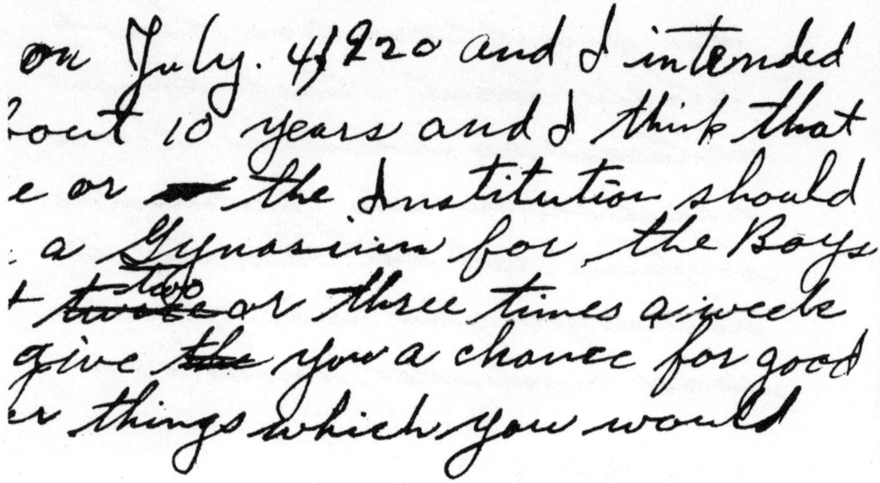

FIG. 150 (7%). Simple schizophrenic

finally, to the degree to which the ductual qualities above defined are found to articulate them as gestures of a tedious and uncertain "screening-off" rather than of "laying hands on," reveal the extent to which reality experience itself has become the central personal problem (figs. 147-149).

On this basis, further differentiation of the schizophrenic group can be undertaken. The graphic products of the *simple type* show accentuated stiffness of the ductus, considerable narrowness, extreme meagerness, displacement of lower extremities towards the left, absence of well-rounded curves and neglect for rounded form altogether, while angularity, visually, may not be prominent owing to the absence of directionally polarizing goal images: the handwriting is "flabby" in a motoric sense while possibly of extreme exactness in the formal sense of executing shapes of the school pattern; in terms of degrees and modes of enrichment, involved elaboration may be combined with a marked reduction in essential structure, so that in the—fairly rare—cases where simple schizophrenics tend to simplify their writing, neglect rather than true simplification may be observed. The tendency towards angular intricacies of the leftward components is particularly high; upper forms show a tendency to decrease in height but may abruptly grow again towards the ends of words in cases where secondary paranoid trends are fairly well-marked; lower extremi-

GRAPHIC EXPRESSION OF PSYCHOPATHOLOGY 189

In short there is nothing wrong with the hospital

Fig. 151 (7%)

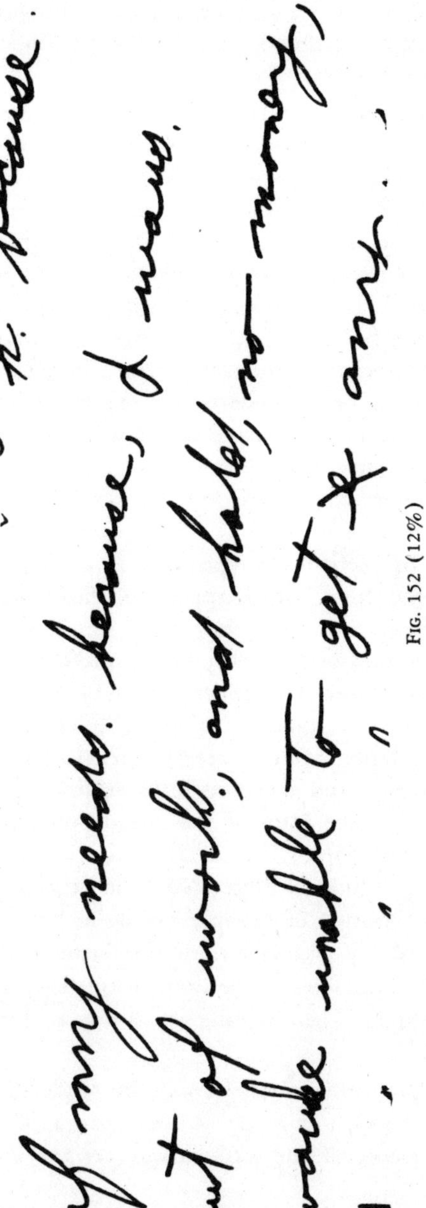

If my needs, because, and because, it is because, out of myself, and half of man, maybe unable to get to one...

Fig. 152 (12%)

FIGS. 151-152. Simple schizophrenics

ties show an inclination not to return to the surface again but to anchor themselves, in a sometimes excessive distance from the writing basis and by way of "tieing knots," at the peripheral points of their extensions (figs. 150-152).

Corresponding with their clinical picture, the handwritings of *hebephrenics* show the disintegrative impact of the illness at its very height and in particular pureness, essentially undiluted by personality trends which, despite their clinical affinity to dementia praecox, can primarily not be defined in its terms. Thus, a high degree of inconsistency in all dimensions, aesthetically amounting to the visual qualities of "torn" and "bizarre," is encountered, contraction is exercised where release would normally be called for, while, vice-versa, movements normally calling for contraction are broken off or led over into uncontrolled distortions frustrating the original contractive intent. Fragmentation is frequent, letter directions are totally unruly, leftward reinforcements and total leftwardness excessive, mannerisms of all kinds are displayed, ornamentation and simplification, pressure and the lack of it may vary with utter arbitrariness, and all proportions are distorted, yet sporadically a mechanical regularity of particularly repetitory, i.e., "dead," precision is encountered— the products of which appear to "float" in the trail like foreign bodies in a liquid. In distinction from simple schizophrenics, furthermore, the graphic trail of the hebephrenics prefers exaggerated curves for the contractive phases of peripheral movements, while the phases of release frequently show angular "splinting"; leftward intricacies are less marked by angularity than they are by narcissistic impulses tending toward rolling movements and secretive little enclosures, which also may leave their imprint in the form of the already previously mentioned conversion of i-dots into loops. The characteristic quality of "hairiness," the impression of a multitude of little thorns or bristles, which is so specific for the graphic picture of hebephrenia is, in the case of this syndrome, not the effect of any peculiarities of the ductus itself but of the aforementioned minute intricacies of the linear formation of the trail which in the typical hebephrenic's handwriting are as tiny as they are innumerable (figs. 153-156).

In *paranoid schizophrenia,* the tendency toward fragmentation, if it occurs—which as a rule it does not—appears more as a mere secondary consequence of the well-marked *peripheral* articulation of the trail and

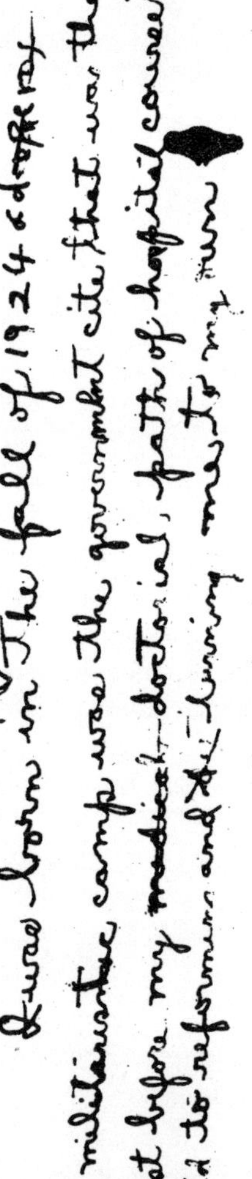

GRAPHIC EXPRESSION OF PSYCHOPATHOLOGY 191

Fig. 153 (17%)

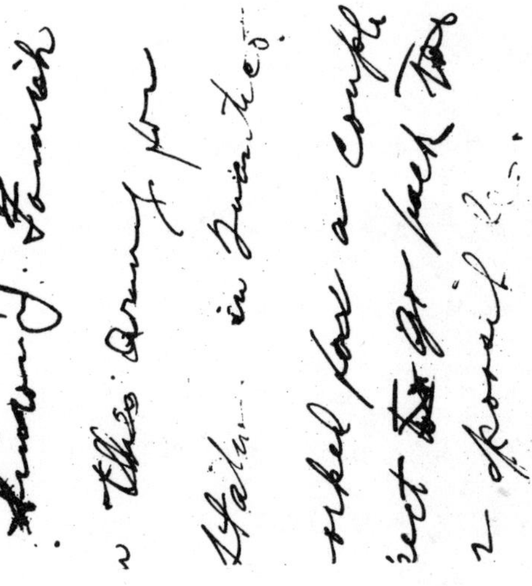

Fig. 154 (31%)

FIGS. 153-154. Hebephrenics

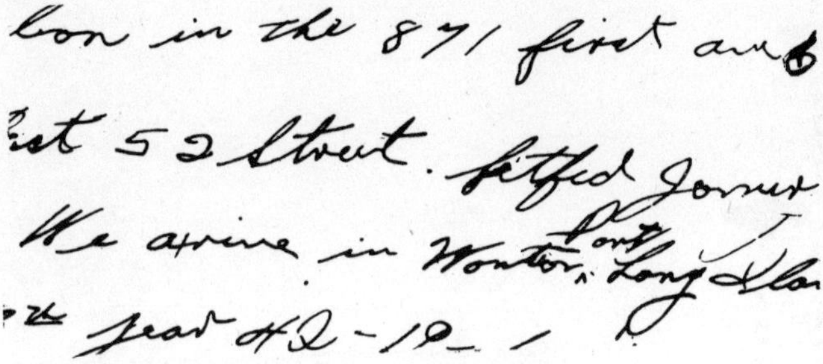

Fig. 155

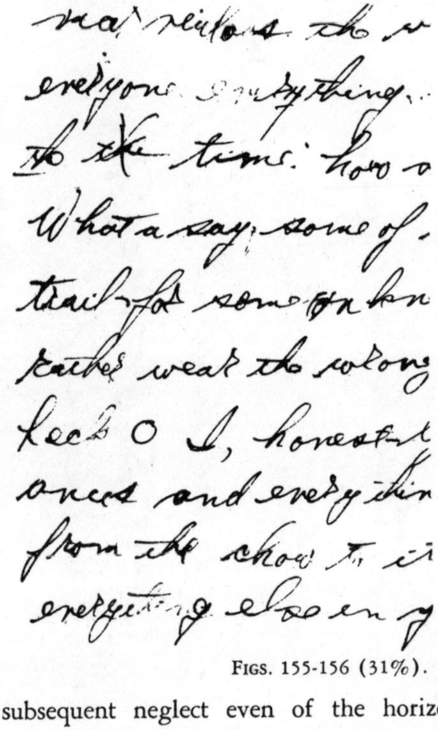

Fig. 156

FIGS. 155-156 (31%). Hebephrenics

subsequent neglect even of the horizontal connection of letters: the paranoid's handwriting, in accordance with his accentuated orientation in the realm of available values, seems continuously to grow—or else to combat a tendency to do so—in the vertical. While this tendency may manifest itself at the expense of the height of the middle zone simply on account of the quantitative changes in proportion it implies, qualitative marks of "shrinking" of the vertical center are at least not prominent in pure cases. On the other hand, narrowness—again particularly of the letter forms—will be found generally increased in coarctated states, but over-ideational conditions as a rule show an expansiveness so generalized that it sometimes may make first glance evaluations exceedingly misleading. Differential diagnosis, systematically undertaken, is nevertheless fairly easy, since the ductus is always extremely stiff; in addition, sharpness, artificial fullness, and, as in all autistic conditions, increases in total leftwardness are in pre-eminence, and the general qualities of curve applying here show a degree of accentuation not matched by any other syndrome. The more the handwriting is found peripherally enriched, and the more the curvedness of the normally straight particles of the long forms accentuates the appearance of the entire trail in a manner of generalized concavity towards the upper left—in pure cases, it looks as though a wind was blowing from behind the trail, swelling the "sails" of the upper periphery and driving the whole structure on—the more delusional activity and receptivity for auditory hallucinations is indicated; degrees of delusional *organization* however depend entirely on the strength of the connecting tendencies rightwardly operative in the movement. A mere accentuation of peripheral movement per se, in conjunction with a high degree of connectedness, thus is characteristic of the general trend toward ideational systematization which is encountered in non-schizophrenic paranoid conditions and character structures as well; its differentiation from the peripheral involvements characteristic of hysteric handwritings is usually not particularly difficult, since peripheral expansion, in both psychotic and non-psychotic paranoids, tends to operate almost exclusively in the vertical; in addition, to the extent to which the paranoid element is in pre-eminence, threading will be absent from the trail. On the other hand, in accordance with the paranoid's total make-up, angularity tends to be rather marked, even though its reign, again in accordance with his inner condition, is found disputed by "bending" tendencies manifesting themselves in the above-stated mark of a generalized curvedness on the part of normally straight particles of the long forms (figs. 157-165). In conjunction with these qualities, the needle-sharp ductus of most paranoid schizophrenic handwritings should make their graphological diagnosis comparatively easy.

Fig. 157 (12%). Paranoid schizophrenia

While the paranoid, in accordance with his auditory preoccupations, generalized speculativeness, and accentuation of ideomotor processes, is primarily oriented towards the experience of *time,* the rule of what previously has been defined as ego-linear constraint is lessened in the *catatonic,* and accordingly his ductus, while being excessively rigid, will show less sharpness than that of the paranoid at least in those phases of his condition which are headed towards excitements and expansions of affect.

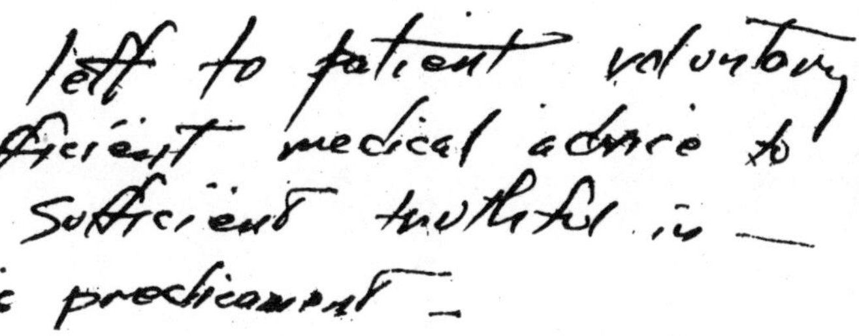

left to patient voluntary
efficient medical advice to
sufficient truthful in
is predicament

FIG. 158 (7%). Paranoid schizophrenia

Paroxysmal, cycloid, and extratensive elements are as distinctly represented graphically as they are clinically, the graphic record is governed by alternations between total centripetal and total centrifugal tendencies, and accordingly the writing field is re-structured. In accordance more specifically with the catatonic's typical ideo-motor impulses pointing in the direction of cosmic and religious identifications—which in themselves imply an alternately oversensitive and overdynamic accentuation of his spatial experiences—temporal progression and its graphic representation, horizontal extension, are relatively disemphasized, i.e., relatively to the entire structure and regardless of their degrees in an absolute sense. As the writing as a whole appears "shrunk" or "expanded," the dimensions of size and of background involvement provide the principal alleys of the catatonic's self-articulation in handwriting.

Therefore, while any of the generally schizophrenic marks and in particular the mentioned autistic reinforcements of leftward impulses of movement may be present in the catatonic trail, the clinically differential element characteristic of it cannot adequately be defined in their terms. Catatonic handwritings differ from the rest of the group by their far

110th (Infant Grand School
8th Grade. Married in 1932 in
Brooklyn N. York. have two Children
both boys. Married in Brooklyn
schools. Wife works as Office clerk.
Army record from 1926 to 1427

Fig. 159 (12%). Paranoid schizophrenia

don't much worry
Helps me a lot. ask for
Hospital they have treated me
good and everything is fine
here. I only hope I can maybe
good news and get home
with my wife and be happy.

FIG. 160 (12%). Paranoid schizophrenic with traits of mania

Fig. 161 (7%). Paranoid schizophrenic with traits of mania

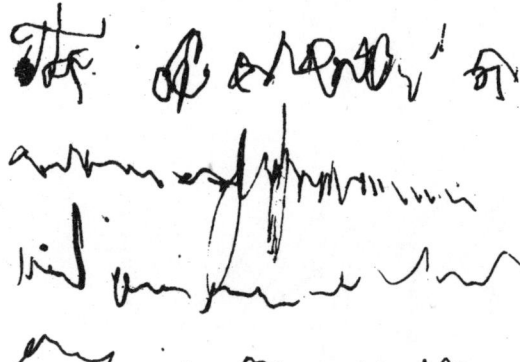

FIG. 162. Delusions about "brain control by radio" in a paranoid patient

FIG. 163. Delusions of grandeur

FIGS. 162-163 (7%). Paranoid schizophrenia

nervous breakdown of hearing voices why
told me was the cause of him going to heaven
and started second work mask by eating
thought-meants to be elevated get hypnotic school
of been tube feeded most of my life.

FIG. 164 (12%). Paranoid schizophrenic with marked systematization

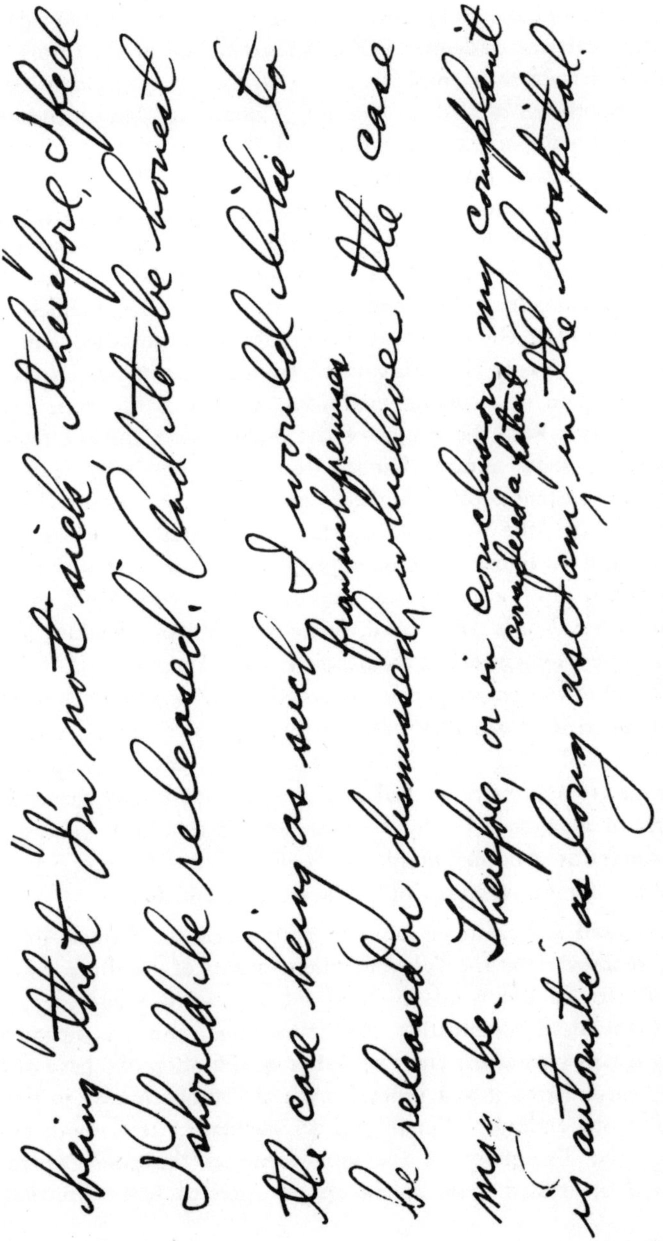

being that I'm not sick, therefore I feel
I should be released. And to be honest
the case being as such, I would like to
be released or demand, whichever the case
may be. Therefore, or in conclusion my complaint
is automatic as long as I am in the hospital.

FIG. 165 (12%). Paranoid schizophrenic with marked systematization greater genuine fullness and curvedness, high pressure, extreme slowness, and resulting extreme unslenderness of the stroke and of the forms themselves which despite their emphasis on round movements seldom tend to show any smoothness of shape. Cracking, "bumping," and mending are in particular prominence, as is a paroxsymal displacement of pressure into movements of release, particularly at the ends of words. The rounding impulse inclines towards gestures of enclosure significantly embracing entire words in their movement, a trend which in turn conditions a "scaled" fluctuation of long form directions, particularly of the upper zone, rather than abrupt inconsistencies, as in the hebephrenics. The enormous rigidity of the movement brings about the so-called long-wave tremor which can easily be distinguished from the tremulous effects both of intracranial and of alcoholic conditions, as well as of severe psychoneurotic anxiety. Both the height of the middle zone and the total size of the writing show abrupt changes, sometimes occurring within the word, in other instances following the line of word succession. In terms of global qualities, the particular structure of the trail can be defined as tending toward a figure-background relationship of "pulsating" concentricity: in phases approaching stupor, tightly contracted, roundly- "armored" little words are placed, sometimes at considerable distance from each other, somewhere at an arbitrary place, frequently in the lower half of the otherwise empty paper, the emptiness of which accentuates the forlorn isolation in which they hide; in the expansive phases, vice-versa, excessive size and a high degree of background involvement are in preeminence, as are aggressive as well as self-aggressive trends characterized by gestures of rage, such as sharp horizontal dashes which, despite their position—in terms of normal graphic periodicity—on the side of "release," usually show abrupt swellings of pressure (fig. 166-174).

Both paranoid and catatonic samples, particularly the former, are characterized, moreover, by the frequent phenomenon of "walling," i.e., an increase in size of the words in their left-rightward phaseology, with vertical quantitative accentuation of the endings, and accompanied by increasing narrowness; apart from the latter qualification, we have already previously encountered it as a general mark of "stubbornness" in the discussion of word endings. Finally, all schizophrenics tend more or less toward specific disruptions of the long forms at the point where the writing basis is crossed, resulting in discrepancies of letter direction be-

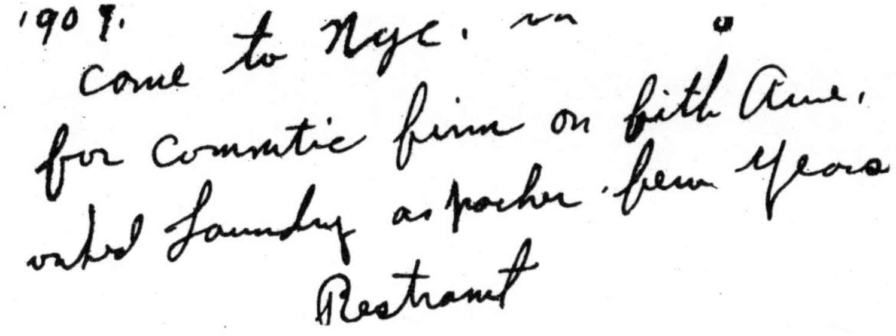

1908.
Came to NYC.
for cosmetic firm on fifth Ave.
worked laundry as porter. few years
Restraint

FIG. 166 (31%)

is trying to put feeling into anything

FIG. 167 (7%)

Joseph F.
111

j J
you came here
I was born June 17. 1914 63 W nron St
Q. 5 27 Cathedral St. Ave

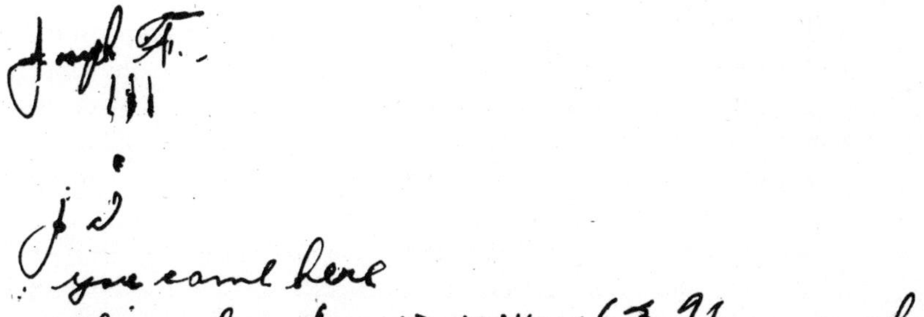

FIG. 168 (31%)

FIGS. 166-168. Catatonic schizophrenics

tween the lower zone on the one hand and the middle and upper zones on the other. While for the group as a whole this discrepancy tends to take the form of *leftward directional* displacements of the lower extremities, their *perpendicular* displacement relative to the angle of slant in the upper

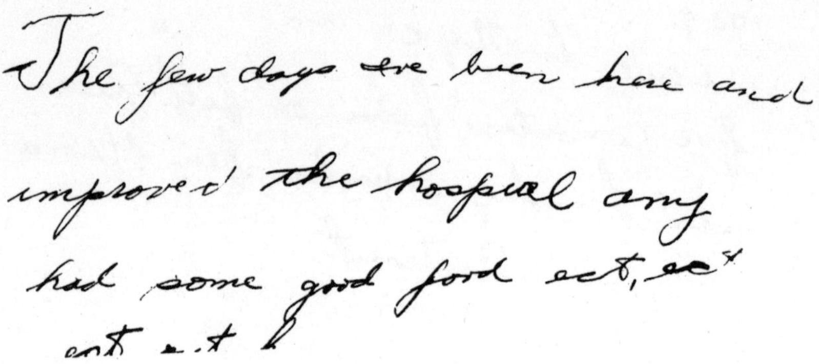

The few days we been here and improved the hospital any had some good ford ect, ect ent ... t

FIG. 169 (45%). Catatonic schizophrenia

sectors of the trail seems somewhat more frequent in catatonic samples, where it is in marked accordance with the total qualities of "concentricity" and weighted-down "heaviness" typical of their movements. A particular prognostic value of this latter trait, of the catatonic's "long-wave tremor," and of the paranoid's above-mentioned propensity for long forms suggesting the effect of a "wind blowing from the upper left," but also of many others of the mentioned characteristics, is evident from their early appearance in pre-psychotic stages of the schizophrenic process where clinical diagnosis may otherwise still be hampered by uncertainties. However, it goes without saying that corroborating marks, of which a considerable number have been named, should always be clearly recorded at the same time, even if their visual articulation is still less far advanced, before differential conclusions are drawn (figs. 175-177).

PSYCHONEUROTIC DISORDERS

The scale of possible graphic expression for anxiety and patterns of reaction to it not jeopardizing the integrity of the ego in its grosser social aspect is as wide as the implied range of disturbed personality structures itself. Traits from both the schizoid and affective graphic syndromes are usually found present in the trail, without however being marked in any decisive manner. In terms of rhythmical qualities, the available scale runs from an extremely low degree of fluctuation, still to be defined more closely, to a combined presence of irregularity and arhythmia; in the latter

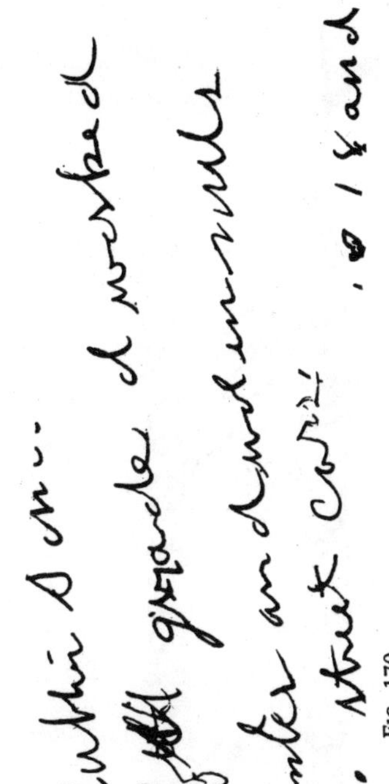

GRAPHIC EXPRESSION OF PSYCHOPATHOLOGY

FIG. 170

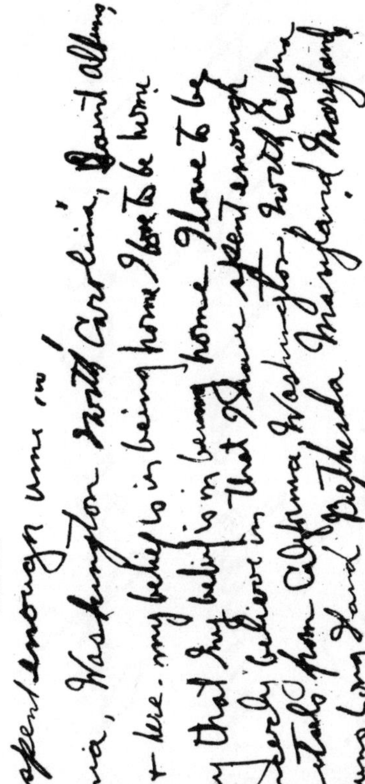

FIG. 171

FIGS. 170-171 (31%). Catatonic schizophrenics

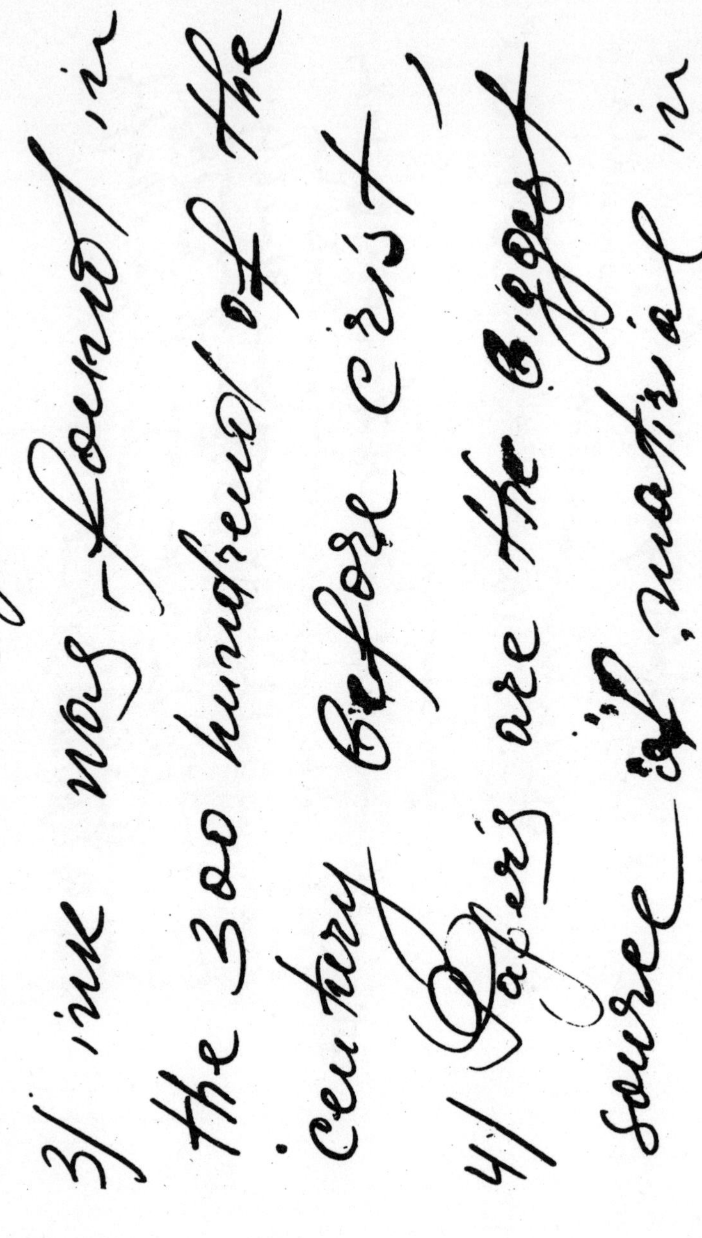

3/ ink was found in the 300 hundreds of the century before crist

4/ Papers are the biggest source of material in

FIG. 172 (17%). Expansive phase

FIGS. 172-173. Writing of a catatonic schizophrenic

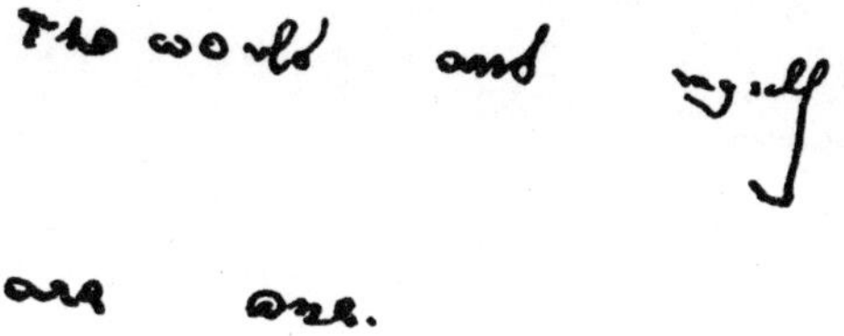

GRAPHIC EXPRESSION OF PSYCHOPATHOLOGY

The world and July

FIG. 173 (17%). Contractive phase

are one.

FIGS. 172-173. Writing of a catatonic schizophrenic

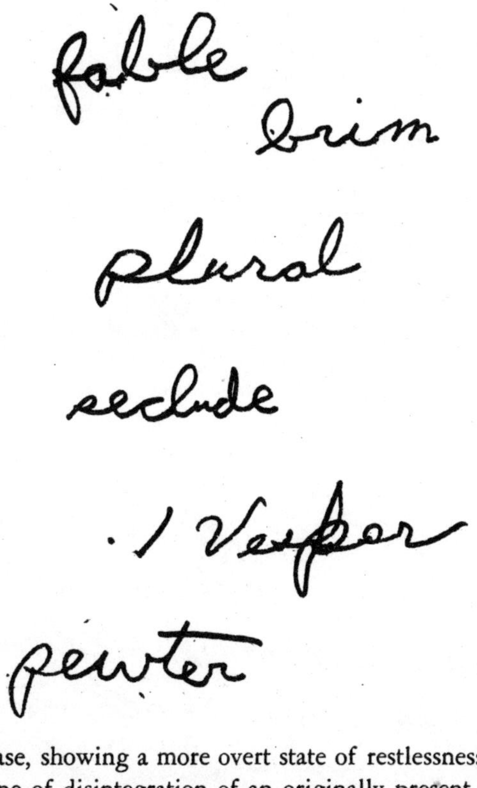

fable

brim

plural

FIG. 174 (7%). Catatonic state approaching stupor

seclude

1 Vesper

pewter

case, showing a more overt state of restlessness, the picture is not so much one of disintegration of an originally present system of temporal articulation as of a continuous failure to attain one. In the overtly constricted cases, on the other hand, the almost total lack of fluctuation cannot be defined in terms of high degree of normal "regularity," since it tends to show a peculiar relative weakness of the pressure cycle. Its presence, in terms of overall properties of visual pattern, is much more easily recog-

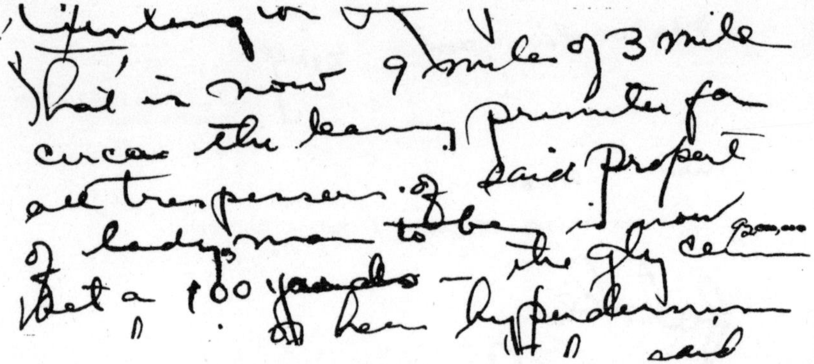

FIG. 175 (45%). Primarily hebephrenic

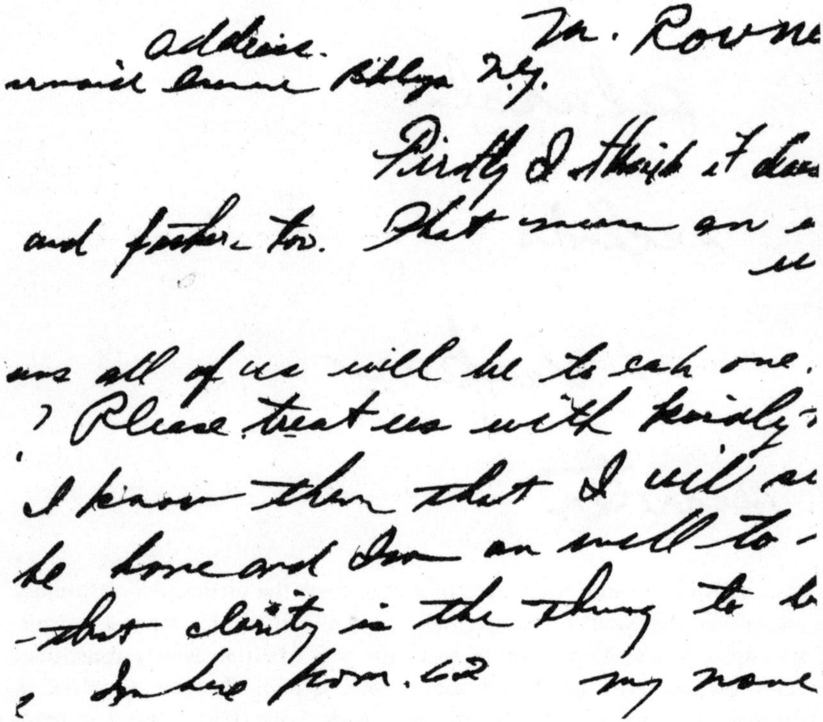

FIG. 176 (7%). Primarily paranoid

FIGS. 175-177. Schizophrenia, mixed syndromes (Cont'd)

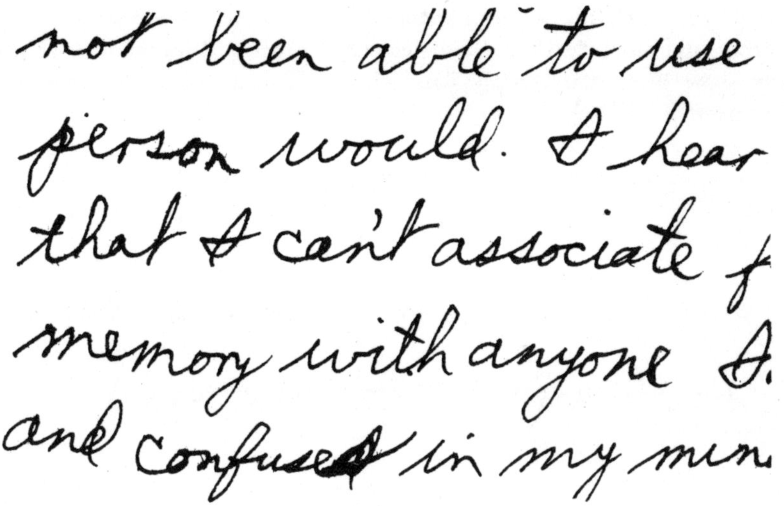

> not been able to use person would. I hear that I can't associate ↓ memory with anyone I. and confused in my min.

FIG. 177 (7%). Primarily catatonic

FIGS. 175-177. Schizophrenia, mixed syndromes (Cont'd)

nized than defined; attempting a definition, one might say that the total rhythmical aspect of highly constricted neurotic samples reflects the dynamic *consequences* of contraction without showing its ordinary temperamental *causes:* the trail is coerced into a pattern of monotony without the force promoting this coercion itself entering its expressive topography.

In consequence of this, the neurotic trail will visually suggest "outside" forces bringing about its constriction by pressing the structure of writing together. In terms of the quasi-spatial aspect of handwriting, the expressive principle operative in this phenomenon can follow either the vertical or horizontal direction (as well as any combination); either version of it we have encountered before, in our analysis of the "shrinking" of middle zones and, subsequently, of narrowness, in both of which qualities *anxiety* was found implied. Since constriction in its proper sense presupposes, psychologically, an impediment of impulse externalization and, graphically, a relative reduction in width, handwritings with low fluctuation unaccounted for by appropriate cycles of pressure will thus fall under the second one of these categories, i.e., will appear "as if" the externally compressing force was operating in the horizontal; accordingly, neuroses involving a strong and more clearly defined element of situational trauma will primarily show horizontal compression, whereas neuroses strongly accentuated by overtly experienced elements of self-conflict, in accordance with our previous analysis of the zonal representation of "super-ego" hypertrophy, will primarily show a relative compression of the middle zone (figs. 178-179).

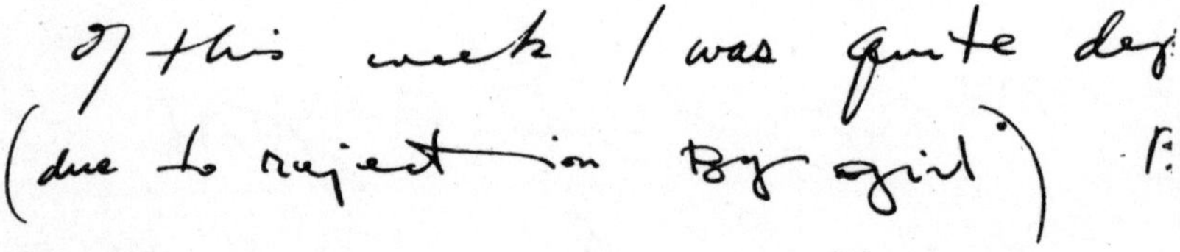

FIG. 178 (31%). Character neurosis, primarily hysterical, with flattening out of the middle zone

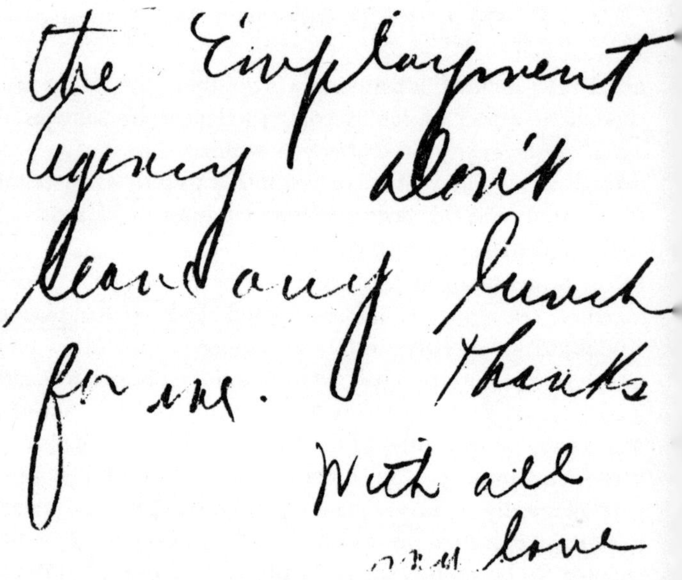

FIG. 179 (7%). Acute anxiety state with strong situational element, graphically "shirking" extension toward the right

FIGS. 178-179. The two prototypes of psychoneurotic compression in handwriting

Since actual conditions seldom follow either principle at the exclusion of the other, the above definitions are primarily to be understood as facilitating directives for orientation and assessment. Sub-specification of clinical types necessarily must involve a large number of differential criteria, many of which have already previously been touched upon in these discussions.

According to the above differentiation of the two types of "neurotic" compression, *hysterics* are recognizable from the reduction of their middle zones, a marked propensity for threading, displacements of pressure into movements of release, particularly at the ends of words, sporadic instances of "lingering" pressure, inclination toward artificial wideness, artificial fullness, peripheral inflations and exaggerations, variations beteween demonstrative simplifications and demonstrative enrichments, and, frequently, an accentuation of the previously mentioned tendency to shift word endings downward which in their cases may in addition be differentiated by a "shoveling" garland-like final stroke, extended from this latter movement, setting a rightward perimetric confine to the entire height of the middle and upper zones, and, in its upper section, swinging back towards the left-hand side, a gesture simultaneously implying the general significance of word endings shifted downward (search for contact with uncon-

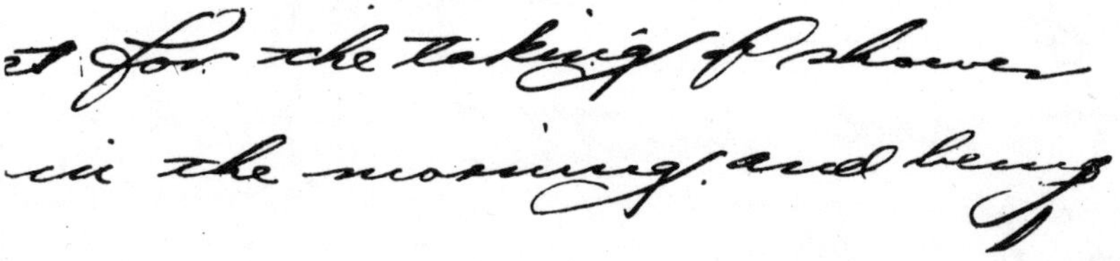

Fig. 180 (21%). Hysteric "embellishment"

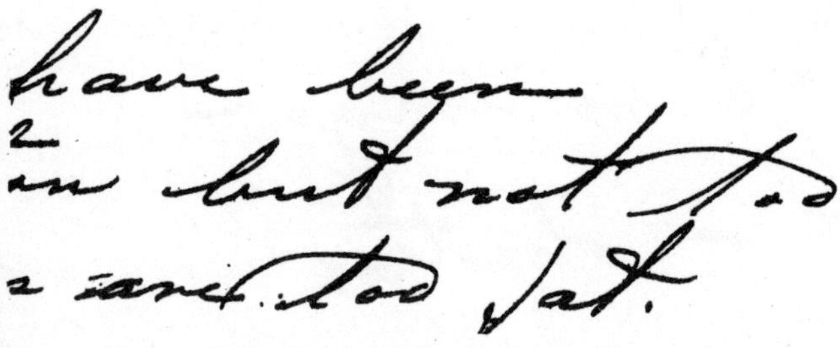

Fig. 181 (7%). Peripheral over-extensions and inflations

scious motivations of others), of leftward endings (contact-avoidance), and of the leftward concave upstroke (traumatization), the gestural profile of which is likewise present in this movement (figs. 180-184).

Fig. 182

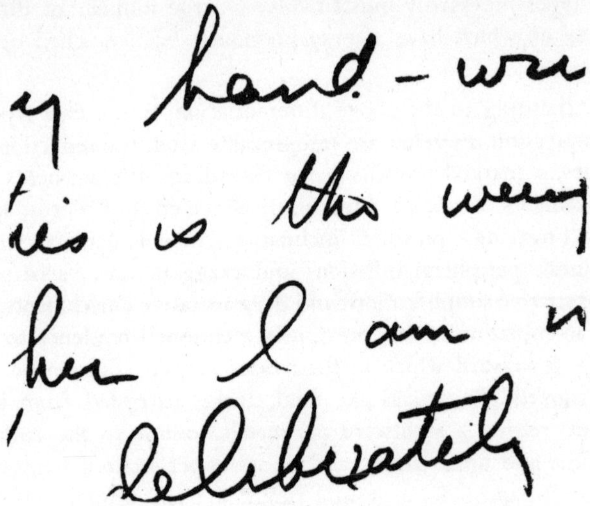

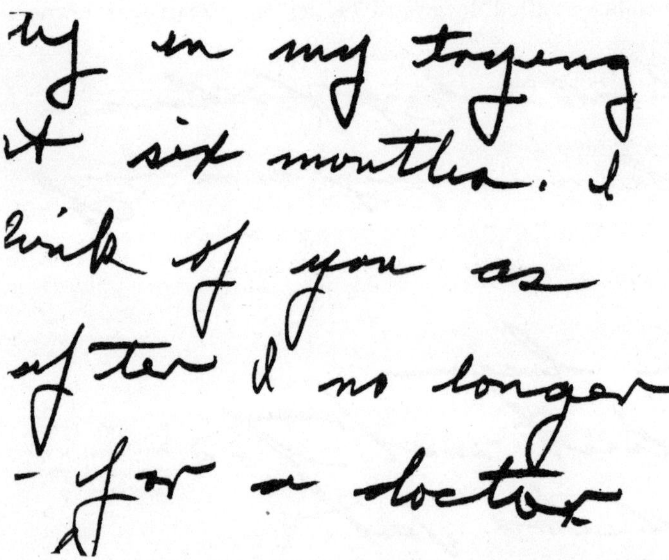

[handwritten sample]

Fig. 183

[handwritten sample]

Figs. 182-183 (7%). Peripheral overextensions and inflations

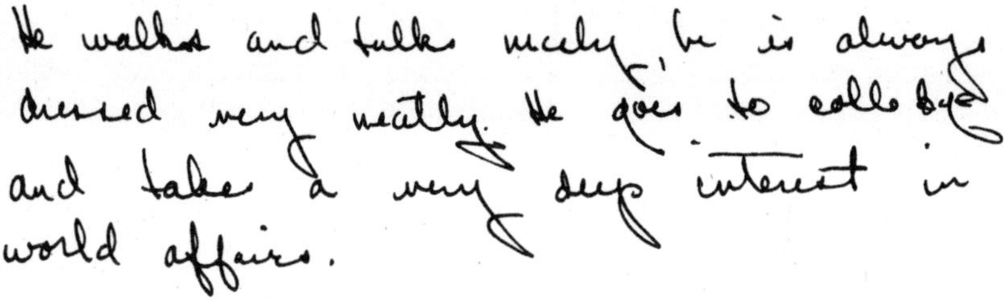

He walks and talks nicely, he is always dressed very neatly. He goes to college and takes a very deep interest in world affairs.

FIG. 184 (35%). Hysteric displacement of affect

Furthermore, in hysteria, there may be the previously discussed "embellishing" type of mending, and the ductus may show a peculiar, occasionally smeary, touch of "dimness" which will the more be displayed the more conversion mechanisms proper are clinically prominent. Like all

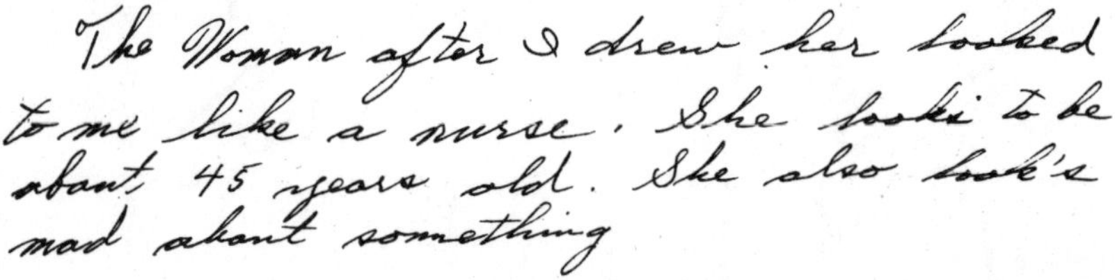

The Woman after I drew her looked to me like a nurse. She looks to be about 45 years old. She also look's mad about something

FIG. 185 (47%)

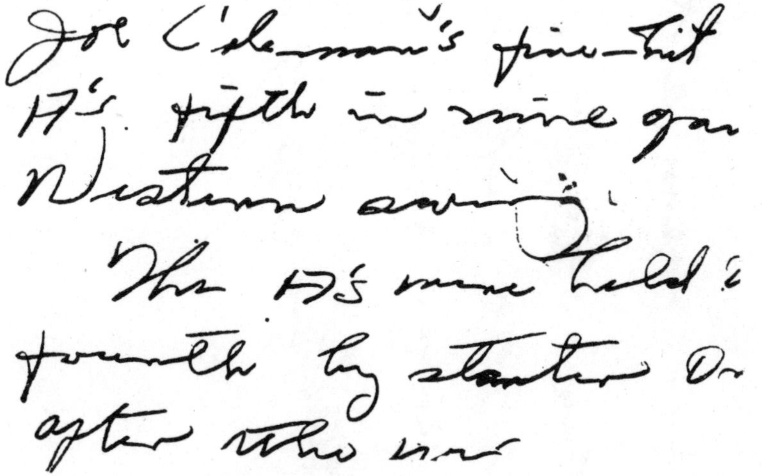

FIG. 186 (7%).

FIGS. 185-186. Conversion hysterics

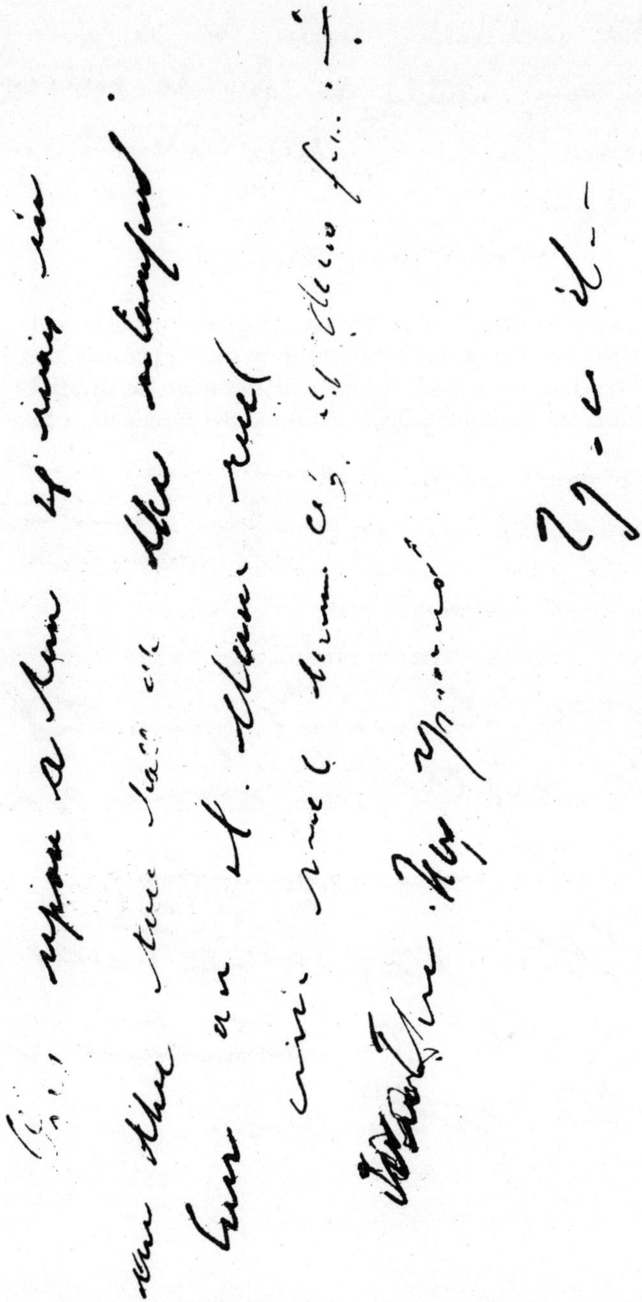

FIG. 187 (17%). Hysteric twilight state

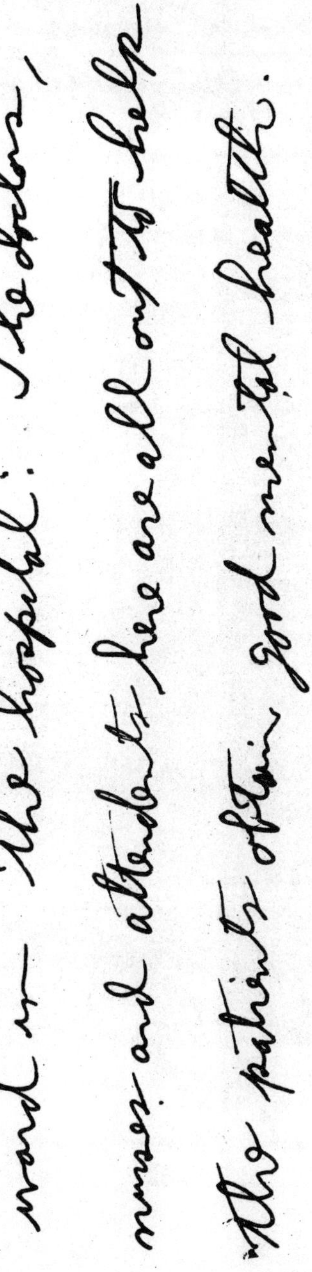

ward in the hospital. The doctors, nurses and attendants here are all out to help the patients obtain good mental health.

FIG. 188 (17%). Conversion hysteric with pseudo-schizophrenic behavior

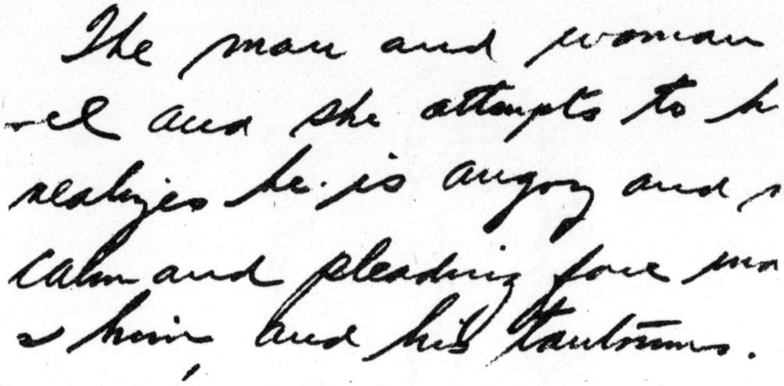

FIG. 189 (7%). Anxiety hysteria with depressions

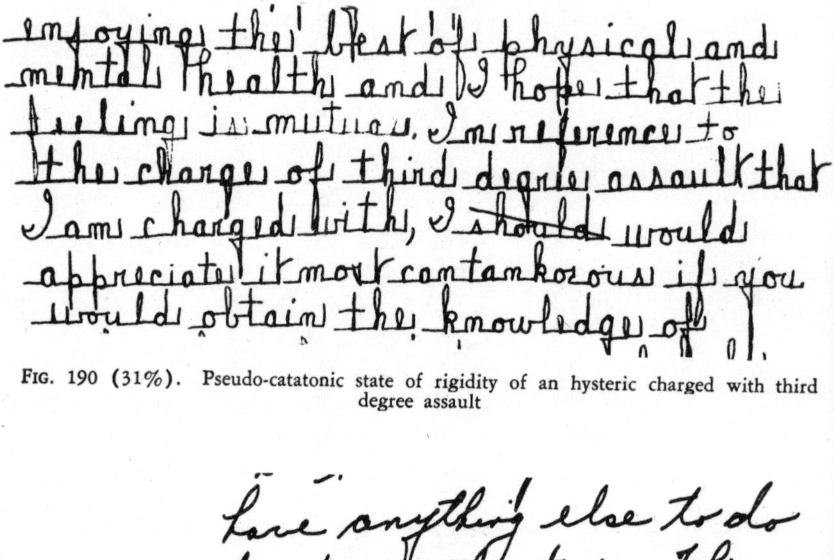

FIG. 190 (31%). Pseudo-catatonic state of rigidity of an hysteric charged with third degree assault

FIG. 191 (26%). His regular writing style

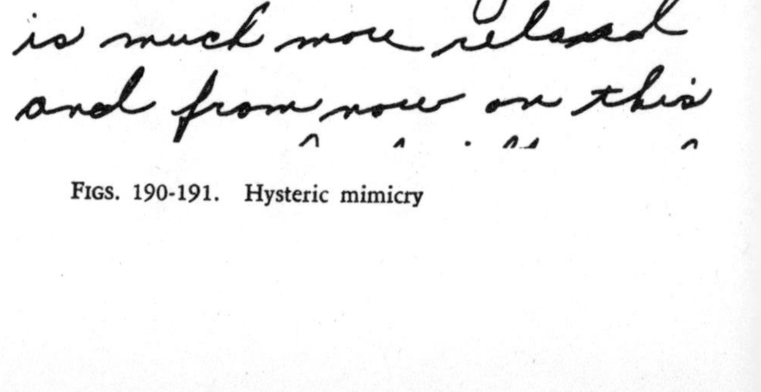

FIGS. 190-191. Hysteric mimicry

proxysmals, but less so than epileptics, the hysterics, moreover, may show abrupt variations both in pressure and in doughiness; the trail of hysteric personalities without clinical symptoms of conversion, on the other hand, usually is characteristically sharp. On higher levels of intelligence and cultural aspiration, finally, there may be displayed a considerable assortment of "coquette" and "elegant" movements of semi-deliberate disruption of the trail, which seem to rely upon the closure effect and more accentuate than disturb the linear rhythm of the writing (figs. 185-191).

While vertical compression, operating at the expense of the height of the middle zone, can thus be defined as the decisive graphic tendency of the hysteric, *pure anxiety states* show a pre-eminent tendency toward horizontal shrinking. In distinction from the corresponding traits of the

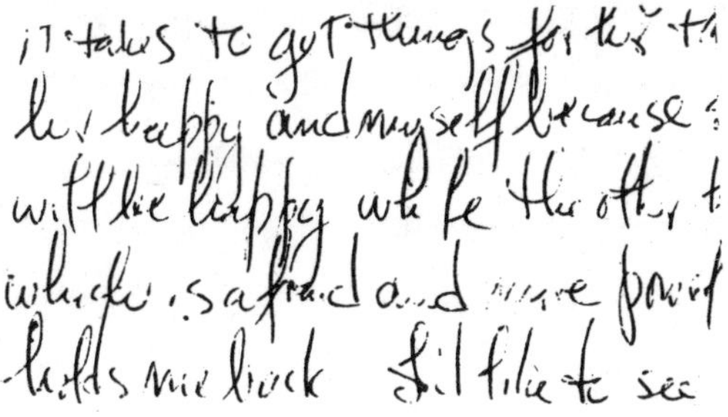

FIG. 192 (31%). Chronic anxiety with depression and obsessional character traits

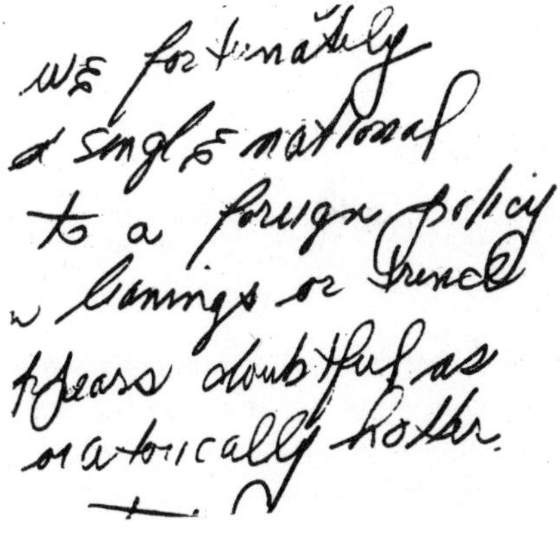

FIG. 193 (31%). Chronic anxiety in a schizoid individual

FIGS. 192-197. Anxiety states

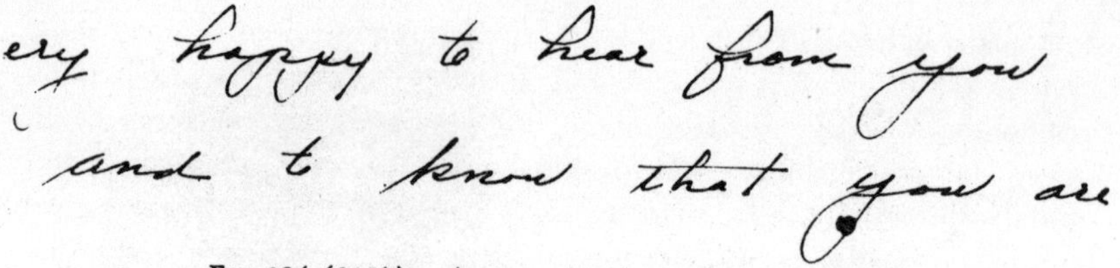

[handwriting sample]

FIG. 194 (31%). Acute anxiety in an obsessive neurotic

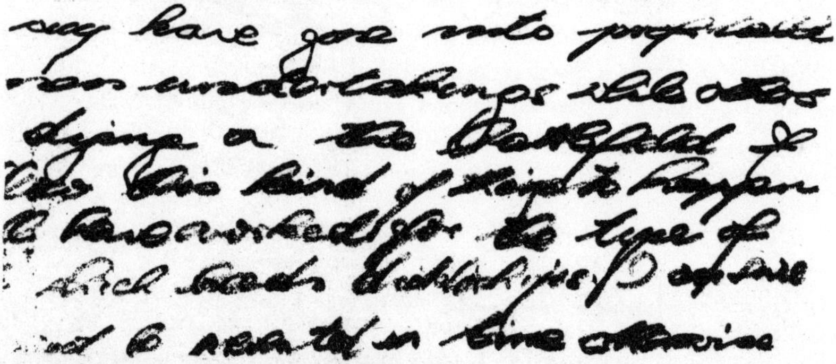

[handwriting sample]

FIG. 195 (31%). Acute anxiety, post-traumatic, with some depression

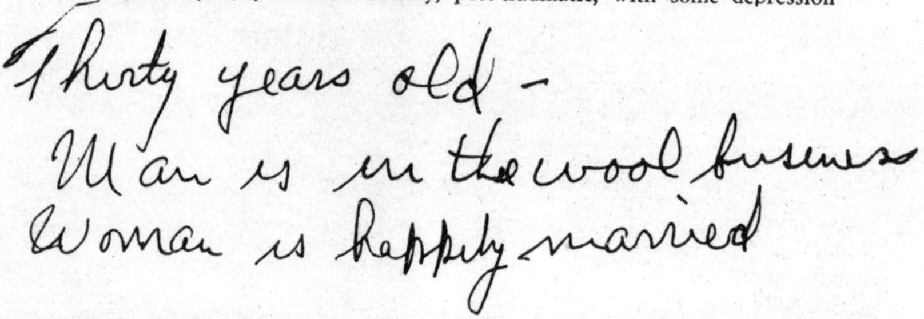

[handwriting sample: "Thirty years old — Man is in the wool business Woman is happily married"]

FIG. 196 (31%). Anxiety hysteria with mild compulsive traits. Note slowness, minute tremors, embellishment (*the*), pressure displacements, inconsistencies in width, letter direction, and extension of lower lengths, and lack of control in the uppermost section of the *T* in *thirty*

FIGS. 192-197. Anxiety states (Cont'd)

writing of fearful and constricted personalities without clinically manifest neurotic symptoms, graphic narrowness in that group is characterized by an exceedingly unsteady and linearly disrhythmicized variation in which movements characteristic of "artificial wideness" may enter the formation of single letters also, while in other sections of the trail downstrokes may appear "pasted" to preceding ones belonging either to the same or

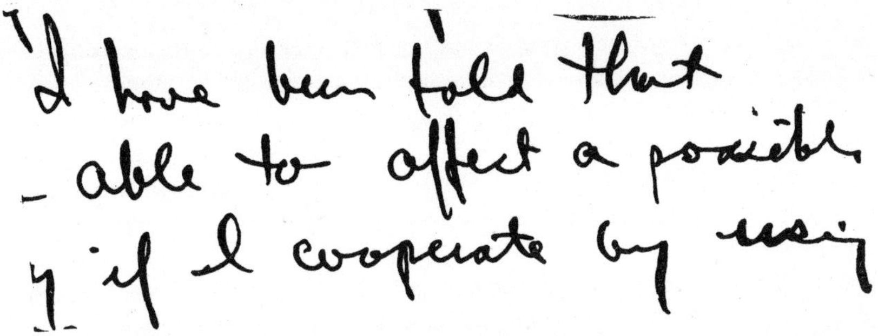

GRAPHIC EXPRESSION OF PSYCHOPATHOLOGY

[handwritten sample]

FIG. 197 (7%). Anxiety state with episodes of petit mal in a highly unstable individual. Note heavier pressure in peripheral movements than in the middle zone, occurrences of "lingering" and of "staccato," doughiness, word-internal threading, general disrhythmization, and appearance of "weighing down" in pressure-accentuated lower lengths of last line

FIGS. 192-197. Anxiety states (Cont'd)

even to different letters. A great variation in total letter direction, rigidity of the ductus, slowness, extreme displays of pressure—sometimes also of extensiveness—in the peripheral extremities, particularly of the lower zone (possibly the most specific graphic mark of this category), unsteady line directions, general predominance of contractive qualities, yet occasional excesses of doughiness, and an accentuation of peripheral movement which, unlike that evidenced in hysteric handwriting, does not necessarily imply a shrinking of the middle zone of the trail, are characteristic of conditions in this group which is frequently marked also by the extreme stiffness and heaviness of its ductus (figs. 192-197).

Among the graphic symptoms of the *psychasthenics,* the frequent phobic reluctance in their lines to proceed toward the right-hand edge of the paper and the related habit to cross the resulting margin by a straight horizontal stroke have been mentioned before. Similar phobias pertaining to rightward extension are numerous in the *obsessional neuroses,* and all find their common link in an extreme narrowness of the trail, in addition to an increase in emphasis laid upon the initial upstrokes of words, an accentuation of pathognomonic signs within the rating area of the general qualities of curve, and a type of peripheral emphasis not tending to operate at the expense of the middle zone, in which an anxious attention to the school pattern, sometimes more marked even than in persons of low educational status, is more frequent than actual threading.

Total constriction of the type defined at the opening of this subchapter is frequent in this group, i.e., the effect of a "regulated" monotony not adequately accounted for by pressure cycles will prevail. In view of the characterological continuum existing between the obsessive and the paranoid, the similarities between their types of relative peripheral emphasis and both's propensities for sharp ductus and related manifestations of egolinear constraint will not be found surprising; differential criteria are provided by the more total contractiveness (also involving its size) of the obsessional trail, by its already mentioned far greater monotony, by the greater total stiffness on the part of the paranoid ductus, by the latter's

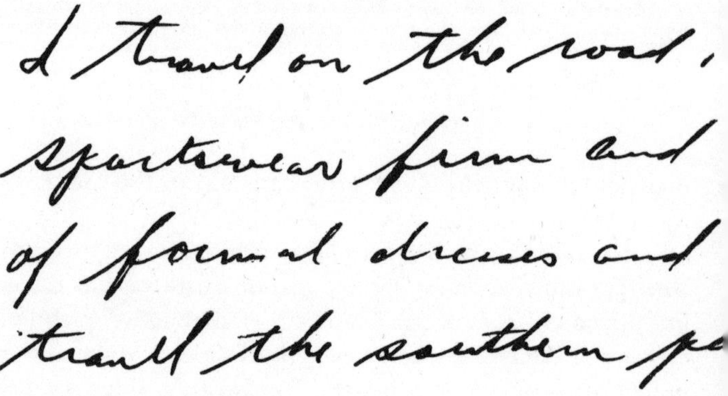

Fig. 198 (7%). Obsessive-compulsive neurosis, obsessive type

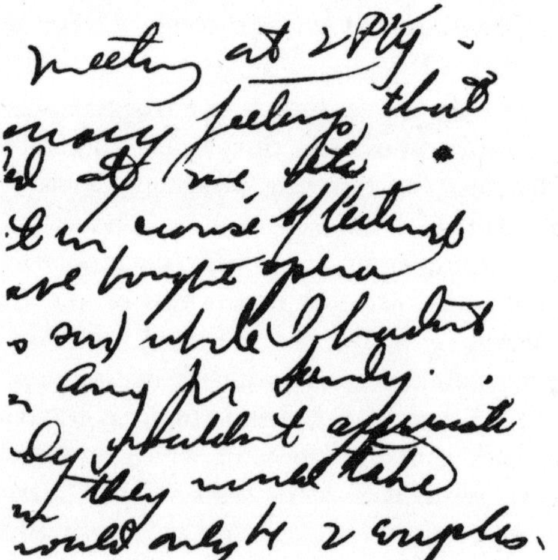

Fig. 199 (7%). Obsessive-compulsive neurosis, obsessive type

Theatre management "On Watch", the latest on RKO. This is America, series of short subjects dealing with the sea. Our armed forces, here been posted as a supplementary attraction to the feature the Return of Jennie.

Fig. 200 (12%). Obsessive-compulsive neurosis, obsessive type generally higher accentuation of pressure, and by the absence in obsessional handwriting of the paranoid vertical "growth" effect as well as of the previously defined specific peculiarities of the paranoid trail in the area of the general qualities of curve, in addition to a considerable number of minor differences. The "compression" shown by obsessional patterns, finally, also seems to tend to reduce to a minimum the relative distances between upper and lower loops and other closed forms within the smaller units of the trail, resulting in an effect of generalized "tightness" which even without an articulate presence of the aforementioned marks will hardly escape the observer's attention (figs. 198-202).

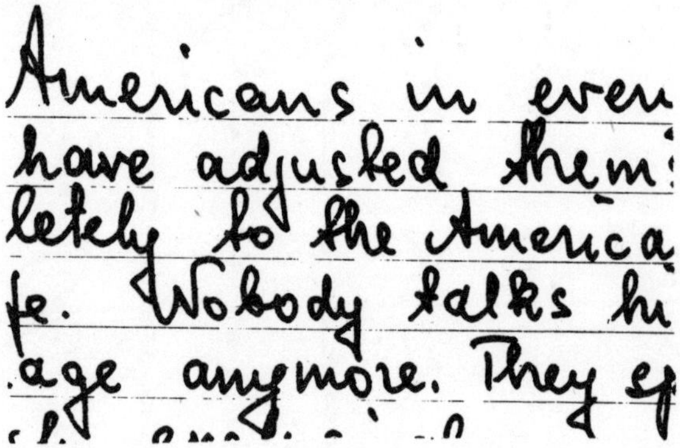

FIG. 201 (7%). Obsessive neurosis with free-floating anxiety

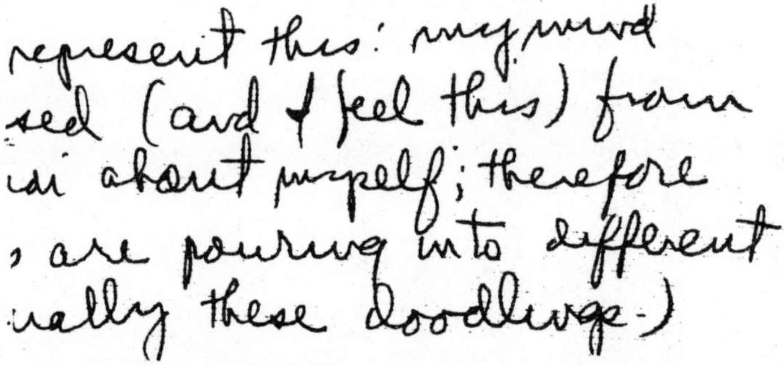

FIG. 202 (7%). Obsessive neurosis with chronic depression

The *compulsive's* handwriting may also show this latter characteristic but will differ from the more specifically obsessional types by the less one-sided appearance of horizontal compression and the more marked one of a global contractive quality tending toward the accentuation of centripetal impulses. Thus, the size of the handwriting tends to be even smaller than in the obsessive group, while both shrinking of the middle zone and narrowness are found accentuated. On the whole, furthermore, obsessional handwriting tends to be more angular, compulsive handwriting rounder, and, as the former to the paranoid graphic type, compulsive handwriting may seem to relate to catatonic patterns from which it can be distinguished by the absence in it of the specifically schizoid and disintegrative tendencies and of the previously defined "concentricity" of the typical catatonic trail. The distribution of pressure, finally, in accordance with the compulsives' closer relations to the paroxysmal types, the psychomotor epilepsies, etc., tends to be far more unruly in their handwritings than it does in those of the obsessives. Compulsive doubters, as well as related "ambivert" character types in the general population, tend to show great

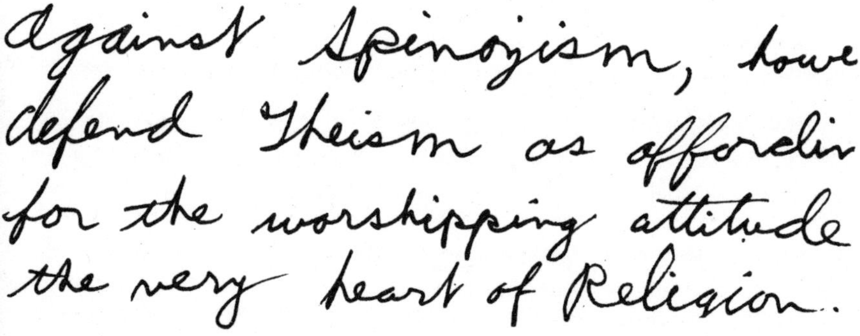

[handwritten sample:] against Spinozism, howe defend Theism as affordin for the worshipping attitude the very heart of Religion..

FIG. 203

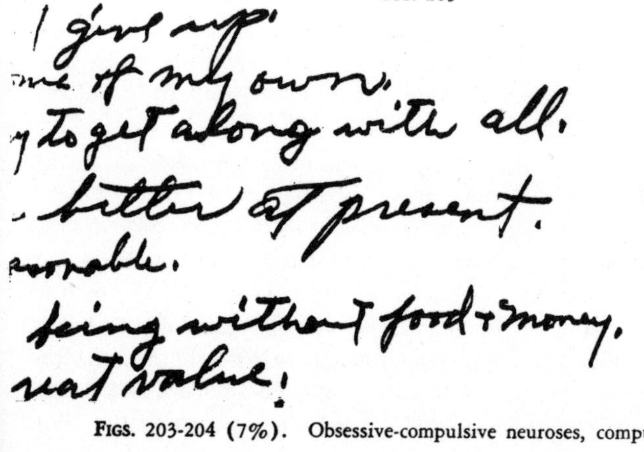

[handwritten sample:] I give up. one of my own. y to get along with all. bitter at present. avonable. being without food & money. reat value!

FIG. 204

FIGS. 203-204 (7%). Obsessive-compulsive neuroses, compulsive type inconsistencies in their handling of the peripheral extremities, a trait which reflects the uncertainties and ambivalences characteristic of their sets of values (figs. 203-205).

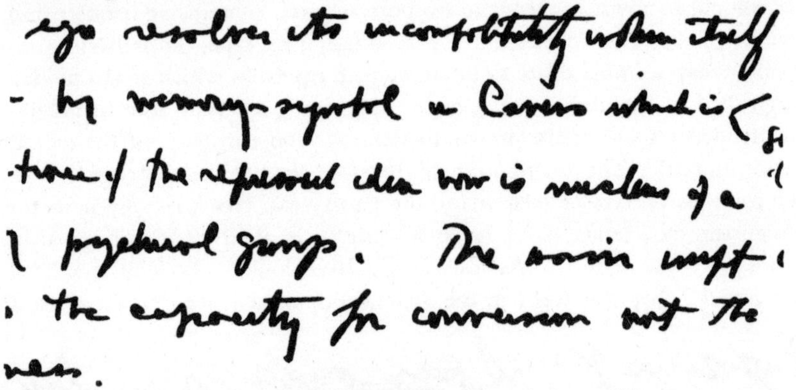

[handwriting sample]

FIG. 205 (7%). Obsessive-compulsive neurosis, compulsive type

Both *anxiety states* and *reactive depressions* (the general graphic physiognomy of the reactive depressions has been touched upon within the context of the affective disorders) can show more or less minute tremors, and in virtually all cases will show a tremulous tendency in the form of a slightly "shivering" quality of the ductus which visually relates to the general effect of doughiness, yet, with some experience, will be distinguished from doughiness, in its more proper sense of an active sensual indulgence in stroke dispersion, without too great difficulties on the examiner's part. Neurasthenias as well as anxiety states with more substantial hysteroid coloring, on the other hand, will generally show a specific frailty of their ductus, which appears as a most revealing mark of their excessive sensitivity (figs. 206-208).

The common tendency of *restless* and *agitated* states toward a combination of a rhythmically distintegrative distribution of the components of movement with a high degree of irregularity in its more proper sense, i.e., of total rhythmical fluctuation, has been stated before, and the combined criterion postulated by this tendency applies outside of the neurotic realm as well as within its boundaries, to obsessional patients with a strong element of moodiness and emotionality, to hysterics and compulsives with more substantial cycloid trends, to agitated anxieties and reactive depressions, and, in particular, to *cardiac neuroses,* in which the above

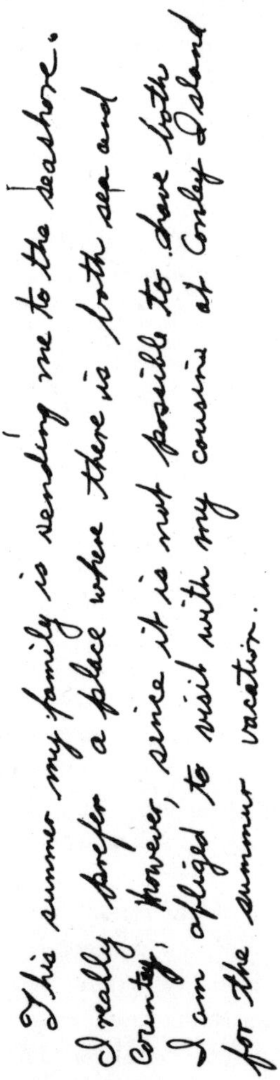

Fig. 206 (31%)

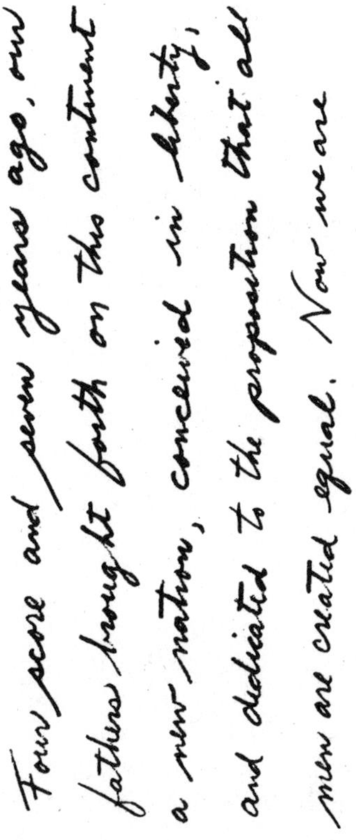

Fig. 207 (43%)

FIGS. 206 and 207. Obsessive-compulsive neuroses, with more generalized compulsiveness

defined total quality seems to result from the simultaneous and mutually contradictory operations of a horizontally compressing and unsuccessfully "regulating" tendency on the one hand and accentuated impulses of "fleeing towards the right" on the other (fig. 209).

INTRACRANIAL DISORDERS

Handwritings of the brain-organics have frequently been touched upon in psychiatric literature. In as far as the conditions reflected, unlike the

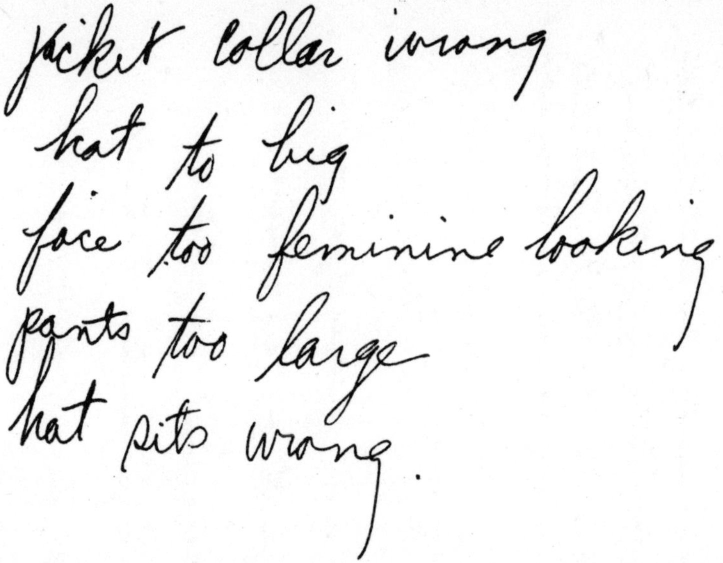

> *jacket collar wrong*
> *hat to big*
> *face too feminine looking*
> *pants too large*
> *hat sits wrong*

FIG. 208 (7%). Neurasthenic woman with traits of somnambulism

psychogenic disorders, cannot be defined in terms of well-established characterological principles, they, properly speaking, do not seem to lend themselves to a system of expression-analysis guided by criteria of total integrative or disintegrative trends of personality structure. Yet, since the distinctions made between organic and psychogenic disorders are based more on the differences between our own cognitive accesses to either of them than on conclusive evidence for the absence of correlated specific organic processes in the disorders called psychogenic, no distinction in principle between the two classes of disturbed personality systems seems suggested, and no sharp borderline between them is indicated by such "central" positions as, for example, presented by the convulsive states. This situation is closely paralleled by the corresponding range of patterns in the typology of handwriting which shows fairly smooth transitions between "true" epilepsies attributed to paroxysmal trends in the personality structure and convulsive disorders clinically traced to lesions in the brain.

Yet, apart from the latter groups, the far more *direct* impact of the disturbances of perceptual and motor coordination in brain disease on the coordinative functions of writing is of an order distinctly separate, on

Fig. 209 (12%). Admixture of hysteria and obsessive neurosis, with marked ideomotor restlessness

FIG. 210 (7%). "Long wave" tremor of a catatonic

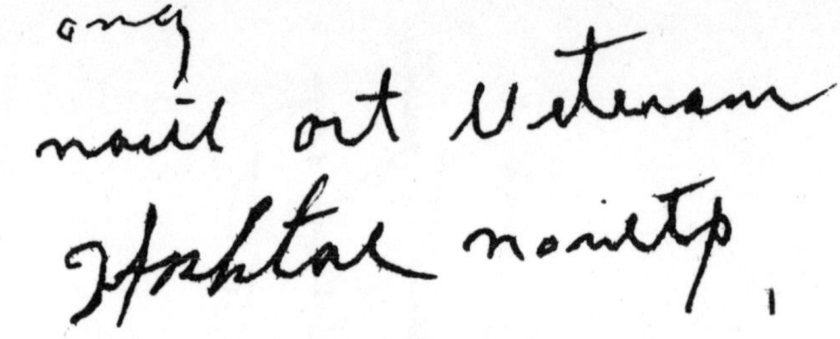

FIG. 211 (7%). Tremulous pressure in underlengths; anxiety state

FIG. 212 (7%). Advanced cerebral sclerosis

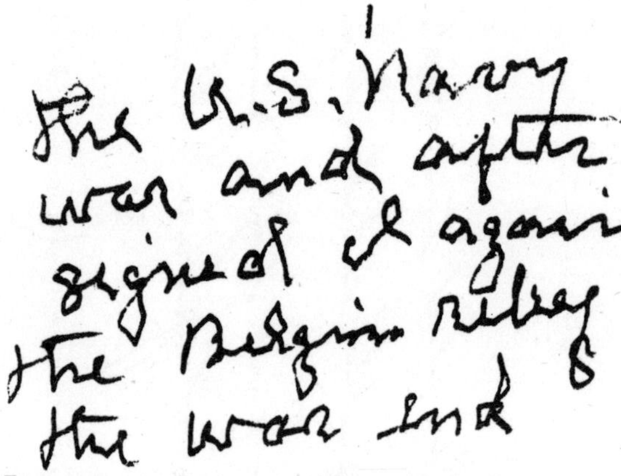

FIGS. 210-214. Psychogenic and organic tremors
FIGS. 212-216. Various Brain Organic Patterns. I

account of the far greater coarseness of the resulting characteristics, from that of any "psychogenic" disturbances. The difficulties of the "organic" patient to master the task of writing are not "gesturally representative" of his global difficulties but are identical with them. While between these handicaps and characterological principles no direct connections exist and while the "organic's" writing difficulties would thus seem to be of greater neurological than psychological interest, they enter the psychological realm by virtue of the functional unity of organisms, i.e., of the necessity for the patient to adjust to them and of his exclusive command for this purpose of modes of adjustment implied in his character structure. Total

FIG. 213 (7%). Brain tumor right parietal region, preoperative

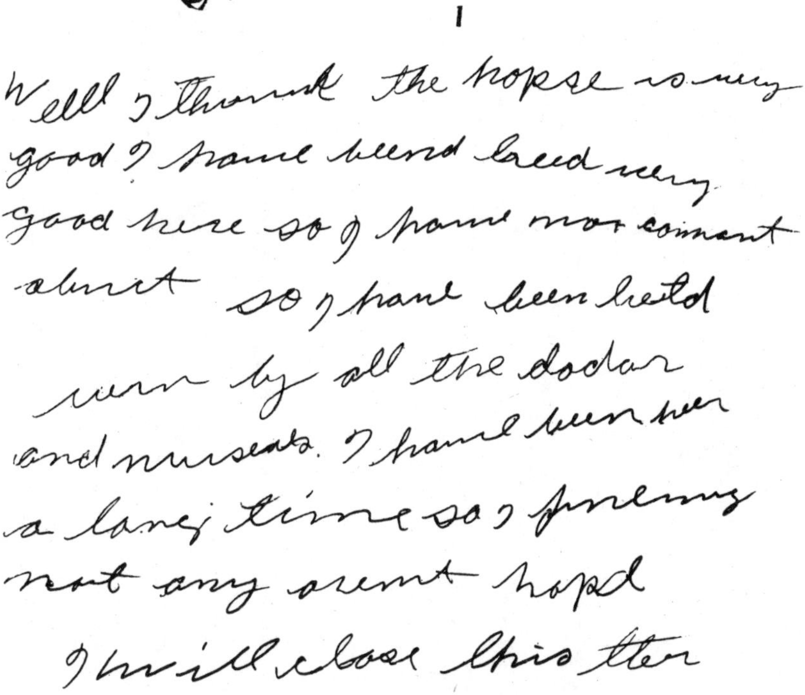

FIG. 214 (44%). Brain tumor, right parietal region, postoperative

FIGS. 212-216. Various Brain Organic Patterns. I (Cont'd)

personality pictures can thus be derived from handwritings of brain-organic patients also, provided that the disease is not so far advanced as to make self-articulation virtually impossible, and accordingly the principles guiding such evaluations, in as far as the characterological aspect is concerned, remain the same as for handwriting in general. Regarding the most prominent types of brain-organic graphic symptoms themselves, the following directives can be given (figs. 210-216).

Cerebral sclerosis and simple senile dementias are characterized by a sometimes extremely coarse yet "regular" tremor often following a pe-

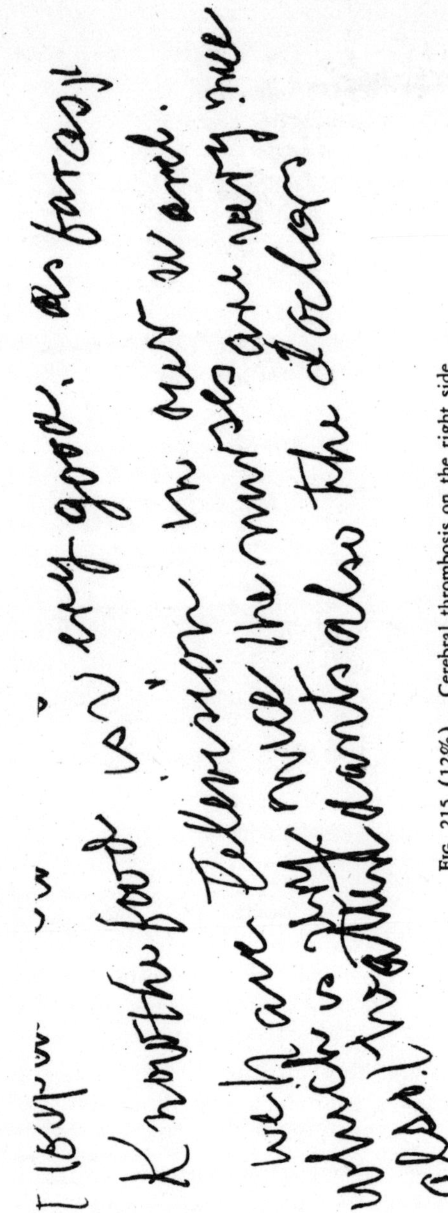

[Handwritten sample 1:] I love...

[Handwritten sample 2:] Know the food in is very good, as far as I
we are Television in our ward.
which is just nice the nurses are very nice
also. Instead dants also the doctor

FIG. 215 (12%). Cerebral thrombosis on the right side

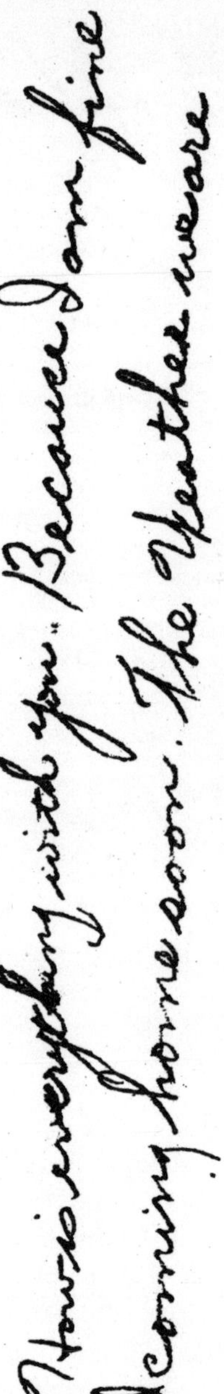

[Handwritten sample 3:] How is everything with you. Because I am fine
and coming home soon. The weather we are

FIG. 216 (17%). Tumor, left parietal region

FIGS. 212-216. Various Brain Organic Patterns. I (Cont'd)
FIG. 215-216. Organic zig-zag, ataxia, and difficulty of size control

culiarly consistent pattern; grosser difficulties of coordination are rare, sporadic instances of graphic ataxia may or may not be present.

Both *cerebral thromboses* and *tumors* tend to show a "shivering" of the ductus far coarser than that found in psychogenic conditions dominated by anxiety. Blotting is frequent particularly in tumor cases, and, as the condition progresses, difficulties in size control tend to become prominent and easily distinguishable from catatonic "shrinking" and "expanding" owing to the absence of corroborating affective accentuations in other dimensions, i.e., of a unifying form principle. Ataxia is prominent and may be found in conjunction with doubling of strokes and marked disturbances in spatial orientation; in cases where this leads to an anxious clinging-to-the-paper, a characteristic zig-zag of the writing basis may result.

Aphasias, in addition to most of the main difficulties of co-ordination, tend to show peculiarly abrupt changes of letter directions and, occasionally, of pressure. Ataxia is particularly well-marked, perseveration in graphic movements frequent. Gross interruptions of the whole trail of writing may occur.

Paretics, beside showing co-ordinative difficulties of the more common types, appear to have a particular propensity for the entanglements of strokes and whole lines. Tremors are particularly irregular, and blotting is frequent. In distinction from the trails of patients with tumors, the writing tends to be fast and flighty.

Focal epilepsy may be marked by coarser co-ordinative difficulties also. Its most pre-eminent feature, however, consistent with that of all convulsive and more or less all "paroxysmally" accentuated disorders, is the tendency toward abrupt changes, particularly of the pressure, which shows no consistent swellings but sudden eruptions within the stroke and equally sudden submersions. Milder movement-perseverative tendencies may be encountered.

All conditions marked by an increase in cerebral pressure, furthermore, are characterized by an extreme slowness and resulting lack of graphic "slenderness," even though other symptoms may not or not yet be ostensive.

Diffuse *nutritional* disturbances of the cortex with or without convulsive corrolaries, finally, can bring about milder degrees of "shivering," more subtle disturbances of the pressure cycles, and occasional ataxias.

FIG. 217 (17%). Paresis in a 52 year old man

FIGS. 217-218. Various Brain Organic Patterns. II

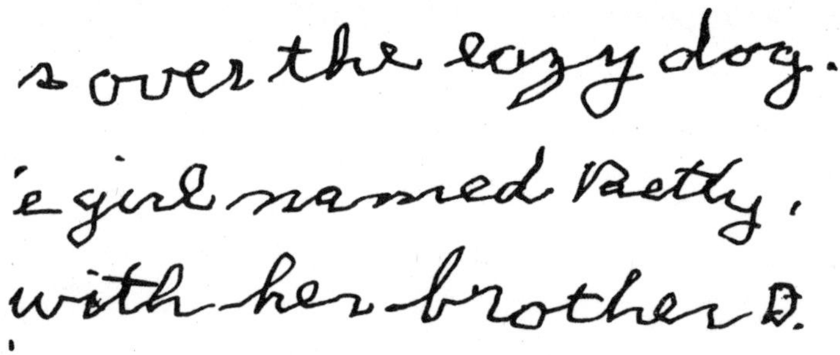

GRAPHIC EXPRESSION OF PSYCHOPATHOLOGY 233

[handwriting sample: "s over the lazy dog." / "e girl named Betty," / "with her brother D."]

FIG. 218 (17%). Feeble-minded woman with diffuse cortical atrophy

FIGS. 217-218. Various Brain Organic Patterns. II (Cont'd)

FIG. 219 (17%) Motor Aphasia, mild

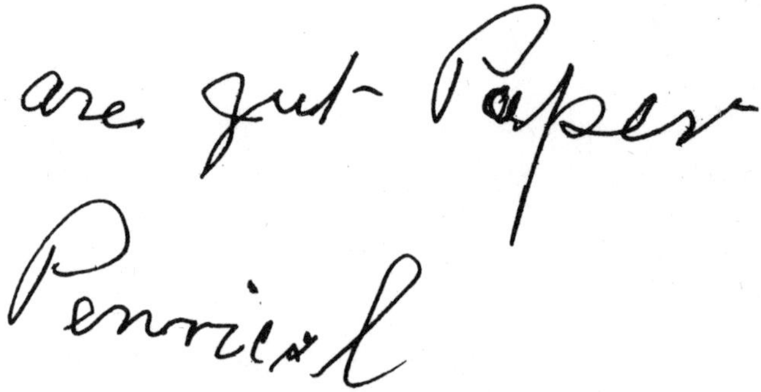

[handwriting sample: "are just Paper" / "Penrinl"]

FIG. 219. Various Brain Organic Patterns. III

While all states of dysfunction of the brain incline to show comparatively coarse difficulties of co-ordination, more specific pattern-types for clinical conditions not named above remain to be defined (figs. 217-219).

MISCELLANEOUS

Since the various different possible criteria for the psychological classification of personality types and personality disorders overlap, group concepts within one typology tend to cut across borderlines between group concepts of another typology. Thus, in the realm of the schizophrenias, the catatonics in some specific aspects show a close relationship to the non-schizoid paroxysmal groups, the epileptics and hysterics. This situation is reflected by the relationship existing between the writing patterns of the named groups in those areas of graphic expression which are

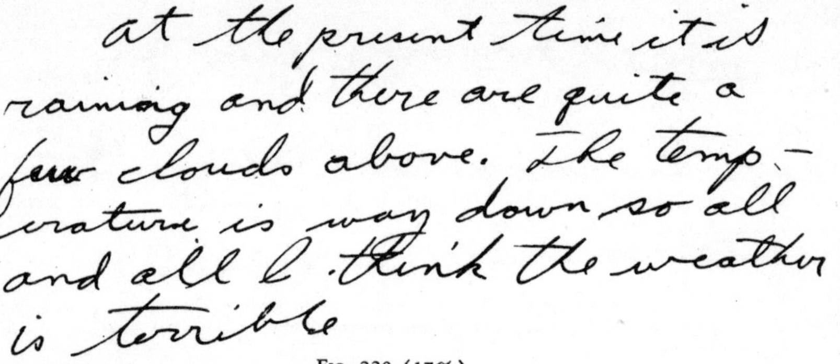

[handwriting sample]

FIG. 220 (17%)

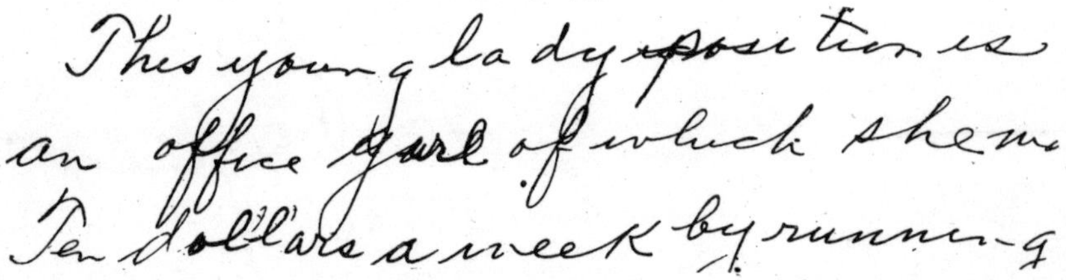

[handwriting sample]

FIG. 221 (45%)

FIGS. 220-221. Idiopathic epilepsy I. Two cases of petit mal

pertinent to the accumulation, repression, and eruption of affect. The catatonic's propensity for the display of high graphic pressure has been mentioned before, as has the unruly, abrupt, and, in terms of the normal contraction-release cycles, "displaced" distributions of pressure characterizing the handwritings of hysteric and convulsive individuals. In true *epilepsy,* and particularly in *grand mal* cases, this tendency often amounts to a quality of "staccato" in the display of pressure which is peculiar for its utter lack of transitional swellings and at times total reversal of the movements of release and of contraction in regard to their receptivity for the manifestation of pressure; in handwritings of the epileptics, more diffuse marks of abruptness may also appear in other areas of graphological inspection such as the longitudinal qualities of the stroke which may arbitrarily, from one part of the text to the next one, vary between high connectedness and high disconnectedness, but the lateral ductual properties seem to lend themselves more specifically to this phenomenon of staccato: entire lines of utter sharpness may alternate with others of an exceedingly muddy quality. A characteristic twilight-like "dimness" or

GRAPHIC EXPRESSION OF PSYCHOPATHOLOGY 235

Fig. 222

Fig. 223

Figs. 222-223 (17%). Idiopathic epilepsy II. "Glassiness of ductus." Patients with grand mal seizures

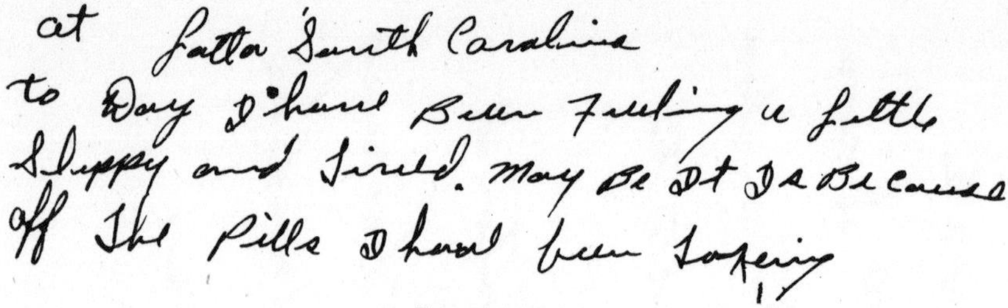

[handwriting sample]

FIG. 224 (45%)

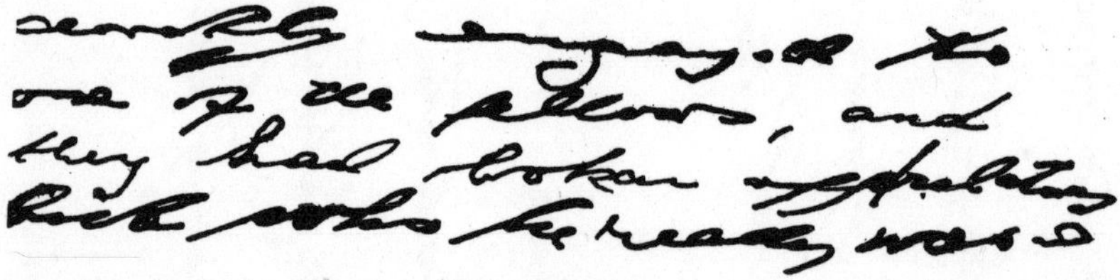

[handwriting sample]

FIG. 225 (7%)

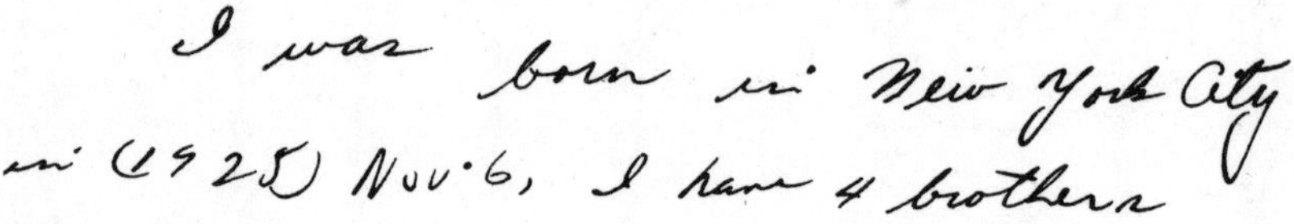

[handwriting sample]

FIG. 226 (45%)

[handwriting sample]

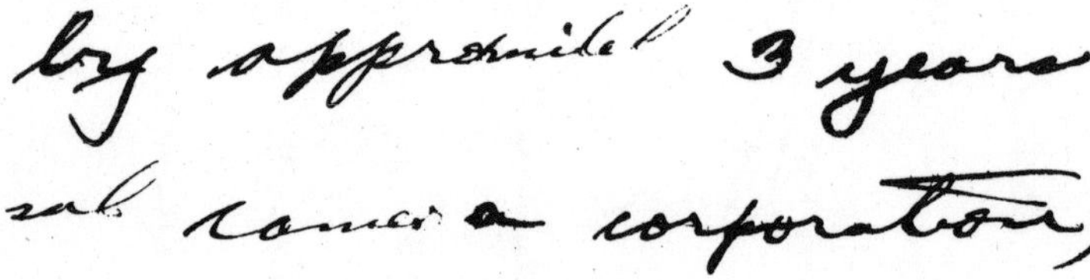

FIG. 227 (7%)

FIGS. 224-227. Idiopathic epilepsy III. "Tumbling" and "staccato." Patients with grand mal seizures

"glassiness" of the stroke, in lighter degrees already marking the trail of conversion hysterias, seems typical of the handwritings of both grand mal and petit mal patients; in addition, in frequent instances of the first group, there are encountered excessive rightward slant and demonstrative tendencies of whole words to tumble below the writing basis, as well as, in both groups, a significant, rightward-concave prolongation of the word-initial upstroke, relating to the peculiar emotional self-intimacy of the epileptoid character. The "disrhythmization" of the schizophrenic and the epileptic's "arhythmia," as appears from the specification of graphic marks for either group, follow the different dynamic principles of disintegration of the concept-unifying functions of thinking for the former and of a primary disturbance in the channelizing of affect for the latter group, with the catatonics presumably representing only one of the possible combined and intermediate positions (fig. 220-227).

A multitude of combinations between the graphic marks of paroxysmal disturbances of affect proper and the various "dashing" characteristics of uncontrolled aggression and self-aggression, of hysteroid "embellishment" and mending, of fluctuations due to mood disturbances, and of impediments and repressions of affect (indicated, apart from the specific conveyances implied in the manners of its distribution, by an unduly high degree of the pressure per se) are encountered in the many instances of emotional lability which can be considered as *"psychomotor"* equivalents of epileptoid conditions (fig. 228). Except for a lesser degree of disinte-

Fig. 228 (45%). Enuresis in handwriting. Note slowness, diffuse losses in directional control and in motor co-ordination, especially of peripheral movements, mild "staccato" of pressure, and specific difficulties with word-internal upstrokes

gration and a lesser accentuation of the leftward particles of movement, they also are frequently found to combine some graphic traits of dementia praecox with the twilight-like ductual characteristics of the paroxysmals. Altogether, it can be said that the lateral and longitudinal ductual qualities of the writing trail, which tend to manifest themselves quite persistently and essentially without regard to the specific implement of writing, present a field for future investigation which seems as promising as it is still virgin. In this connection, we may mention the many successful

238   HANDWRITING ANALYSIS

early ventures which these ductual qualities and many related aspects of handwriting have already enabled graphologists to make into the field of somatic illnesses. In itself, the extension of expression-analysis over the entire structure of organismic functioning seems as justified in principle as the characterological and biological aspects of this structure seem interdependent. The vigor or frailty of handwriting reflects the vigor or frailty of the writer's health per se. The tendency of *glandular disturbances* towards specific disturbances in the areas of pressure displacement and of ductual dispersion have been noticed: e.g., *hyperthyroid conditions* as a rule show up by way of highly distinct and occasionally blot-

FIG. 229. "Knots" in the writing of a hyperthyroid patient

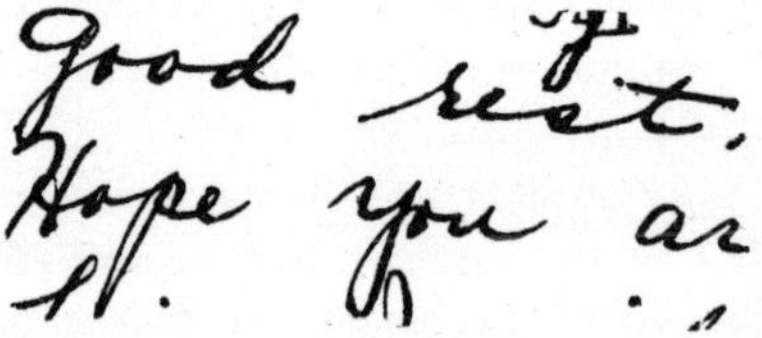

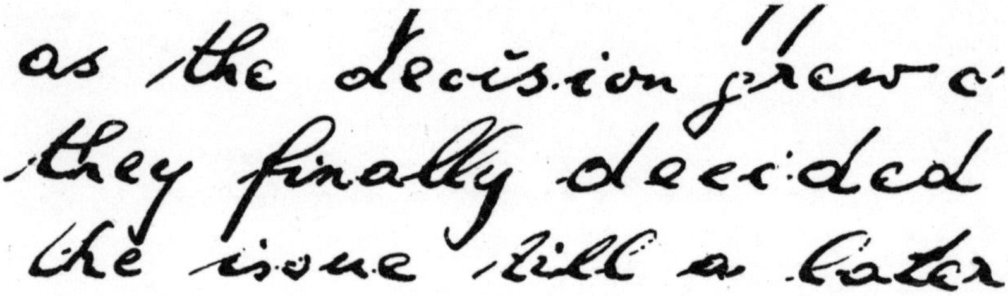

FIG. 230. "Dotting" in a case of cardiac disease

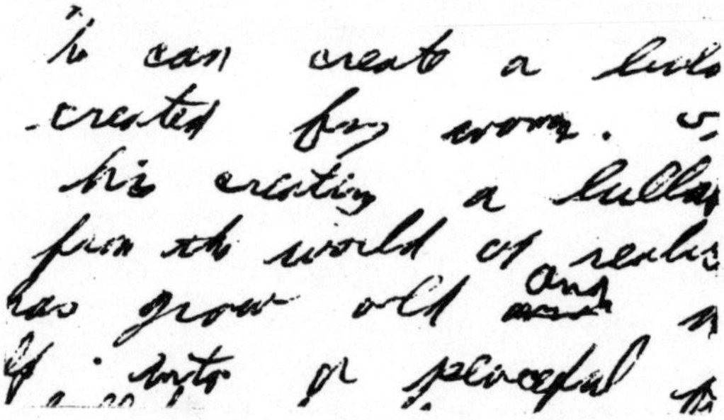

FIG. 231. Multiple pathology of the cardio-vascular and endocrine systems

FIGS. 229-231 (7%). Somatic illness in handwriting

FIG. 232 (7%). "Indented" alcoholic tremor

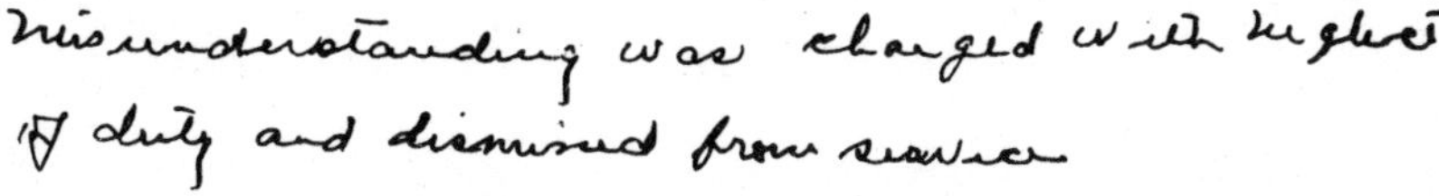

FIG. 233 (45%). Chronic alcoholism, simple

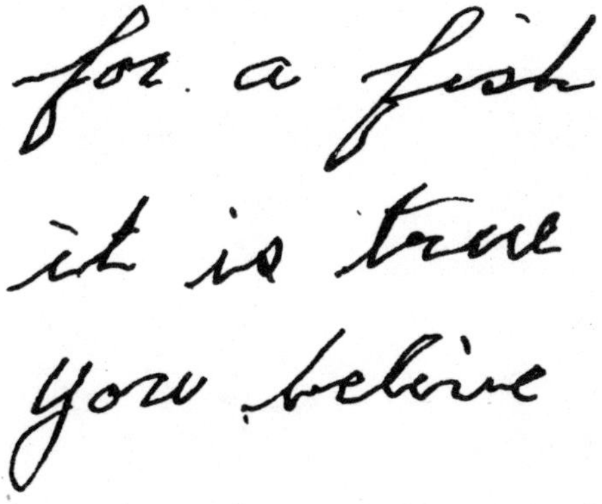

FIG. 234 (7%). Chronic alcoholism with diffuse cortical atrophy in an unstable individual

ting "knots" of pressure which are sharply demarcated and in which the trail momentarily seems to get stuck. Graphically unwarranted dots between words reflect an increased physiological need of the writer for frequent moments of rest. Specific frailties and incomplete ataxias marked by partial dotting of the course of strokes have been found indicative of *cardiac diseases* at sometimes very early and clinically still entirely undetected stages, and systematic attempts to use handwriting in the exploration of the "psychology" of *cancer* which have been made in Hungary have yielded stimulating preliminary results (figs. 229-234).

Alcoholic conditions tend to manifest themselves by combinations of an *"indented"* type of tremulousness with smeariness of the ductus, the total effect of which usually is easily recognized and distinctly demarcated from the ductual expressions of any other disorders unless of course they also are present in the person afflicted, in which case, as in all cases of this kind, a merging of pathognomonic qualities will ensue. Investigations into the graphic articulation of other types of addiction are still in progress. Regarding the gestural physiognomy of the *psychopath*, his propensity for a combined presence of irregularity and low rhythmical in-

FIG. 235. Chronic instability with traits of depression

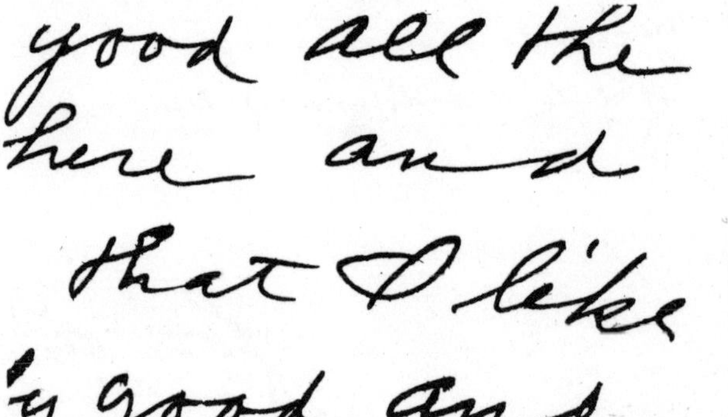

FIGS. 235-236 (7%). Psychopathic personalities

tegration has been stated earlier; differentially important, here, is the usually high degree of graphic marks of impulsivity, the overextension of the middle zone, the relative disemphasis on peripheral accentuation, particularly in the upper zone—the lower one may show horizontally inflated

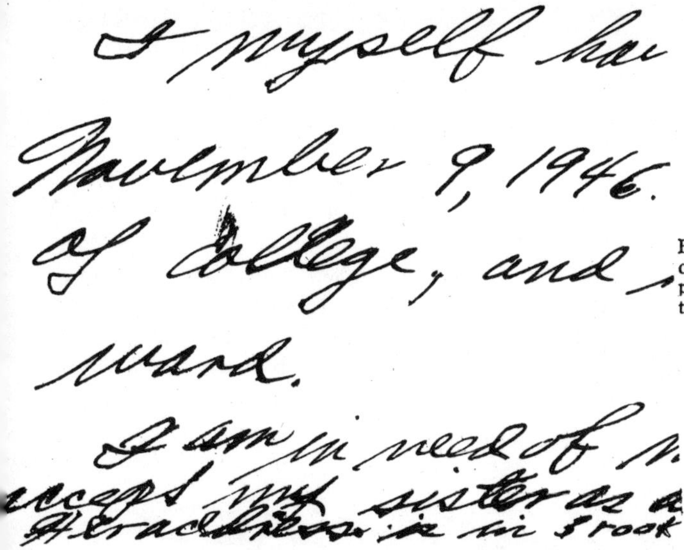

[handwritten sample]

FIG. 236. Psychopath with paranoid character traits

FIGS. 235-236 (7%). Psychopathic personalities (Cont'd)

loops—and, most decisively, the low level of form quality. The potential scope of personality classification according to criteria of social role naturally reaches far beyond the limits of this study which, in that realm, has only been intended to supply the characterological keys required for such classification (figs. 235, 236).

Handwritings of the *feeble-minded,* which sometimes may show a superficial resemblance with brain-organic traits, can easily be distinguished from the latter on the basis of the presence of unifying form principles still operative in their generalized clumsiness, as well as of remnants of higher previous levels of form quality which may still be recognizable in "organic" patterns. Global criteria for the assessment of intelligence levels have before been presented in the discussions in this book on the levels of form quality, of the speed of writing, and of simplification and elaboration, respectively. The actual assessment of intellectual capacity and effective intellectual ability in the individual case will have to be guided by a consideration of structural differences between types of intelligence, which are closely related to characterological ones, as much as of total differences in intellectual scope.

The presence of specific *sexual* deviations in personality functioning can often be inferred from particular combinations of indicators, never from any single one. Thus, homosexuality, which psychologically represents a considerable and strongly divergent variety of possible lines of self-articulation, cannot be concluded even from a massing of signs of attitudes more proper to the opposite biologic sex than the writer's own, but requires additional graphic indications of specific difficulties in external and self-adjustment in order to be concluded. The frequent combination of "scaling" in long-form directions of the upper zone and within single words with marked variations in the total peripheral extensions of these upper extremities and with an ostentatious overall tendency toward rightward slanting in the handwritings of persons with strong *exhibitionistic* impulses may nevertheless be mentioned here, since its gestural conveyance of "self-exposure" appears to be particularly manifest (fig. 237).

FIG. 237 (40%). Exhibitionism in handwriting

Adjustment difficulties of childhood and of the adolescent age offer a particularly fruitful field for graphological inquiry. Many specific disturbances of early puberty with possible serious consequences in later stages of the individual development can graphologically be detected a considerable time before they may become manifest and more or less inveterate. Rapid sample-to-sample increases in narrowness and total leftwardness, crowding, inconsistencies in ductual qualities and in the display and distribution of pressure, more specific "symbolic" manifestations of adolescent rigidity, like "stubborn" triangularizations of lower loops, "opinionated" downward-directed t-bars, to speak in terms of the sometimes too specific definitions of the older graphology of signs, and many other graphic indications of unhealthful developmental trends warranting efforts at an early correction before "petrefaction" sets in allow of subtle yet possibly decisive changes in policy on the educator's part.

Since clinical graphology is only in its beginning stages, the need for continuous awareness of the many dangers to the left and right of his course on the part of the investigator imposes itself with special emphasis. In view of the multitude of "overlapping" concepts in psychopathology and of the further complication of this multitude by discrepant criteria of psychological focus on the part of the different schools of thought now existing, the fact that the characterological and expression-analytic principles presented in this book pertain to *prototypical* positions between which the reality of clinical cases extends in all directions should continuously be kept in mind by psychologists training themselves in the graphological method. The obvious dependence of their work on ample graphic material in the individual case, in order to be successful, need not be stressed. The frequent advisability of comparing present and past samples produced by the same patient and of follow-up studies suggests itself both from the point of view of learning and of greater clinical proficiency in the graphological evaluation of personality changes. Finally, no graphological assessments in the psychodiagnostic realm should persist in the mistake of the early nosologists and their present day disciples to "build the roof prior to the house"—i.e., to think in terms of "labels," even if these labels themselves are highly differential, and to "diagnose" mental illness in the individual case before a total and strictly individualizing characterological basis for such diagnosis has graphologically been developed. Global analyses of the personalities of his patients the clinical graphologist should therefore consider as the only sound foundation possible for his diagnostic work and as his most obliging indebtedness to the future development of his method.

SOME ABNORMAL SAMPLES AND THEIR ANALYSES

Graphic patterns of the more prototypical psychiatric syndromes usually cause the student of graphology relatively much less difficulty than do handwritings of mental patients—sometimes cases which are comparatively light but at the same time highly resistive to therapy—whose personalities and clinical conditions lend themselves to multiple interpretations and whose diagnoses therefore, as they are seen by many diagnosticians and are subjected to many case conferences, show a tendency either to vary over the years or to be perpetually regarded as "problem cases" or both. The difficulties of assessment presented by the clinical picture thus are simply reflected in those presented by the graphic one.

The following ten sample analyses which shall illustrate the clinical application of the graphological method were therefore selected with special regard to the representativeness of most of them for this very kind of situation. All ten studies were derived from the handwriting samples alone, with the writer's sex, age, and handedness as the only additional data placed at the graphologist's disposal; and all ten have this in common that they refuse to use nosological terminology as a necessarily adequate concept system for the categorization of actual cases of abnormal personality structures, states, and trends.

All ten were confirmed by psychiatric impressions and case studies and were given credit for shedding light on a number of clinically still unelucidated points (fig. 238).

Sample I
(Male, age 28, right-handed)

The handwriting (fig. 238) shows signs of severe emotional trauma in a highly hostile and distrustful, yet at the same time polite and well-mannered and even mildly effeminate subject of superior to very superior intelligence who is morbidly self-conscious and self-observing. Deeply uncertain of his own identity and life role, he has been unable to accept any definite system of values by which to orient himself, even though fairly much personal ambition, as well as a vague and general flair for "aristocratic" attitudes, is noticeable; the latter trends, however, are likely to aggravate rather than modify his experiences of frustration. The lack of direction in his formation of, and approach toward, his life goals per-

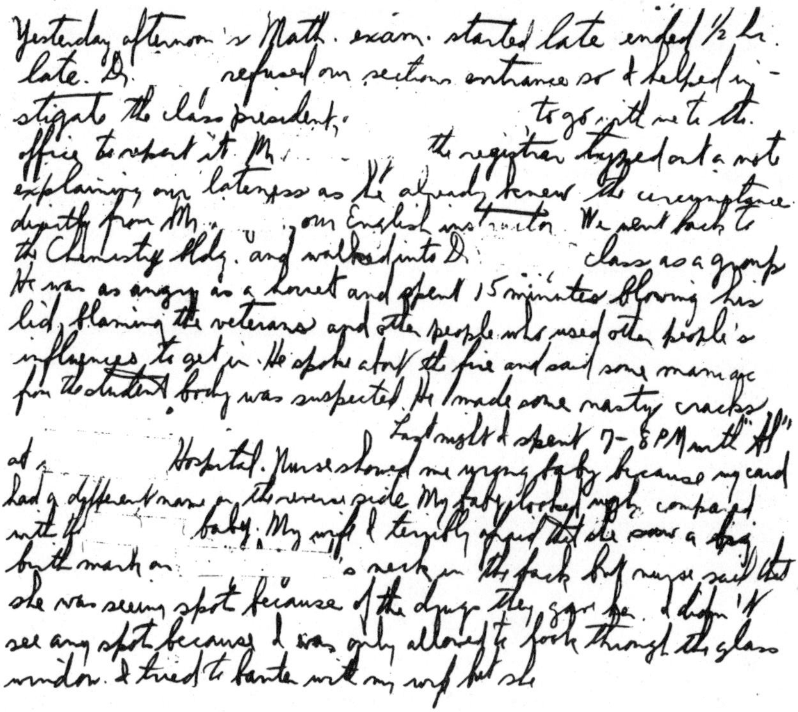

FIG. 238 (45%). Case 1 (names deleted)

meates all personality strata and lines of functioning; whatever he tackles, his focus is centered on his own emotional experience of it rather than on the object per se. The consequences are a repression of his spontaneity which absorbs most of his energy and leaves little for external pursuits and emotional engagements; a state of restless discomfort which drives him into accelerated ideational and verbal activity; a hypochondriacal depressiveness which accentuates the negative in all experiences and inclines towards the assumption of "martyr" roles; an excessive personal touchiness and resentfulness—he is always ready to feel offended by someone or something, and the basic tenor of his attitude always seems to imply that the world owes him something and is missing out on its obligations; finally, an overscrupulousness which is aesthetically rather than morally oriented: he is self-critical and even self-torturing, not by virtue of any particular ethical aspirations or standards but on the basis of a compulsive insistence upon exactitude and a craving for perfection which, in his direct experience, is encountered by him more as a coercive ego alien than as a spontaneous and positive urge. He dislikes to assume obligations but is very conscientious about obligations once accepted. The otherwise obsessional pattern is not free from hysterical elements: he has a marked ability to manipulate—in as far as he does not repress—his own affects, and there should be some tendency toward headaches and related lines of somatization. At the present time he is markedly depressed and experiences a general slowing down of his psychomotor functions which sharply contrasts with his restlessness and which exceeds his habitual hesitancy and indecision; suicidal ideas should play their role from time to time, but at least in his present phase of development are not to be regarded as too serious. His suspiciousness, on the other hand, often assumes excessive forms and may sporadically interfere with his interpretations of reality though at present he cannot be considered actually and positively psychotic (fig. 239).

Sample II
(Male, age 26, right-handed)

The writer (fig. 239) is an ambitious, argumentative, very "touchy," deeply hostile and perpetually high-strung, easily excitable individual of superior intelligence, with obsessional fears and marked contact difficulties, who is constantly on the defense, is unable to relate himself spontaneously to his environment, is given to ruminations and speculations with a definite paranoid over-ideational tinge, and is of sometimes considerable flightiness. The flightiness has a distinctly paroxysmal character, as the slightest irritation suffices to induce a mild "twilight" state in which the patient is apt, to a certain extent, to lose his orientation, particularly in regard to the temporal order of events and to specific memory materials. His logical and ideational stubbornness—when he is in more "normal conditions"—markedly contrasts with his basic insecurity, his emotional dependency on the environment, and his unproductive self-centeredness which alternates between self-pity and self-repression and, in a manner characterized by frequent self-references, distorts his interpretations of reality and his judgmental functions at large. His ideational and behavioral over-activity is rather hypomanic and, in one of its aspects, appears as a continuous movement of self-escape conditioned by the ambivalent semi-repressive ex-

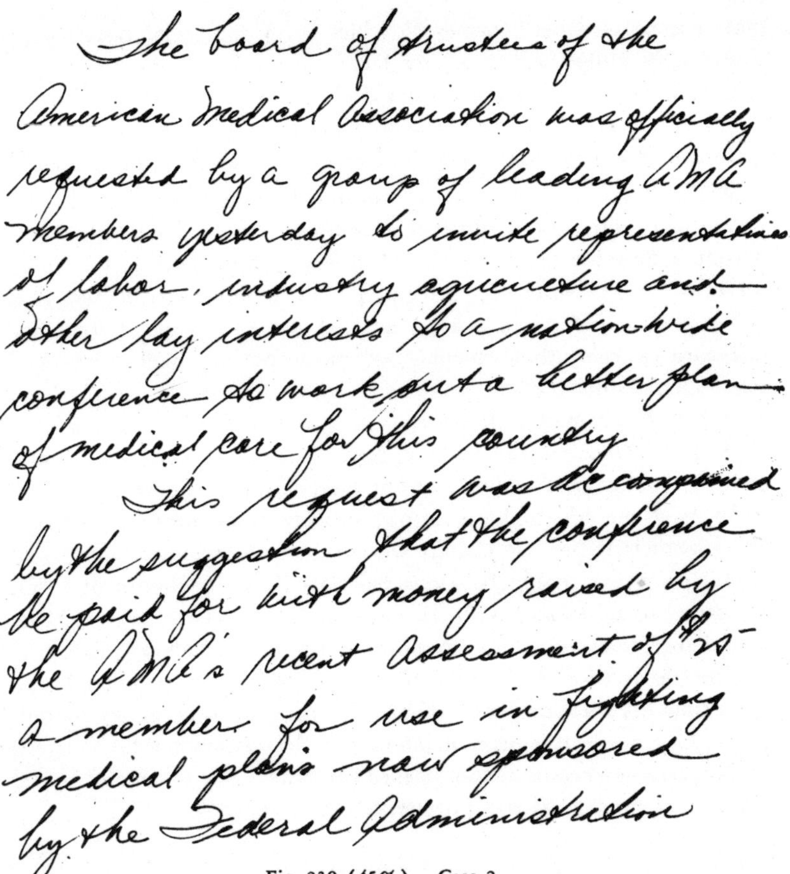

> The board of trustees of the
> American Medical Association was officially
> requested by a group of leading AMA
> members yesterday to invite representatives
> of labor, industry, agriculture and
> other lay interests to a nation-wide
> conference to work out a better plan
> of medical care for this country
>   This request was accompanied
> by the suggestion that the conference
> be paid for with money raised by
> the AMA's recent assessment of $25
> a member for use in fighting
> medical plans now sponsored
> by the Federal Administration

Fig. 239 (45%). Case 2

perience of homosexual urges centered on his self-identification with a passive, feminine role. Directly experienced fears deriving from this basis are likely to be of short duration but of panicky intensity, especially since the above characterized paroxysmal trend activated by them has a deeply upsetting effect on the patient. Sexual preoccupations, involving both sadistic and masochistic desires, but particularly the latter, prevail throughout his scope of conscious impulse experience; his heterosexual wishes should primarily focus on masculine women but only sporadically should assign "maternal" roles to them; his day-dreaming, however, is more preoccupied with themes of achievement and social rank than with sexual ones altogether; to a very large extent, he suppresses this entire sphere, and his active pursuits should be marked by a rigid and insistent, if not very successful, search for order, cleanliness, and justice, and by a stiff adherence to preconceived—and very ill-conceived—"principles."

With all his intellectual capacities and propensities, he is deeply deprived of experiences of spiritual integration, has no sense of humor and, despite a flair for psychological, motivational speculation, is a poor observer of others. Since his "principles" (including his principles of right and wrong, of justice, etc.) are conceived in hate and self-defense and in disregard of facts, they not only are sterile but are likely to bring him into innumerable conflict situations in which he likes to assume the role of a persecuted martyr; however, more seriously trying experiences are likely to be frequent and to have badly exciting effects on him in view of his low tolerance for shocks of any kind. Despite the strongly paranoid trend, however, his thinking is not positively dissociational or delusional, and superficially he is in contact with reality. A psychotherapeutic attack on his condition should be successful only if the environmental field is structured in accordance with the necessity to protect the patient from potential incentives of panic. A position for him involving demands for responsible decisions and judgments should therefore be avoided; yet at the same time his vocational role should also make allowances for his intelligence, his considerable need of intellectual stimulation and his unquestionable capacity—when in a more relaxed condition—for systematic procedure along lines predefined and predetermined by others.

Sample III
(Female, age 27, right-handed)

Oscillating between feelings of insecurity and of euphoria, the writer (fig. 240) lacks a stable direction not only in her momentary emotional

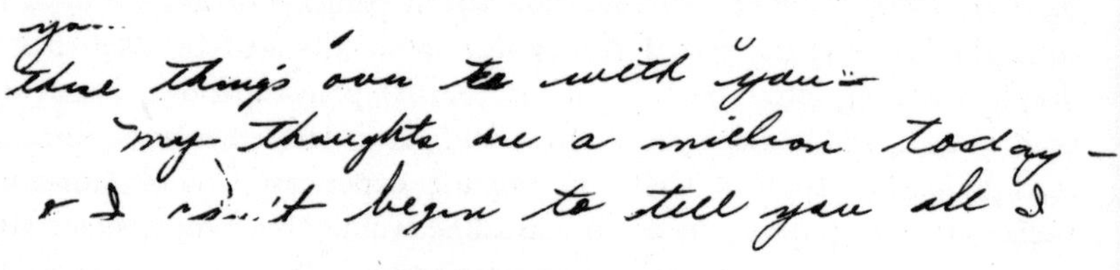

Fig. 240 (45%). Case 3

experiences but in her motivations and values and in the concepts of her life role as well; she has not only not succeeded in consistent goal formations but has been defeated in many previous attempts at attaining them. A relatively better constancy exists in her thought processes which show impulses of flightiness but also a tendency to keep them in check. She is given to worrying and intermittent depressions and in almost continuous need of reassurance, which tends to mount proportionately to her restlessness.

Her thinking, nevertheless, is markedly superficial and overassociational. Her assessments of her own strength show the typical faultiness of a cycloid affective disorder: of low basic vitality, she alternately overestimates her forces and, following the slightest setback, gives up and either sinks into depression or engages in a new undertaking in the initial phase of which a new misjudgment of her energies—as well as of her situation in the environment—develops. While her emotional and instinctual immaturity is not compensated by substantial experiences in the intellectual sphere— she is of bright normal intellectual capacity with quite unmaterialized superior potentialities—a certain noblesse and idealism, with nostalgic adolescent-like day-dreaming about erotic partnerships and with aspirations for "higher" forms of life, are unmisrecognizable.

Despite the apprehensiveness of her thinking which tends to act as a stabilizer to the over-ideational trend, she often finds it impossible to co-ordinate and organize her thoughts. On the other hand, the violent mood swings to which she is subjected and over which she not only has no power of control but which leave her with a distinct feeling of powerlessness are relatively concealed as far as her external behavior is concerned, and she should, on the whole, not appear too manifestly overactive, except on closer personal contact and under a more longitudinal observation. Her "worrying" and her external controls—which are very adaptive to the "expectations" she senses on the part of others—betray the presence of an hysterical element in this basically manic-depressive character. She is oversensitive, and, in her depressive intervals, morbidly self-conscious without being capable of any genuine insight. Moreover, in the depressive phases, she is hypochondriacal, given to all kinds of catastrophic anticipations, and markedly suggestible. The latter trend, together with her generosity and general lack of caution whenever she engages in any actual undertaking should involve the definite danger for her to be exploited easily—her worries and disillusionments, with all their momentary intensity, will almost always come too late.

Her present condition can be defined as a mild manic-depressive psychosis but the existing remnants of control are rather substantial in a clinical sense. In a social sense, she is in evident need of a protective, stable, and understanding environment, which at the same time should avoid either overstimulation or monotony. To the extent of her intellectual capacity as stated, the patient's effective abilities are unimpaired, and, as far as her vocational aptitudes are concerned, she should make a fairly satisfactory teacher of preparatory school subjects involving limited responsibilities and requiring a didactic rather than practical approach.

Sample IV
(Male, age 22, right-handed)

The patient (fig. 241) is an unspontaneous, self-conscious, and delib-

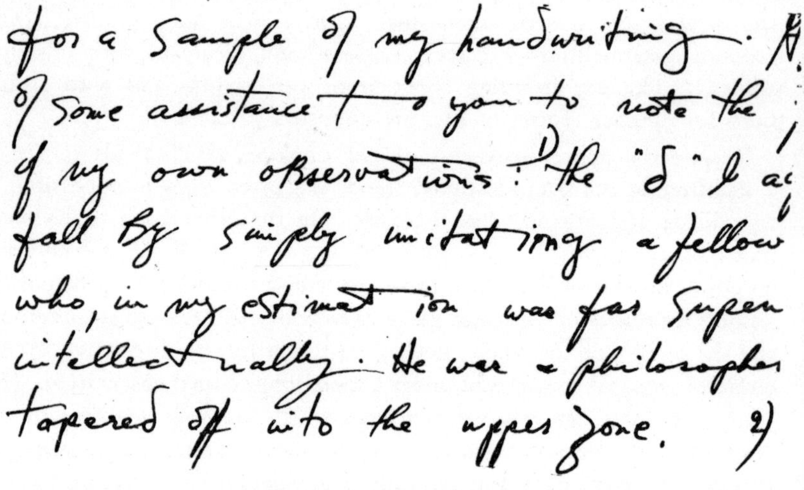

Fig. 241 (31%). Case 4

erate but, at the same time, restless and ideationally agitated individual, strongly given to ruminations, day-dreams, and theoretical speculation. He hates himself for being an introvert thinker, wants to externalize all the time, and closely watches the environment's reactions to him; he depends on them in his self-evaluations and has no stable set of values of his own.

His aspirations, therefore, have a touch of the exhibitionism of an actor and he keeps trying to put them to work; behaviorally, they are toned down by both his inhibitions and his flair—which is quite genuine—for poses of modesty and compliance and for noble and distinguished attitudes; the latter, however, are not likely to hold up in any really threatening situation for any length of time.

As already implied, there is no stable direction behind his deliberations and he is likely to lie a great deal in order to cover this up. He suffers from feelings of meaninglessness, guilt, disintegration, and discontinuity and needs an extensive number of inveterate little compulsive habits to conjure these away. Given to perpetual self-observation, he is exposed to terrible uncertainties in which he is constantly trying to have others share, and is interested in outside reality only to the extent to which he is able to relate his external observations to the all-important observation of his own conflicts. A tendency toward hairsplitting dialectics is noticeable. Despite much superficial spreading of his intellectual interests over many fields, there are few real topics of thinking and fairly much perseveration or at least repetitiousness in arguing them out with himself and with others. Ideas about matters out of his personal sphere are vague, but nevertheless are usually on the right track—which he fails to follow up. His speculations are intuitive and have little ultimate consequences in his life. His spiritual aspirations have a tendency to bluff others as well as himself, and this is facilitated by the fact that, while incapable of being systematic, he is nevertheless a good logician. He is of superior to very superior, clinically unimpaired intelligence, a fact which helps him toward a sometimes considerable efficiency in his lying.

With his uncertainty in respect to goals and his constant self-preoccupations, his life philosophy points in the opposite direction. He has a strong craving for doing something, whatever that may be, for its own sake and makes all kinds of far-reaching plans. These, once they have been made, give him such a feeling of security and even of elation that he immediately begins to take life leisurely and postpones carrying them out until they have become outdated, whereupon a new project will be produced. In other instances, apprehensions about external security, interpersonal relations, etc., will interfere with the realization of his plans. The most obstructing factor, however, appears to be his excessive self-pity. Together with his compulsiveness and with the touchiness of his ego, this should lead to a peculiarly stuffy, pseudo-dignified artificiality of his behavior and to related masquerades of affect on his part, all of which, however, are only fleeting or even episodic; he "plays" with attitudes, not knowing his role in the world.

He should have a very inconsistent economy, being alternately greedy and wasteful. Basically an egotist, with self-centered and quasi-masturbatory practices in every realm of life, he is nevertheless genuinely devoted to the lofty if vague ego-ideals which he has come to form, and secretly believes he has a mission in the world, even though he does not know the cause, and an obligation to accept the martyrdom which it is likely to entail. The element of masochism in this attitude should find its correlate in his instinctual impulse experiences—which are likely to be bi-sexual. An unresolved oedipal conflict is evident, but in the present preoccupations of his consciousness the father should be more in the background, and feelings of ambivalence should be centered upon the figure of the mother. He hates himself for his dependence on her, yet this dependence is strong enough to exert itself even in his hatred, which is heavily tinged with feelings, not only of self-pity but of powerlessness as well.

This experience of powerlessness is linked up with a number of somatic fixations and preoccupations which, despite the preponderantly hysterical structure of the character, exceed the range of either simple conversion processes or hypochondriasis. Graphic traces of early cardiac neurosis are present in the sample.

Sample V

(Female, age 34, right-handed)

The writer (fig. 242) is under the dominance of momentary emotional impulses which not only continuously fluctuate but to a large extent are mutually contradictory and frequently paralyzing. She quite desperately attempts to keep up a consistent attitude, to be orderly, steady, conventional, and reserved in a casual and normally friendly way, but experiences extreme sensations of discomfort when trying to enforce such control upon herself. To these sensations she reacts with precipitate impulses of expansion and generosity, impulses to seek adventures, attachments, activity, which in turn are being antagonized by her phobic shyness in the face of real life situations where she almost invariably reaches a point of actually

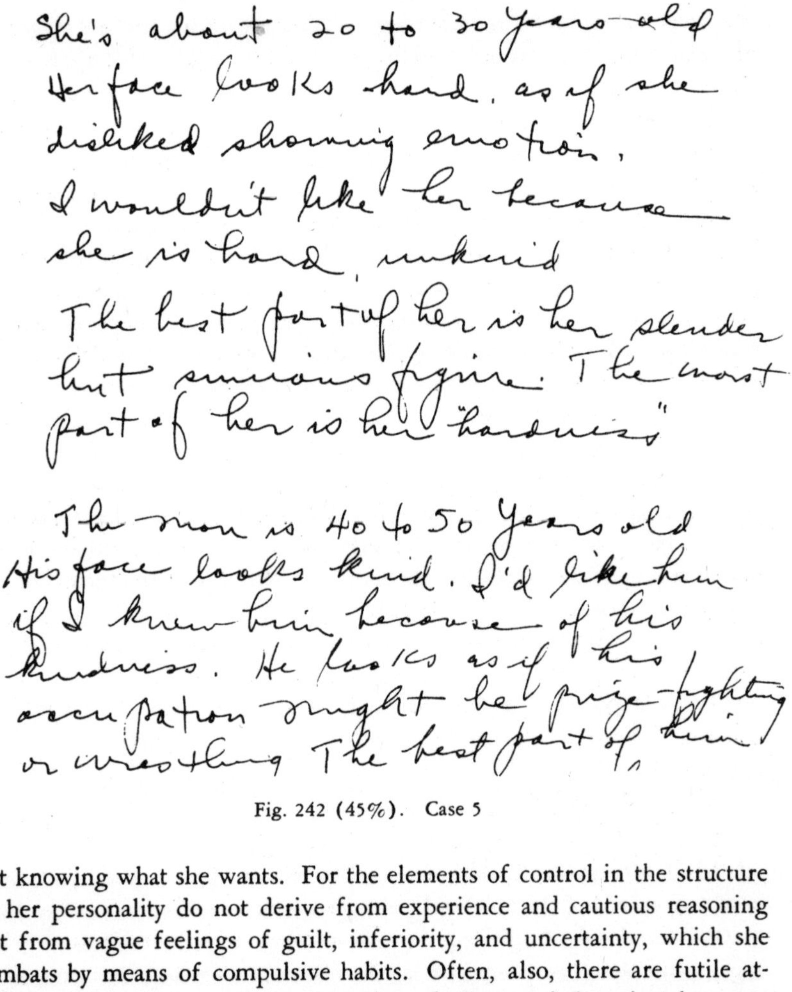

> She's about 20 to 30 years old
> Her face looks hard, as if she
> disliked showing emotion.
> I wouldn't like her because
> she is hard, unkind
> The best part of her is her slender
> but sinuous figure. The worst
> part of her is her "hardness"
>
> The man is 40 to 50 years old
> His face looks kind. I'd like him
> if I knew him because of his
> kindness. He looks as if his
> occupation might be prize-fighting
> or wrestling. The best part of him

Fig. 242 (45%). Case 5

not knowing what she wants. For the elements of control in the structure of her personality do not derive from experience and cautious reasoning but from vague feelings of guilt, inferiority, and uncertainty, which she combats by means of compulsive habits. Often, also, there are futile attempts on her part to rebel against these feelings, rebel against her own social and cultural standards, against her self-consciousness, against everything that represents the environment she comes from and the values imbedded in its structure; antagonism toward her mother—who, in view of this constellation, should have been a discouraging factor in the development of her femininity—is particularly likely.

While she thus identifies with a feminine existence, her actual attitude whenever she yields to her emotions remains aggressive and self-aggressive in a masculine way, although this aggressiveness, again, will largely remain theoretical and deprived of effective consequences in altering her life pattern. Her day-dreams are likely to focus on herself as an object of desirable masculine aggression, while aggressiveness of herself, not as an actual attitude but as a consciously exercised role, appears far more repressed. Despite her compulsive tendencies, her strong needs for self-preservation, her general contact shyness, and her inclination toward temporary outlets of tension by way of speculating and theorizing about her situations, there are emotional states following periods of depression where she becomes over-susceptible to any kind of external stimulation, easily swayed by it, and, almost without knowing how, will glide into situations which she is unable to handle. Quite intelligent whenever in a structured situation involving a set goal, a predefined task, anything directing her, she is of the poorest judgment whenever it comes to her own basic life problems and undertakings and decisions involving her existence as a whole. Her plans can be quite orderly but in view of her instability will most frequently be unrealistic because she will not carry them out and ultimately is aware of this already at the time of making them. Her observation is particularly poor. Her thinking is given to illusions, flighty and, in a markedly speculative way, superficial, although having pretty good *logical* power at its disposal; it is primarily motivated by noble and generous impulses, alternating, at times, with petty apprehensions about her security.

The emotional stalemates brought about by the two conflicting aspirants for leadership in her personality functioning, compulsive control on the one hand, emotional expansiveness with a manic tinge on the other, often result in episodes of emotional paroxysm which are believed most likely to take the form of agitated depressions here and there climaxing in a rage, while at other times she is likely to tyrannize her environment by extreme moodiness, although she even then does not really mean evil and even in moments of greatest tension and distress will subjectively tend to preserve the highest standards of self-identification.

While her verbal thinking retains a thin coating of logical consistency, its actual motivations and evaluations, owing to constant interferences on the part of her repressed aggressiveness, are so extremely contradictory from one minute to the next that relationships to schizophrenic thinking are evident. While episodes of emotional paroxysms will show her suspicious, over-sensitive in regard to her social role, and generally engaged in ideations of a distinctly paranoid tinge, she is too totally unstable to be able to cling to lines of ideational systematization with any degree of steadiness; extreme emotionality and frustrated extratensive needs prevail, and the combination would therefore suggest a manic-trend interacting with a schizophrenic one. Up to the present time, these trends are not likely as yet to have led to any permanent clinical condition or impairment: at the time of writing, the patient was acutely moody, and her thought processes were disturbed and very mildly disassociational but she was not manifestly psychotic. Prognosis in her case must depend on the extent to which environmental security can be provided for her, and to which she can be kept from misjudging her resources in entering new enterprises and engagments. This not only applies to her emotional makeup: despite sporadic experiences of seeming surplus energy, her physical health is believed to be comparatively frail.

Sample VI
(Male, age 40, right-handed)

The writer (fig. 243) is of superior capacity and unimpaired effective intelligence in all "structured" situations where the overall direction of his attack on the task or problem at hand is given. Where it is not given, where, in situations challenging his entire existence, he has to depend on his judgment, he will not be able to avail himself of his capacity to any degree commensurable with its native strength but will react in an overemotional fashion or, defending himself against the tides of his affect, will act in a rigid and constricted and frequently persevering manner, without being able to make allowances for changes in the situation. Accordingly, he is a poor observer and, despite his marked ideomotor restlessness, his imaginative life is lacking in vigor, clarity, and direction.

Overly dependent on the social environment and anxiously observing its responses to his actions and attitudes, his mood swings, though sometimes excessive, are on the whole more reactive than autonomous. The depressions are brief but sharp and are accompanied by experiences of total disillusionment, and it is in these moments that he most painfully feels his lack of a valid and convincing identification with any life role or goal. In order to give some meaning to his frustrated existence, he will

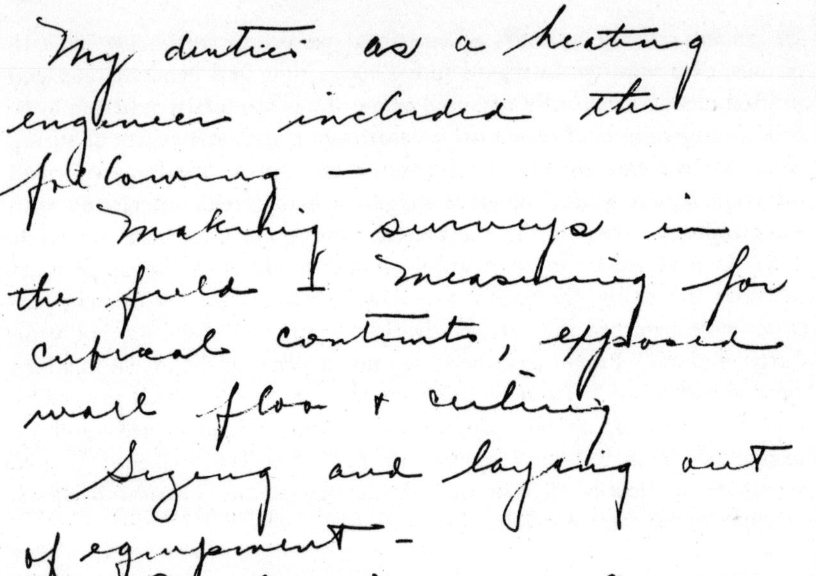

> My duties as a heating engineer included the following —
> Making surveys in the field & measuring for cubical contents, exposed wall floor & ceiling
> Sizing and laying out of equipment —
> Analyzing complaints and calling on customers in the field
> Figuring heat loss & heat gain of buildings both residential and commercial
> Contacting dealers, builders and architects from a promotional standpoint

Fig. 243 (45%). Case 6

then incline toward self-accounts, self-historical interpretations of his past experiences and motivations and will endeavor to look at himself with the eyes of a case worker writing his biography rather than with any viewpoint that would reflect his own feelings. Another frequently preferred reaction to his depressive experiences is a stubborn and very aggressive identification with certain theoretical positions, in the defence of which he can be very blind. He has excellent logic and good mathematical sense but comparatively poor reality testing, so that his sometimes very speculative deductions are frequently based on false premises, among which suspicious projections of all kinds of evil motives into others usually play a substantial, at times even dominant, role.

His deliberate assumption of a socializing attitude—he is a very courteous person—his emotional overreactivity and his extreme sensitivity—which is personal touchiness rather than emotional empathy and refinement—have little to do with true engagements and externalizations of positive affect. He is a resentful, egotistical, vengeful, suspicious, often cruel and markedly cunning person who hides his aggressive deliberations and sneering negativisms and carefully prepares his attacks on the environment behind a facade of vague and noncommittal politeness. He loves to take advantage of sometimes rather small and trivial opportunities to punish or exploits others, and one of his most powerful and persistent lines of motivation is distinctly parasitical in nature; he is the typical domestic tyrant. Combined with this we find exhibitionist and theatrical needs which however are screened through intellectual controls and, socially, will seldom manifest themselves too grossly; however, it goes without saying that, with all this personality background, the writer is as sensitive to flattery as he is to criticism and that he will not easily let any opportunity to "exhibit" himself go by. When not under stress, more gentle and even generous impulses will manifest themselves, and the writer will then appear as a rather soft and good-natured person, qualities most closely corresponding to his ego-ideal.

While he can be heterosexually engaged to a quite considerable extent and has fairly strong conscious needs for an orderly family life, his homosexuality, the repression of which has never been quite successful and which is tinged with sadistic wishes, has kept troubling him. While his homosexuality thus appears to be more strongly interlinked with his aggressivity, his heterosexual relationships are marked by a passive and dependent, unsacrificing type of tenderness implying a predominant element of self-love and clearly betraying an unrelinquished mother-fixation on his part.

Escapes from this conflict are indicated primarily along the line of alcoholic addiction, potentially of other narcotic dependencies also. The patient's relationship to alcohol is very clearly characterized by signs of overindulgence on the one hand, a low narcotic threshold on the other.

In brief, he can be defined as a paranoid personality who suffers from alcoholic addiction and is showing potentialities for a psychotic break but is not overtly psychotic at the time of writing.

Sample VII
(Male, age 31, right-handed)

The writer (fig. 244) is of very superior intelligence, is strongly inclined toward logical operations, and insists upon his own independent ideas and unconventional evaluations, which combine a good deal of dogmatic tenacity with a considerable amount of emotional opposition and ag-

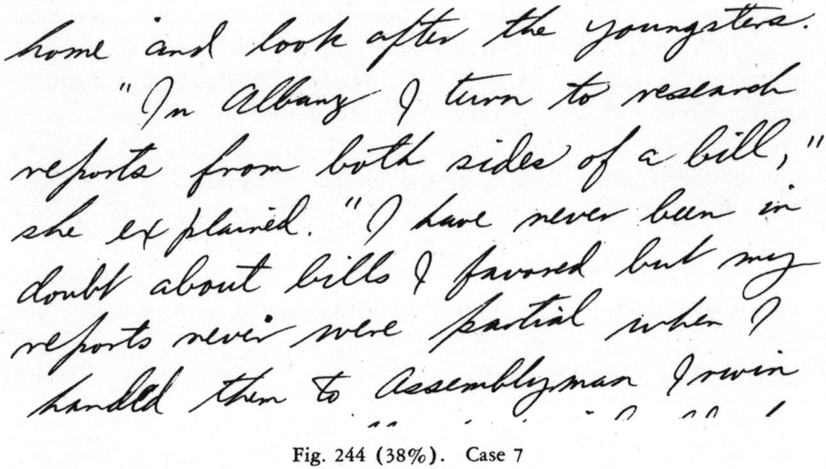

Fig. 244 (38%). Case 7

gressiveness. Much of the latter only comes out in "theoretical" situations, while in ordinary interpersonal situations the writer will rather show social dexterity and a pleasant although slightly too effeminate smoothness of attitude—which can be understood as a reaction of fear of his own aggressiveness as well as of craving for the affection of others. He is exceedingly sensitive and may display in stressing situations an amount of touchiness and irritation likely to be anything but "smooth"; aggression in a situation of this kind is not likely to be confined to theorizing attitudes but may find its outlets in the form of sporadic rages and tantrums. He is very suspicious and perpetually inclined to detect "schemes" of some kind on the part of people very close to him—much less on that of strangers. He is dependent on others, and on female partners in particular, in all situations involving any responsible decisions, any challenges to his judgment and to his ability to keep a straight and steady course; he shows himself rebellious against such authority, such self-imposed system of external dependencies, whenever his situations in the environment tend to become more stable, easy, and remunerative.

A continuous conflict seems to be going on between his rather noble and magnanimous, "aristocratic" values and aspirations, which at least disclose a substantial need for inner freedom on his part, and the petty apprehensions and suspicious worries in which he will seem to get stuck from time to time. Somatic displacements of affect are not outside of his scope, either, but are more likely to lead to diffuse disturbances of organ systems than to clearly delineated hysterical conversions; he is on the whole more obsessional than paroxysmal, yet his ideationally accentuated introversion, his indulgence in speculative fantasies, etc., is balanced by a genuine need for a verbalizing and intellectualizing type of sociability which he operates with the expectation—of which he has no awareness—of gains in recognition and affection. No psychotic trends are indicated. The writer is the prototypical perpetual neurotic: while his creative capacities are not ever allowed to grow and win freedom of action, neither are his self-destructive trends, as he is far too absorbed in "little" preoccupations (or escapes from them) ever to generate impulses of lasting consequence or of incisive power.

Some compensatory absorption of disturbing affects is provided by his compulsiveness which inclines toward "magic" habits rather than towards the generalized overorderliness of the simple compulsive character. With the latter he even has very little in common: a marked inability of his to "live according to plan" is rather obvious; on the other hand, however, he possesses fairly much "theoretical" conscientiousness and sense of obligation and at the present time is very much bothered by his failure to live up to his ego-ideals.

Sample VIII
(Male, age 25, right-handed)

The patient's conflict (fig. 245) is centered on experiences of guilt from which he is in a constant restless flight. This flightiness should strongly betray itself in his manner of verbal behavior which is likely to combine rapid changes of topics with a resistance against tackling anything in any but the most superficial fashion and with a judgmental attitude which is strictly based on his most fleeting emotions. The patient feels inferior and inclines to use his social contacts to allay this feeling; this he does by means of a self-demonstrative stubbornness which is actually meant as a policy of maintaining his position in the face of a world which he vaguely suspects of operating against him.

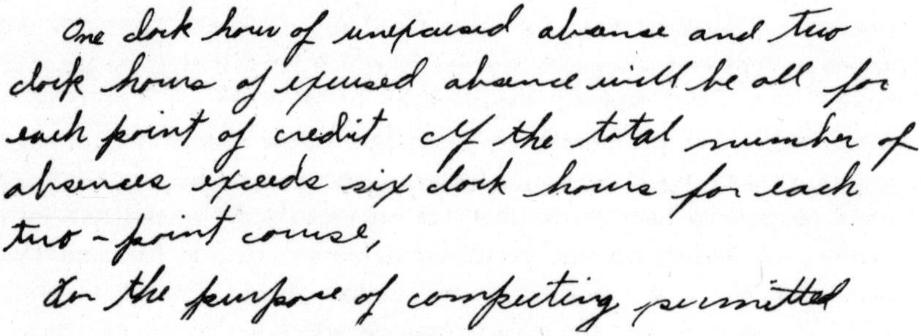

Fig. 245 (45%). Case 8

He is given to sudden emotional blockings which are colored with anxiety and are frequently followed by outbursts of negative affect. The self-expression which he experiences only in action never lasts very long and does not hold up in the face of real obstacles not to be run over by means of persuasion; yet his yielding to such obstacles will always have an undertone of offended protest. He is inclined to display more self-confidence but at the same time less ambition than he actually possesses. In his instinctual life, he represses passive homosexual needs and experiences overt exhibitionistic ones; heterosexually, he is quickly aroused but cannot continue long in any relationship and nurtures a "functional" view of love life which is tinged with cynicism; almost all experiences in this realm should be precipitate and unsatisfactory. His precipitateness often gets him into situations which frighten and disgust him, and he will then try to escape the consequence of his undertakings almost in the last minute, soon to rush into another one. This abruptness in the pattern of his life course causes experiences of discontinuity which he is likely to ward off by a number of little compulsive rituals. Intermittent headaches are likely to be incurred. The patient is of bright normal capacity and his effective intelligence is unimpaired.

Sample IX
(Male, age 26, right-handed)

The handwriting (fig. 246) displays a morbid depression with very severe anxieties in a shut-in individual of excessive sensitivity, badly injured self-esteem, very high spiritual aspirations, and a basic attitude of paranoid "protesting" against the meanness of the world, who attributes a deeply secret meaning, unrecognized by the common crowd, to his existence as a lonesome, disillusioned thinker, and takes a tragic pride in his "fate," while at the same time suffering deeply from almost unbearable feelings of gloom.

Under their impact, the continuity of his inner experience is giving way, and this disintegrative process is farther advanced than his still main-

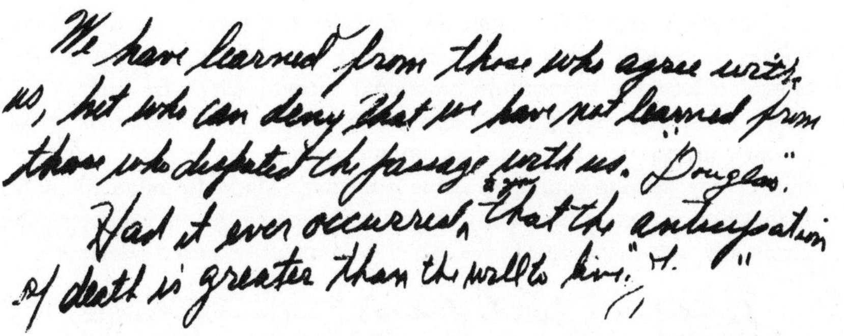

Fig. 246 (45%). Case 9

tained superficial coherence of thinking betrays; grossly dissociational ideations are still covered up, but there already is a twofold manner of experiencing his self-identity. While the two "egos" are still linked together by a continuous "mono-dialogue," in which the two are "arguing it out," the argument is no longer yielding anything new on either side, the positions are fixed, and, in becoming more immobile, are losing their independence and are turning into quite concrete and self-contained ego-images with which he is alternately identifying himself, although he still retains enough reality contact and corresponding survey over himself in his social role to stay dimly aware of the duality.

In brief, he is suffering from a true and almost "classic" schizophrenic psychosis, which, differentially, is marked not only by paranoid ideations but more and more also by generalized rigidity with paralyzing fears, approaching a point where somatic manifestations of catatonic stiffening are among the possible symptoms to be reckoned with. A long preceding record—which may or may not be documented—of both obsessive and compulsive manifestations is likely, and oedipal constellations must have prevailed in his childhood. Messianic forms of self-identification already are well-marked and, supported by enormous upsurges of affect, should here and there penetrate the thin wall of rigid behavioral control which he is still maintaining. Hospitalization seems imperative and prospects are poor.

Sample X
(Male, age 24, right-handed)

The writer (fig. 247) combines superior, if not very superior, potenialities of creative intelligence with a lack of intellectual discipline that closely reflects the tremendous emotional turmoil which he harbors and which constantly "spills over" into consciousness in the form of inconsistent and mutually contradictory impulses which prevent the crystallization of any definite course or stable direction. Markedly retarded in his maturation processes, unrealistic in his approach to the environment, and constantly self-preoccupied, his general immaturity nevertheless is con-

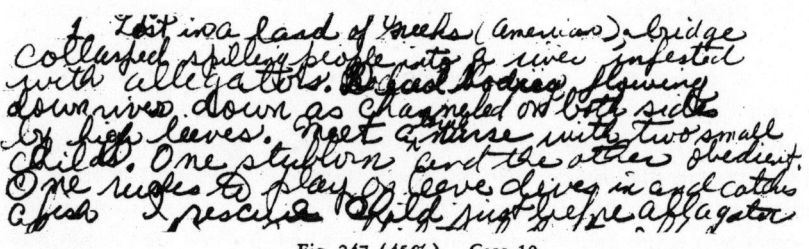

Fig. 247 (45%). Case 10

trasted by spiritual and moral aspirations which imply a remarkable astute awareness of values, very much spontaneous idealism, and enough real or potential originality of ideas to constitute, in all the chaos, a solid core of personality formation which should be quite possible to work with therapeutically.

At the present time, he should be distractable, disorderly, forgetful and extremely sluggish in his work, yet not illogical in his thinking, the motivations far more than the formal elements of which appear "torn" by the constant upsurge of powerful archaic images. He is a typical dreamer, given to lyrical and speculative contemplation, exceedingly narcissistic, yet no egotist but full of natural goodness, alternately tending to identify himself with "noble" masculine and "idyllic" maternal roles: it is essentially the latter polarity which constitutes his inner alternative and, in consequence of it, his general state of indecision, which is not likely ever to be overcome as such but which he should be capable of transforming into pools and incentives of creative activity providing his education and interests in external reality can be sufficiently stimulated to keep him going.

Danger points for future greater maturation are the sweeping intensity of his unchannelized instinctual urges which range all the way from crudest narcissism via overt homosexuality—with some traits of sadism—to sporadic occurrences of heterosexual desire; the corresponding impact of anxiety; the extreme moodiness; and, finally, an undertone of traumatization and resentment (when feeling offended he can be quite quarrelsome and argumentative) which tends to foster hypochondriacal self-observation and "suspicious" projections rather than the spontaneous "lyrical" introspection of which he is capable. Since he experiences his own inner needs as a perpetual threat as well as a perpetual enticement, in order to be provided with sufficient strength to meet these forces, he needs environmental assertions of his ego in the form of social successes badly. The entire constellation, in conjunction with his marked depression and with a tendency toward outbreaks of aggressive emotion in the form of rages and tantrums, points toward potentialities of a psychotic break which primarily would be characterized by alternations of depressive rigidity and hypomanic expansion with "cosmic" projections, i.e., the psychotic development within his scope would probably take a medium course between the catatonic and manic-depressive, with only secondary, if any, paranoid coloring. The excellent basic personality factors which could serve to ward it off have been pointed out in the beginning. His present acute depression should be marked by some agitation. One of the greatest difficulties for therapy would be to make him gain more self-understanding without fostering his self-observation. Opportunities for mature associations, for inspiring experiences in literature and the arts and for integrative rhythmical activities should be provided.

SUMMARY

Graphology was defined as the psychological analysis of handwriting for the purpose of exploring and describing personality. Three different approaches at the present time—an impressionistic, an atomistic, and a systematic one—were distinguished, the development of the third one of these, in addition to a discussion of its clinical applications, was proposed, and the history of handwriting analysis was presented in an outline. The concept of expressive movements as psychological indicators was traced to the necessity of viewing personality as a functional unit or system in which a unifying qualitative principle governs the entire scope of organismic action. Three dimensions of personality functioning were differentiated, and criteria of handwriting analysis were grouped according to their roles as representatives of these three aspects. This led to a differentiation of the total motivation operative in handwriting into purposive and expressive goals, and to the consideration of diversions of the inner focus toward the self as a third and only potentially operative motivating factor.

Questions of methodology and objectification were discussed, objections to the method were faced, the necessity to validate graphological findings on a basis of total configurative evaluations of personality, rather than of quantification of single graphic traits, was pointed out, and matching experiments were recommended for this purpose.

A definition of basic concepts followed. Handwriting in its total motoric aspect was defined as governed by cycles of muscular contraction and release. Handwriting in its total symbolic aspect was defined as governed by the spontaneous conversion of the field of writing into a quasi-spatial realm in the writer's and reader's inner order of experiences. Handwriting in its total interpretative aspect was defined as governed by the principles of ambivalence and of interdependence, the first one implying a consideration of the level of form quality, the second one a synoptic consideration of multiple differential criteria applying to identical areas of functioning.

The discussion of the graphological method proper was based on the three global considerations of the level of form quality, of the rhythmical qualities, and of the overall arrangement. The first one of these was defined as the combined degree of aesthetic balance and of originality of form. The second one of them was derived from a psychological analysis of the graphic contraction-release cycle as one specific appearance of the self-articulation of systems, determined by the simultaneous operations of the two principles of repetition and of change, in the dimension of time. The necessity of an early focus in the course of the graphoanalytic attack on the overall arrangement was argued on the basis of practical considerations of procedure.

Handwriting then was considered in accordance with the principal properties of graphic movement themselves, and the system of the dimensional concepts of rating as specific aspects of the writer's expressive profile in terms of qualities of gesture was derived. Extension, velocity, and impact were defined as representatives of the writer's total scope of self-experience and of aspiration, i.e., of his temperamental qualities, and the interpretative basis for each of them was developed. Between the place in the dimensional system occupied by them and the one occupied by dimensions governed by directional criteria, the lateral and longitudinal qualities of the ductus were encountered, and the establishment of a basis of interpretation for them was followed by one for the vertical extension of handwriting which was defined as representative of the writer's orientation in the realm of available values. The horizontal dimension of the writing movement was then considered according to the static rightward-progressive aspects of the word body as well as to the general dynamic criteria of the relative width, the relative slant, and the total relative right- and leftwardness, and was defined as the dimension of impulse externalization and of intercourse with the environment. As a specific dynamic criterion and particular area of crystallization for the writer's "typical gesture," the forms of binding were classified and interpreted according to their prototypes; considerations of the broader static aspect of writing as provided by the directional qualities of the line concluded the discussion of the horizontal dimension. Beyond the scope of the temperamental, ductual, and directional aspects of handwriting, the types and degrees of background involvement were focused upon. An analysis of the general qualities of curve followed the discussion of the last named dimension, which itself was differentiated according to the three criteria of graphic amplitude, of enrichment, and of total spatial dispersion. Finally, the signature in its particular position as a social representative of the person, those special "signs" of the older graphological school the overall interpretations for which have survived the

SUMMARY

holistic revisions of its system, and miscellaneous matters pertaining to the graphological inquiry were taken up.

For the work of interpretation, knowledge of the writer's age and sex was defined as imperative, of his cultural background, as desirable; to these considerations, there was attached one of possible special circumstances of the graphologist's situation in the face of his objects of inquiry, and the advisability of information regarding the writer's handedness was postulated. In order to facilitate interpretative operations and in particular to help in the detection of early states of discrepancy between a writer's modes of external and of self-adjustment, graphic qualities were then grouped according to their psychological articulation on either the sides of contraction or release, as well as to their accessibility to conscious modification. The graphology student's presumable main difficulties were considered and a procedural order of turns for his first approaches to samples of handwriting was formulated. Practical demonstrations of the method in its general applications followed this presentation of the graphological system itself.

Preceding a study of the clinical applications of the method, the expression-analytical concepts of personality were related to those of psychiatric nosology and present day thinking; based on an inquiry into the logical nature of a prominent psycho-diagnostic concept, analysis of the mental patient's specific gestural profile as representative of his individuality in a strict sense, such as proposed by clinical graphology, was found to be directly suggested by the present situation of diagnostic work in psychiatry itself. The various pattern principles of graphic expression applying to the existing standard groups of classification of the mentally ill were then characterized, and, for each of them, directives for subspecification of clinical cases were developed. Except for the specific affinity of the depressed states to a reinforcement of the downward impulse, accentuated by supporting reinforcements of pressure and by reduction in speed, the affective psychoses were found to be characterized, primarily, by extreme degrees of total rhythmical fluctuation and by accentuations of the rightward impulse of writing, secondarily by possible attempts of the person to resist these trends. The schizophrenic psychoses were found dominated, primarily, by tendencies toward rhythmical disintegration frustrating the unification of the trail of movement, secondarily by specific reinforcements of the leftward impulse. The psychoneuroses were found dominated in their graphic expression by impulses of compression operating in either an overall vertical or overall horizontal direction, or in any combinations of these. Intra-cranial disorders were found characterized by grosser failures in perceptual and motor co-ordination. Paroxysmal trends of personality were related to specific disturbances in the area of the ductual qualities as well as of the pressure cycles of writing.

Subsequently, a number of miscellaneous clinical, characterological, and procedural matters pertinent to the graphologist's work were taken up, and the practical application of the method to the tasks of mental diagnosis was shown.

BIBLIOGRAPHY

Allport, Gordon Willard and Vernon, Philip E. *Studies in Expressive Movement.* New York: The Macmillan Co., 1933.
Angyal, Andras. *Foundations for a Science of Personality.* New York: The Commonwealth Fund, 1941.
Arnheim, Rudolf. "Experimentelle psychologische Untersuchungen zum Ausdrucksproblem," *Psychologische Forschungen,* XI (1928), 1-32.
Becker, Minna. *Graphologie der Kinderschrift.* Freiburg: Niels Kampmann Verlag, 1926.
Biäsch, Ernst. "Graphologische Bemerkungen über die Bindungsform," *Psychologische Rundschau,* I (1929), 230-34.
Binet, Alfred L. *Les révélations de l'écriture d'après un contrôle scientifique.* Paris: F. Alcan, 1906.
Bleuler, Eugen. *Lehrbuch der Psychiatrie.* Berlin, 1930.
———. *Textbook of Psychiatry.* Edited by A. A. Brill. New York: The Macmillan Co., 1936.
Bobertrag, Otto. *I: die Graphologie zuverlässig?* Heidelberg: Niels Kampmann Verlag, 1929.
Breitkopf, A. "Grossbewegungen und Kleinbewegungen. Ein Beitrag zu einer vergleichenden Ausdruckslehre," *Zeitschrift für angewandte Psychologie,* LVIII (1939), 1-92.
Crépieux-Jamin, J. *L'âge et le sexe dans l'écriture.* Paris, 1925.
———. *Les bases fondamentales de la graphologie et de l'expertise en écritures.* Paris: F. Alcan, 1921.
———. *L'écriture et le caractère.* Paris, 1888.
———. *Les éléments de l'écriture des canailles.* Paris: E. Flammarion, 1923.
Erlenmeyer, A. *Die Schrift.* Stuttgart: Bonz, 1879.
Fischer, O. *Experimente mit Raphael Schermann.* Vienna, 1924.
Hull, C. L. and Montgomery, R. P. "Experimental Investigation of Certain Alleged Relations between Character and Handwriting," *Psychological Review,* XXVI (1919), 63-74.
Jacoby, Hans. *Handschrift und Sexualität.* Berlin and Cologne: A. Marcus and E. Weber, 1932.
Klages, Ludwig. *Ausdrucksbewegung und Gestaltungskraft* . . . Leipzig: J. A. Barth, 1923.
———. *Einführung in die Psychologie der Handschrift.* Stuttgart: W. Seifert, 1924.
———. *Graphologisches Lesebuch.* Leipzig: J. A. Barth, 1930.
———. *Grundlegung der Wissenschaft vom Ausdruck.* Leipzig: J. A. Barth, 1936.
———. *Handschrift und Charakter.* Leipzig: J. A. Barth, 1936.
———. *Prinzipien der Charakterkunde.* Leipzig: J. A. Barth, 1910.
———. *Die Probleme der Graphologie.* Leipzig: J. A. Barth, 1910.
Koehler, Wolfgang. *Gestalt Psychology.* New York: Liveright Publishing Corp., 1947.

Koffka, Kurt. *Experimental-Untersuchungen zur Lehre vom Rhythmus.* Leipzig, 1908.
———. *Über Vorstellungen.* Leipzig, 1911.
Kraepelin, Emil. *Psychologische Arbeiten.* Leipzig: Engelmann, 1898.
Langenbruch, Wilhelm. *Praktische Menschenkenntnis auf Grund der Handschrift.* Berlin: Kameradschaftsverlag, 1929.
Meyer, Georg. *Die wissenschaftlichen Grundlagen der Graphologie,* 3rd edition. Jena: G. Fischer, 1940.
Michon, Jean-Hippolyte. *Système de graphologie.* Paris, 1875.
Munroe, Ruth L. "Three Diagnostic Methods Applied to Sally," *Journal of Abnormal and Social Psychology,* XV, No. 2 (April, 1945), 215-28.
Munroe, Ruth and Stein-Lewinson, Thea, and Schmidl-Waehner, Trude. "A Comparison of Three Projective Methods," *Character and Personality,* XIII, No. 1 (Sept. 1944).
Preyer, Wilhelm, *Zur Psychologie des Schreibens.* Leipzig: L. Voss, 1919.
Pulver, Max. *Symbolik der Handschrift.* Zurich: Orell Füssli, 1931.
———. *Trieb und Verbrechen in der Handschrift.* Zurich: Orell Füssli, 1934.
Roman-Goldzieher, K. "Untersuchungen über die Schrift der Stotterer, Stammler, und Polterer," *Zeitschrift für Kinderforschung,* XXXV (1929), 116-39.
Saudek, Robert. *Experimental Graphology.* London, 1925.
———. *Experiments with Handwriting.* London: G. Allen and Unwin, Ltd., 1928.
———. "The Methods of Graphology," *British Journal of Psychology,* VII (1927), 221-59.
———. *The Psychology of Handwriting.* London: G. Allen and Unwin, Ltd., 1925.
———. "Writing Movements as Indicators of the Writer's Social Behavior," *Journal for Social Psychology,* II (1931), 337-73.
———. "Zur Psychologie der Amerikanischen Handschrift," *Zeitschrift für Menschenkenntnis,* VI (1931).
Die Schrift. Fachblatt für wissenschaftliche Graphologie. Bruenn, 1935-39.
Seesemann, K. "Bewährungskontrolle graphologischer Gutachten," *Zeitschrift für industrielle Psychotechnik,* VI (1920), 104-08.
Stein-Lewinson, Thea. "Dynamic Disturbances in the Handwriting of Psychotics; with Reference to Schizophrenic, Paranoid, and Maniac-Depressive Psychoses," *American Journal of Psychiatry,* XCVII (July, 1940), 102-35.
Theiss, Herbert. "Zur experimentellen Graphologie," *Zeitschrift für Menschenkunde,* V (1929), 237-45.
Tittel, Käthe. "Untersuchungen über Schreibgeschwindigkeit," *Neue psychologische Studien,* XI, no. 1 (1934), 1-54.
Trey, Marcel de. *Der Wille in der Handschrift.* Bern: A. Francke, 1946.
Vértesi, Etel. *Handschrift und Eigenart der Krebsgefährdeten; ein Beitrag zur Dispositionsforschung.* Budapest: Brüder Tisza, 1938.
Wagner, Lutz. "Der Unterschied männlichen und weiblichen Selbstgefühls in der Handschrift," *Zeitschrift für Menschenkunde,* X (1934), 129-43.
Walther, Johannes. "Die psychologische und charakterologische Bedeutung der handschriftlichen Bindungsarten," *Neue psychologische Studien,* XI, no. 3 (1938), 63-158.
Werner, Rudolf. "Über den Anteil des Bewusstseins an den Schreibvorgängen," *Neue psychologische Studien,* XI, no. 2 (1937), 1-72.

Wertheimer, Max. "Über Gestalttheorie," *Symposion*, I (1925).
Wieser, Roda. *Der Rhythmus in der Verbrecherhandschrift*. Leipzig: J. A. Barth, 1938.
Wolff, Werner. *Diagrams of the Unconscious*. New York: Grune and Stratton, 1948.
———. *The Expression of Personality; Experimental Depth Psychology*. New York and London: Harper and Bros., 1943.
Zubin, Joseph and Stein-Lewinson, Thea. *Handwriting Analysis, a Series of Scales for Evaluating the Dynamic Aspects of Handwriting*. New York: King's Crown Press, 1942.

INDEX

Affective psychoses, 169-173, 267
Age in handwriting, 134-135, 267
Aging, 134-135
Alcoholism, 202, 239
Allport, G. W., 12
"Ambition" stroke, 124
Ambivalence and interdependence, 24, 265
Amplitude, see Fullness and meagerness
Angle, angularity, 77-82, 88, 90, 96, 135, 182, 186, 188, 223
Angyal, A., 7, 71, 72
Anxiety, free-floating, 51, 158, 159, 222
Anxiety hysteria, 217
Anxiety states, 210, 217-219, 224, 228
Aphasia, 231, 233
Arcade, 77, 81-83, 89, 90, 183, 186
Arch, see Double arch
Artificial fullness, see Fullness, artificial
Artificial wideness, see Wideness, artificial
Ataxia, 231, 239
Atomistic approach in graphology, 2, 14, 15, 265
Autonomy, trend toward, 71-73

Background involvement, 102-116, 202, 266
Basic concepts, 20-24
Becker, M., 5, 269
Bender-Gestalt test, 125
Bergson, H., 34
Binding, forms of, 76-91, 266
Blockings, 43
Brain tumor, 229-231
Busse, H. H., 5

Cancer, 239

Cardiac disease, 238
Cardiac neurosis, 224
Catatonia, 105, 181, 195-202, 204, 223, 228
Cerebral sclerosis, 228-229
Cerebral thrombosis, 230
Character neuroses, 210
Children's handwriting, 134
"Chthonic" character, 63
Closure effect, 54, 217
Compulsive neurosis, see Obsessive-compulsive neurosis
Connectedness and disconnectedness, 51-55, 234
Conscious modification, 138-140
Contraction-release scale, 138-140
Contraction versus release, 20-21, 27, 32-33, 35, 36, 181, 209, 219, 220, 234, 265, 266
Control, dominance of, 21, 35
Cortical atrophy, 233, 239
Couvé, R., 12
Cover strokes, 87-88, 95
Crépieux-Jamin, J., 4, 269
Crowding versus distinctness, 36, 111-116
Cultural background, 135-136, 267
Curve, general qualities of, 117-118, 222, 266
Curving versus angularity, see Angle, angularity
Cyclothymic (type), 182

Dementia praecox, see Schizophrenia
Depression, 93, 222, 240, 267
 (agitated), 181
 (cyclic), 173-179
 (involutional), 179-181
 (reactive), 179-181, 224

INDEX

Dimensions of rating, 39-133
Disconnectedness, see Connectedness and disconnectedness
Dispersion (ductual), see Doughiness
Dispersion (linear), see Distinctness
Distances and margins, 111-116, 266; also see Margin emphasis
Distinctness, see Crowding versus distinctness
Double arch, 86-87
Doughiness and sharpness, 46-51, 213, 219, 224, 234
Ductus, qualities of, 46-55, 266, 268
Dynamic aspects, general, 65-73
Dynamic aspects, specific, 76-91

Ego articulation, 83
Ego-emphasis, 21, 74-76
Ego-linear constraint, 49; also see Doughiness and sharpness
Elaboration and simplification, 106-110, 211, 241, 266
Embellishment, 129-131, 237
Emotion, dominance of, 21, 35
Enrichment, see Elaboration and simplification
Enuresis, 237
Epilepsy, 226
  (idiopathic), 233-237, 268
  (focal), 231
  (psychomotor), 223, 237, 268
Epistemology, 11-19, 26-27, 168-172
Erlenmeyer, A., 5, 269
Exhibitionism, 242
Expressive movements, 2, 3, 7-10, 39
Expressive versus purposive goals, 9, 134, 265
Extension, velocity, and impact, 40-46, 266

Feeblemindedness, 233, 241
Flightiness of ideas, 54
Fluctuation, see Integration (and fluctuation)

Form quality, level of, 24, 25-27, 28-32, 72, 241, 265
Fragmentation, 54
Fullness versus meagerness, 102-106, 202, 266
Fullness, artificial, 105, 211

Gait, 10
Garland, 77, 83-84, 89, 91, 93, 96, 112, 173, 211
Gestalt psychology, 3, 6
Glandular disturbances, 238
Grand mal, see Epilepsy
Graphology, history of, 1-6, 265
Graphology of signs, 4

Handedness, 136-137, 267
Handwriting identification, 1, 40
Hebephrenia, 54, 137, 190, 202
Homonomy, trend toward, 71-73
Homosexuality, 143, 242
Horizontal dimension, 63-102, 266
Hull, C. L., 11, 12, 18, 269
Hyperthyroid states, 238
Hypomania, 176-179
Hysteria, 75, 181, 193, 211-217, 219, 227, 233, 234

I-dots, 124-125
Impact, see Extension, velocity, and im-impact
Impressionistic approach in graphology, 1-2, 265
Initial upstrokes, 121-123
Integration (and fluctuation), 27-36, 267
Interdependence, see Ambivalence and interdependence
Interpretative aspect, total, 24-27, 265
Intracranial disorders, 202, 225, 268
Isomorphism, isomorphic, 3, 7
Klages, L., 1, 2, 5, 6, 11, 12, 33, 39, 78, 139
Koehler, W., 78
Kraepelin, E., 169

von Kuegelgen, G., 12
Langenbruch, W., 5, 269
Level of aspiration, 41-43
Line directions, 92-102, 219
Lower zone, 56, 57, 61

Manic-depressive psychosis, 38, 169, 173-180, 181, 183
Margins and distances, 111-116
Margin emphasis (versus margin neglect), 36-38; also see Distances and margins
Majuscles, 74-76
Meagerness, see Fullness versus meagerness
Memory, 54, 55, 106
Mending, 129-131, 202
Meyer, G., 5, 11, 270
Michon, H., 4, 5, 11, 122, 125, 270
Middle zone, 22, 23, 36, 56, 57, 58, 59, 61, 105, 130, 192, 210, 211, 217, 219, 240
Minuscles, 74-76
Mirror writing, 137
Montgomery, R. P., 11, 12, 18, 269
Motoric aspect, total, 20-21, 265
Munroe, R., 12, 270

Narcissism, 137
Neglect, see Ornamentation and neglect
Neurasthenia, 224, 226
Nutritional disturbances of cortex, 231

Object emphasis, 21
Objectivity problem, 11-19, 168-172, 265
Obsessions, obsessional, 51, 219
Obsessive-compulsive neurosis, 218, 219-224, 227
Ornamentation and neglect, 106-110
Overall arrangement, 36-38, 265, 266

Paranoid trends, 51, 105, 122, 128, 186, 188, 241
Parasitism, 84
Paresis, 231, 232

Paroxysmal character, see Hysteria, Epilepsy
Peripheral zones, 22, 23, 56, 105, 127, 130, 190, 203, 211, 212, 219, 224, 237, 240
Personality dimensions, 8, 265
Petit mal, see Epilepsy
Physics, 171
"Platonic" character, 63
Positivism, 16
"Power" stroke, 124
Pressure, 14, 15, 40-46, 167, 202, 207, 211, 219, 222, 231, 234, 237, 267
Preyer, W., 5, 270
Proprioceptive reflexes, 80
"Protection" stroke, 124
Psychasthenia, see Obsessive-compulsive neurosis
Psychiatry, 168, 170, 171, 172, 267
Psychoneurosis, 202, 204-205, 267
Psychopathy, 35, 240, 242
Pulver, M., 5, 12, 270
Purposive goals, see Expressive versus purposive goals

Quasi-spatial experience of writing field, 21-24, 265

Regularity, see Rhythm and regularity
Release, see Contraction versus release
Rhythm and regularity, 27-37, 204, 207, 237, 240, 265
Rolling, centrifugal versus centripetal, 151
Roof-tile arrangements, 97, 102
Rorschach test, 13, 17, 18, 85

Sample as a whole, 25-38
Saudek, R., 5, 12, 270
Schizophrenia, 38, 75, 105, 169, 171, 172, 173, 181-204, 205, 206, 207, 208, 209, 237, 267
  (catatonic), see Catatonia
  (hebephrenic), see Hebephrenia
  (paranoid), 190-194, 202, 204, 223
  (simple), 188-190

Schizothymic (type), 182
Schmidl-Waehner, T., 12, 13, 270
Script, 137-138
Seesemann, K., 12, 270
Senile dementia, 229
Senility, 54
Sense of economy, 68
"Sense of humor" stroke, 124
Sex in handwriting, 135, 267
Sexual deviations, 242
Sharpness, see Doughiness and sharpness
Sherrington's phenomenon, 80
Signature, 118-121, 266
Simplification, see Elaboration and simplification
Size, 40-46
Size control, 231
Slant, 65-73, 203, 266
Somnambulism, 226
Special signs, 118, 121-133, 266
Speed, 40-46, 202, 219, 241, 267
Static aspects (line), 92-102, 266
Static aspects (word), 73-76, 266
Stein-Lewinson, T., 5, 12, 270
Suicidal tendencies, 127
Super-ego, psychoanalytic concept, 61, 130, 131, 210

Supported forms, 88, 96
Symbolic aspect, total, 21-24, 265

T-bars, 123, 242
Temper tantrums, 123
Thread, 77, 84-86, 91, 92, 94, 95, 128, 186. 211
Total interpretative aspect, see Interpretative aspect, total
Total motoric aspect, see Motoric aspect, total
Total right and leftwardness, 65-73, 266
Total symbolic aspect, see Symbolic aspect, total

Upper zone, 56, 57, 61

Velocity, see Extension, velocity, and impact
Vernon, P. E., 12, 269
Vertical dimension, 56-63, 266
Vitalistic school of thought, 34

Walther, J., 5, 270
Wideness, artificial, 71, 136, 211, 218
Width, 65-73, 209, 266
Wieser, R., 5, 270
Wolff, W., 6, 270

Zubin, J., 5, 270